HOW TO WIN CAMPAIGNS

100 STEPS TO SUCCESS

WEEK

EARTHSCAN

London • Sterling, VA

*For Amazon, Willow and Sarah, and for all the campaigners
who have given their safety, lives, freedom or comforts to try
and make the world a better place.*

First published by Earthscan in the UK and USA in 2005
Reprinted 2005

Copyright © Chris Rose, 2005

ISBN-10: 1-85383-962-0 paperback
ISBN-13: 978-1-85383-962-7
ISBN-10: 1-85383-961-2 hardback
ISBN-13: 978-1-85383-961-0

Typesetting by Mapset Ltd, Gateshead, UK
Printed and bound in the UK by The Bath Press
Cover design by Yvonne Booth

For a full list of publications please contact:

Earthscan
8–12 Camden High Street
London, NW1 0JH, UK
Tel: +44 (0)20 7387 8558
Fax: +44 (0)20 7387 8998
Email: earthinfo@earthscan.co.uk
Web: **www.earthscan.co.uk**
22883 Quicksilver Drive, Sterling, VA 20166-2012, USA

Earthscan is an imprint of James and James (Science Publishers) Ltd and publishes
in association with the International Institute for Environment and Development

A catalogue record for this book is available from the British Library

Library of Congress Cataloging-in-Publication Data

Chris Rose, 1956–
    How to Win Campaigns : 100 Steps to Success / by Chris Rose
        p. cm.
    Includes bibliographical references and index.
    ISBN 1-85383-962-0   (pbk.) — ISBN 1-85383-961-2   (hbk.)
    1. Social action. 2. Communication in social action. 3. Social marketing. 4.
Persuasion (Psychology) 5. Publicity. I. Title.
HN18.R628 2005
659–dc22

                                                        2005003302

The paper used for the text pages of this book
is FSC certified and totally chlorine-free.
FSC (the Forest Stewardship Council) is an
international network to promote responsible
management of the world's forests.

Mixed Sources
Product group from well-managed
forests and other controlled sources
www.fsc.org Cert no. SGS-COC-2121
© 1996 Forest Stewardship Council

CONTENTS

LIST OF FIGURES, TABLES AND BOXES

Figures

Tables

Boxes

LIST OF ACRONYMS AND ABBREVIATIONS

BSE   bovine spongiform encephalitis ('mad-cow disease')
CAMP CAT channel, action, messenger, programme, context, audience, trigger
CFCs   chlorofluorocarbons
CLEAR   Campaign for Lead-free Air
ECF   elemental chlorine-free paper
FAIR   Fairness and Accuracy in Reporting
FoE   Friends of the Earth
FSC   Forest Stewardship Council
FTSE   Financial Times Stock Exchange
GM   genetically modified (food)
HCFCs   hydrochlorofluorocarbons
HFCs   hydrofluorocarbons
ICLEI   International Council for Local Environment Initiatives
IPCC   Intergovernmental Panel on Climate Change
MIPIGG   Multisectoral Initiative on Potent Industrial Greenhouse Gases
MMR   measles, mumps and rubella vaccine
MSC   Marine Stewardship Council
MSF   Médecins Sans Frontières
NGO   non-governmental organization
NASA   National Aeronautics and Space Administration
NVDA   non-violent direct action
OSPAR   Oslo and Paris Commission regulating the disposal of wastes in the North East Atlantic
POPs   persistent organic pollutants
PR   public relations
TCF   totally chlorine-free paper
UNFCCC   United Nations Framework Convention on Climate Change
WRI   World Resources Institute
WTO   World Trade Organization
WWF   Worldwide Fund for Nature

ACKNOWLEDGEMENTS

I am particularly grateful to Simon Bryceson and Rick LeCoyte who fought off stupor to wade through several whole drafts of this text and made many helpful suggestions. I also wish to thank many others who helped significantly, including Richard Sandbrook for helping me get started, Robin Grove-White for suggesting how to get it finished, and Jonathan Sinclair-Wilson and all his staff at Earthscan. Jackie Potter retyped many sections, and Pat Dade deserves special thanks for allowing me extensive access to his research on value modes at Cultural Dynamics. My apologies to those I have omitted to credit, misquoted or misrepresented. To all those who generously agreed to be interviewed and whose thoughts now don't appear – I am sorry, I hope to write another book, in due course. Most of all, I owe a great debt to my long-suffering family who put up with me during the five years it took to put an incoherent jumble of ideas into book format.

INTRODUCTION

There are but two powers in the world, the sword and the mind. In the long run the sword is always beaten by the mind.

Napoleon Bonaparte

There are two forces in the world today – US military power, and world public opinion.

Time Magazine, 2003

Every day, millions of people are touched by campaigns. It is important that campaigns succeed. Lives may depend upon the outcome of campaigns over access to health, medicines, clean water or to justice. The survival of nature depends on the success of campaigns to change policies and industries that are destroying our atmosphere, oceans, forests and other 'public goods'. If campaigners for education, child rights and fairer trade are to fail, then the poorest of the poor will be condemned to a more miserable future.

Yet most campaigning does fail, and there is remarkably little effort to learn why, or to analyse and replicate the campaigns that are successful. This book cannot provide a comprehensive answer but it collects together some campaign 'tools' that have a track record of helping campaigns work. It is good that thousands, perhaps millions, of people devote their lives to campaigns, it is tragic if their efforts are mostly wasted, and a scandal if that could be avoided.

Campaigns mostly involve communication: a conversation with society. This differs from the communication we carry out one to one with our friends or colleagues. This communication is used to persuade large numbers of people to act as a matter of urgency, so many campaign techniques are those of influencing people without having to stop and make friends first, and in this respect campaigning is like PR or public relations. But unlike PR, campaigning is an expression of popular democracy; it creates new channels of influence for the public, in the public interest. Campaigns work in the public interest by borrowing power from the people for good causes. In a world where politics are increasingly professionalized[1] and lean increasingly towards promotion of private economic interests, campaigning has often become the common politics of the people.

Advertising campaigns sell things, electoral campaigns get politicians elected, but the sorts of campaigns this book is about bring neither money nor formal power. Instead, they harness a collective will and effort as an engine of change for public benefit.

What sway campaigns have depends upon the scale and intensity of their public support. This is their source of energy and an inbuilt test of legitimacy. Generally the rich and powerful do not campaign – they do not have to. Many campaigns are a reaction against an abuse of power.

For most voluntary non-governmental organizations (NGOs), their only resource to secure real change is public persuasion. Business has money, government has law but campaigns have only public support. Communication is the campaigners' instrument for change, not simply a way to publicize an opinion.

The best campaigns seem to communicate themselves. Others go down in a blaze of publicity but achieve no real change; many more struggle on in obscurity. A high failure rate is to be expected. Campaigning is a high-risk venture. In business, most new enterprises will fail. In nature, few species of wildlife reaching a new land will ever become established – most, as with campaigns, will die out.

In business or ecology, though, we expect to know the reasons for success and failure. We have studies and colleges devoted to the subject. Much the same is true of politics – getting elected is not generally regarded as an accident. Yet with campaigns the reasons for success and failure are often treated as an impenetrable mystery.

Such explanations as are given often descend into glib circularities such as 'to be effective, campaigns must communicate effectively' or effective campaigns need to be 'well planned, adequately resourced and engaging for the public'. This is about as useful for planning real activity and expenditure as saying that in order to be healthy, people must not get diseases and should avoid getting ill.

Campaigns are wars of persuasion. Use of communication is often the key to success or failure. By itself, public concern is rarely effectively focused: hence this book is mostly about how to use communication to enlist and focus the support of others. While there are lots of books about issues, this one is about the tactics and strategies of campaigning and communication, looking as much as possible at underlying principles.

Even though it is evident that most campaigning relies on communication, and some organizations excel at it, many NGOs ignore it in favour of issue knowledge. So a route map or strategic advice on how to organize it is hard to come by. Some 'campaign manuals'[2] contain valuable advice, but most tend towards details of individual communication practices or specialisms such as lobbying at international negotiations,[3] or domestic issue-by-issue advice.[4] The more recent 'grass-roots' and direct action-based campaign groups have produced a lot of useful websites, but these too tend to be either practical (how to encase your arm in concrete) or polemical (why capitalism must be defeated). Useful new web resources appear all the time: www.environmentaladvocacy.org for example. I try to list them at my website www.campaignstrategy.org. Please send me your ideas at mail@tochrisrose.idps.co.uk.

The commercial marketing and public relations literature is large, but campaigns for corporates are very different because they don't have to appeal to anyone's better nature. They rely on self-interest and normally start from the position of an insider. 'Social marketing' uses a number of similar techniques for non-profit purposes but generally does not challenge power or vested interests, or even seek specific outcomes.

Even some voluntary campaigning organizations, which rely so much on communication, don't treat it with the seriousness it deserves. Many managers and directors believe that communication is a low-value extra, something 'handled' by the press office, while other staff are given little or no training in it. All politicians are said to be susceptible to the conceit that they are economists. The NGO equivalent is to assume that everyone can communicate. One commentator[5] has put it like this:

> *Communications is seen as 'soft'. While programme development and practice are seen as requiring expertise and the thoughtful consideration of best practices, communications is an 'anyone can do it if you have to' task. It is time to retire this thinking. Doing communications strategically requires the same investment of intellect and study that these other areas of non-profit practice have been accorded.*

Today most managers are at least dimly aware that they *ought* to have a 'communications strategy'. It's seen as good practice. Unfortunately even many campaigners also think that a communications strategy equals a media strategy. In reality using the 'media', that is press, radio, television and so on, may not be the most effective way to communicate.[6] As a consultant and campaigner for over 20 years, I've lost count of the number of directors who assess the success of campaigns by weight of press clippings, and campaigners who are better able to tell you about how the media is covering their campaign than what effect that campaign is having in terms of change.

The mistaken assumption that communications simply means media is more likely where an organization has a specialist media department, while other departments may not be called 'communications' although that is mostly what they do – for example 'campaigns', 'marketing' or 'public information'.

Campaigning is a mongrel craft drawing from many other disciplines, so it's no surprise that lawyers tend to think campaigning hinges on making arguments, scientists want to progress campaigns by research, writers and academics by publishing, and teachers may believe education is how to change the world. Each can play a part in campaigns, it is true. Yet effective campaigns are usually better executed by showing rather than arguing, by motivation rather than education, and by mobilization rather than accumulation of knowledge. Doing this to order means planning communication like a composer or film director.

There is no absolute right answer to effective communication. Communication strategy for campaigns is like chess but with your opponents changing all the time, and with rules that are a matter of opinion. My general advice is:

- Keep it short and simple
- Be visual
- Create events
- Tell stories about real people
- Be *pro*active – don't just respond
- Get your communication in the right order
- Communicate in the agenda of the outside world – don't export the internal agenda, plan, jargon or 'message'.

Easy to say; harder to do.

A common pitfall is to get stuck arguing over 'messages'. It's best to avoid discussing 'your message' altogether and instead focus on the elements that are often critical to the success or failure of communication. The Context, Action, Trigger, Channel, Audience, Messenger and Programme all need to be got right (see Chapter 1) – discuss these and the 'message' will often emerge.

Effective campaigns, and effective campaigning organizations need a structure. Composers use concertos or symphonies. Campaigners can use communication strategies. Done badly, these can be dull plans, tick-box exercises and lists of impossible aspirations. Done well they can be fun, inspiring, lyrical and useful. Campaigns should also be exciting – an adventure. Aim to conduct your campaign like an opera – a political opera, painted in dramatic polarities.[7]

A communications strategy is about planning and knowing what you communicate, who to, why, and what can make it effective. It is using communication instrumentally – as an instrument to make change happen. It needs mechanical inputs such as identifying particular audiences or channels, but should also flow from your values, from the essence of your organization and cause, from the heart as well as the head.

Communications strategies can exist at many levels. For campaign groups the three most important are:

1   organizational – the whole communication of the organization;
2   campaign – for example, a campaign on child labour;
3   project – for example, around a specific European Union Council decision.

At a micro-level, campaign communication can literally be a conversation. At organizational level, it is an indirect 'conversation', a relationship built up over years. Your campaign communication may be carefully conceived all on its own, but it will arrive as part of a compound mosaic of impressions and information received from many sources. Everything your organization says or does – be it intended as communication or unintended – and anything said about it, will be added into the mental mix.

Maybe it includes direct engagements such as an encounter with a street money collector, or a campaign team, or even helping in a campaign activity. What were the people like? How were you treated? Who else was there? It all forms an impression, the result of a lot of fragments.

Impressions that count are mostly the result of events, things that happen: the equivalent of a few 'snapshots'. We 'make sense' of them by filling in the 'missing gaps' and explaining fragments by using other information, maybe about the issue in general, or our own life experiences. That way we make an overall picture that adds up. Campaigners can make deliberate use of this habit of 'first we see, then we understand' (see 'framing', Chapter 1).

The steps to change determine the campaign strategy, and that in turn needs to determine communications. Here's a shorthand way[8] to link communications to a campaign strategy:

- Locate decision – locate the action (often a decision) you want to achieve. What decision do you want made, and by whom?
- Identify mechanism – what mechanisms will get you the decision? What is the best way to get to the people you wish to influence?
- Determine audience – who do you need to convince/affect to get your mechanism into operation? If you do not reach the target audience, the mechanism will not operate, no matter how good the campaign materials are. Getting the mechanism to operate may require you to influence a different audience from the ultimate target
- Work back to proposition – what is the best way to motivate your audience? Tailor the original arguments/communications that you want to use for your target audience. What angle will your target audience respond best to?
- Define activities and materials – knowing the decision you want, the mechanics of that decision, what will motivate your target audience – you can now decide the appropriate materials for the campaign.

This book has no academic pedigree but shares practical lessons learned from successful campaigns and repeated failures, in the hope that it may help campaigns be less frustrating, more rewarding and above all, more effective. A lot of the examples are from Greenpeace, simply because they were ones I had easiest access to. They all illustrate principles that can apply to any campaign. A well-resourced book of campaign case studies could cast the net far wider.

The essentials of campaigning have a history as long as human communications itself – perhaps from the first time that someone questioned the direction of a group or tribe and said to others: 'Come with me – let's go this way instead.' An alternative objective, a call to action, the need to get attention, to reach the right audience with the right message at the right moment – these are some of the fundamentals.

The pages of this book mostly contain 'thinking tools'. Using them doesn't require any equipment, any qualifications or even any money. They apply to any topic and from the scale of a one-person one-street project, up to the major campaigns of pressure groups, advocacy organizations involving hundreds of people.

Campaigns did not begin with pressure groups, marketing or 'modern' advertising. History is littered with the antecedents of campaigning. Plenty are military, for at their root, campaigns are about power and contested 'outcomes'. Many campaigners like to name *The Art of War*[9] by fifth century Chinese General Sun Tzu, as their favourite text, though fewer seem to put his principles into practice. As a copywriter Shakespeare penned many effective calls to action, 'once more unto the breach, dear friends, once more' being one of the better ones.

To campaign effectively it is not enough to be concerned, or even to spread that concern to others: instead one needs to motivate people to take action, and that requires a solution which looks feasible, as well as a problem that is compelling. Good campaigning involves figuring out when to work on the problem, and when to work on the solution (Chapter 5). Nor is campaigning necessarily punitive – any campaigner whose objective is to punish the opponent is unlikely to achieve an early surrender or to win many friends. Campaigning is a business for those who want to get even, not mad. It's the marketing of motivation.

Campaigning is not always a particularly polite or noble business, and some may baulk at the thought of using techniques that in some cases were developed for the darker arts of politics, war or commerce. In fact, these days campaigns are pilfered by government and business far more than the other way around. All I can say is that my sympathy lies with those who ask: 'Why should the devil have all the best tunes?'[10]

What campaigning gets you

The essential difference between campaigning and 'advocacy' is public engagement. A campaign needs public support to succeed, and it is a form of politics for the public. There are many reasons people campaign, most of which boil down to righting an injustice. Organizations campaign because it works: it can get you change which goes beyond business as usual, the fruits of persuasion that cannot be bought or obtained by mere argument, protest or admonishment. Here are some reasons why campaigning can work:

• It creates gearing – multiplies the impact of efforts at change by enlisting the help of many people, thereby making it possible to achieve particular changes more quickly, or bigger changes altogether

- It sets agendas – it aligns the public about what needs to be done
- If action-based, it is a more powerful form of communication than just dialogue based on opinions
- It can remedy a democratic deficit, compensating for the corporatization and professionalization of politics and the consequent spiralling lack of trust in the formal political system
- Politics respond more and more via the media and less directly to the public, so having a dialogue in society is more and more important in creating political backing for a proposal
- Trust in the media, especially paid-for messages is declining, so communication with a clear personal endorsement, such as through participative networks, is more persuasive
- For the time being, NGOs – and this includes many campaign groups – are generally more trusted than most other elements of society, such as businesses, politicians and paid-for scientists
- It is established as a way of raising and testing injustices and action-deficits, and is now almost indispensable in trying to protect 'public goods'[11] because politics have broadly become the promoter of private interests
- Atomization of society has raised the importance of mass and networked media as a way of being heard
- Globalization of communications technology and narrowcasting has increased the opportunity to be heard if you are organized but reduced it otherwise, and made achieving 'cross-over' between 'unlike' segments of society more difficult, eroding 'common values'
- It creates a community and ecology of action – it means people are 'not alone'
- It gives agency – greater influence over the world.

Politics and business are converging with the form and techniques, although not the purpose of campaigns. As societies become driven less by survival needs and more by need to fulfil potential, they increasingly deal with things for which there is no direct market price, and this is the territory of campaigns. Equally the public communication techniques of campaigning become more salient in a 24/7 global 'public conversation world' in which, as public affairs executive Simon Bryceson says: 'politicians cast themselves in a "perpetual campaign", competing to stay in line with "public opinion"' (personal communication, simon@bryceson.com).

What campaigners need to know

For strategy, campaigners need to understand power. You may have a good argument or a cause you care about, but why should anyone listen or take notice? An interests analysis (see Chapter 4) should identify who is in control of what and who is benefiting from the status quo. It should help you answer the question: 'Why hasn't the change I want already taken place?' Posing a threat to established power or interests will make people take notice. Remember what Stalin responded when told that the Vatican opposed his actions in World War II: 'How many divisions does the Pope have?'

For engagement, campaigners need to understand motivation – their own, and that of others. If this is not well understood, it's unlikely that sufficient people can be motivated to lend the necessary support. Frequently it is not a question of which 'facts' are presented or what 'argument' is made but the terms in which a case is made – what 'the issue' is framed as, whether it meets the psychological needs of an audience, and whether factors such as the channel, messenger or context are right. Effective campaigning is rarely the result of a blind experiment which people come flocking to support. More often it results from identifying key audiences for change and then finding out what will motivate them. Neither 'education' nor 'changing minds' often come into it (see Chapter 10).

To engage in the business of public politics – and play out issues of who is right and wrong, and where society should be heading – campaigners need to understand 'the media' and the ritualized hidden formats of news reporting. To lure and feed the media machine, campaigns require events, the stuff of news and politics. The capacity to create events which lead observers to conclude they support the campaign, and then to act, marks out truly effective campaign groups from those that simply protest.

To make use of public sympathy and support, campaign groups need to organize themselves, with engagement mechanisms and supporter communication. They need to be able to analyse and achieve simplicity without simplification, to create compelling propositions (Chapter 6) which capture the problem, solution, responsible parties, consequent benefit and action needed, in a succinct phrase or image. To reach large numbers of people they need to think visually and use visual language (Chapter 5).

To compete for scarce human attention campaigns need to offer agency – more sway over the world – and to offer solutions not available via formal politics or the market. To persist and endure, campaigns need both organization and a vision, as well as a brand (see Chapter 11).

Campaigners need to identify what needs to be done or how the world should be different, what would have an effect in making that happen, and how to do it. They then need to assemble the forces and mechanisms to make the necessary changes happen. It is pretty easy to reach stage one: to specify what a better world would look like. It's harder to uncover the truth about the politics and dynamics of potential change. And it's very much harder to put together a campaign machine capable of making that change a reality. Yet it is only at this third level, that campaigns transform from being protests, well-publicized arguments or demonstrations of wishful thinking, into agents of change. It is also only then that they are taken seriously by opponents.

There are suggestions and techniques for all of the above in this book, though many are necessarily mere sketches of what is required. All this requires strategy, method and calculation but the most powerful campaigns also reach the heart by clearly coming from the heart as well as the head (see 'the glass onion', Chapter 11).

To do this, campaign groups need to be able to operate on principle as well as by strategy, and to achieve that, they need to understand, express and use their own values. Campaigns can change politics and power structures by strategy calculated from an understanding of interests, and in this they are like PR operations by major companies, or politics. But they can also change the same targets through the shaping pressure of values, formulating new concerns and norms, and from this territory professional politics and commerce are largely excluded.

The two processes – influence by changing interests and by changing values – are linked because it is events and conversations in society that gradually surface and coalesce values as new norms, often over decades or generations.

Campaigners also need to understand the issue of their campaign – which this book is not about – but it is a great mistake to assume that this is the most important thing. Too much focus on the issue, instead of on changing the issue, is almost invariably a recipe for failure.

John Muir and seven principles of campaigning

To my mind, the first 'modern' campaigner was John Muir. In the 19th century he used the media, and personal action, to mobilize support in a cause that changed great events in the US, with reverberations that have spread around the world.

Muir was an irascible Scot from Dunbar who emigrated to the US as a child. He lived drama and adventure, activism, science and politics. He was a one-man 19th century David Attenborough, Petra Kelly and tree-hugger rolled into one.

John Muir was for Nature with a big N, science, beauty and learning. Muir confounded his Calvinistic parents who believed maths to be the devil's work by learning in secret. After failing at farming, his family trekked west to an unsuccessful get-rich-quick opportunity – the California gold rush. Later, Muir had the first recorded 'wilderness experience' when he spent the American Civil War in the Canadian forests after losing an eye in a spinning accident. 'Going out,' he wrote just before he died, 'I was really going in.'

As a communicator, Muir connected personal action with 'global' responsiblities. He walked across the US and began his journal with his address: 'John Muir, Earth, Planet, Universe' – perhaps the best known self-declaration of citizenship of nature by a Westerner since the Celts.

As an activist, Muir climbed into the Yosemite region in the forests of the Sierra Nevada with a Chinese and a Spanish-American. Together they helped fight off loggers of giant redwoods at Mariposa Grove above Yosemite, including use of muskets. The massive redwoods – some fallen as the loggers left them, others still towering like giant, tufted icebergs of wood – are still there today.

Scaling many famous peaks for the first time, Muir proved glaciers actually moved and convinced President Theodore Roosevelt to back conservation, create national forests and expand national parks.

Muir used his adventure writing in east coast magazines and newspapers such as *The New York Tribune* to reach a wider mass public, arguing for Nature in the face of wholesale railway-driven development. That way he met a lawyer, who helped take the cause 'to the Hill' to seek legislation in Washington. So Muir combined the components of subsequent environmental 'campaigns': communication, inspiration, definition of an issue at individual and global scales, use of ethics and law, politics, journalism and the media to play out a struggle between the public conscience and private interests.

Muir founded the Sierra Club, and then split from it over its support for a dam at Hetch Hetchy in Yosemite Valley. The San Francisco authorities blamed a lack of water – rather than their lack of a fire brigade and proper planning – for the fires that followed the great San Francisco earthquake. Hence, they needed a dam. It was the environmental cause célèbre of its day.

Others later split from the Sierra Club to form Greenpeace and Friends of the Earth.

Muir's work largely inspired the global national parks and conservation movement. So no emigrant child from Dunbar: no Rainbow Warrior no World Heritage Sites – perhaps even no defence of the ozone layer. Despite his achievements, Muir is largely unsung as a hero or significant social figure.[12]

Why seven principles? It seems a good number.[13] Ideally, a campaign needs to:

1   Be multidimensional: communicating in all the dimensions of human understanding and decision-making. Political, emotional, economic, spiritual, psychological, technical, scientific, maybe more. Even if it begins in one, it must be able to translate into the others. It must understand the intuitive and personal (for example flowing from psychology and culture), and the counter-intuitive (for example from science) and be able to deal in both

2   Engage by providing agency – it needs to give its supporters greater power over their own lives. It must offer a credible, feasible and atttractive way to make a new and additional difference (see Chapter 2)

3   Have moral legitimacy, which it gets not by whom it represents but by meeting a need. Campaigners and their supporters have to be convinced the campaign is needed to make something happen in society which ought to be happening but which is not. The more widely shared this feeling becomes, the greater the moral authority of the campaign and the more that can be done. Most campaigns are planned in the mind, won in people's hearts and rationalized again in the mind

4   Provoke a conversation in society (see Chapter 3). I say they provoke a conversation rather than conduct it because, to be really effective, campaigns often need society to rethink its views and actions on a particular issue. When campaigns achieve 'cross-over' or a self-sustaining chain reaction of participation, then of course the campaigning organization has lost 'control' and the 'issue' is no longer its property, but it has probably succeeded in changing that society forever. Start talking with society, end by society talking to itself

5   Have verve, élan, infectious energy. It may feed aspirations, or provide security but above all, it needs an inspired vanguard. If your campaign doesn't excite you, then it probably won't engage others

6   Be strategic. It must plan a way to assemble enough forces to change what it wants to change. It must involve a battle-winning strategy at one level, and a war-winning strategy composed of a series of battles (see 'critical paths', Chapter 4)

7   Be communicable, first verbally, as a story – which enables it to be passed on, remembered, perhaps mythologized, not forgotten, mused over, rekindled, reinvented; second, visually: both as emotionally powerful framing images, and as 'evidences'. These visual signs are short cuts to understanding. Campaigns that can be communicated like this can be literally understood without words so have no trouble crossing over languages or, for the most part, across cultures. They also become 'semiostic' – people read their own meaning into the images, enabling a campaign to unite rather than to divide.

With qualities such as these, a campaign can resonate, spread and survive setbacks, able to reinvent itself and grow 'reflexively'. Even if crushed, oppressed or deserted by supporters, such a campaign may live on as an inspiration and rise again. When campaigns are successful in these terms they can offer some people a lifestyle or belief system, and in some cases organizations, individuals and the campaigns become indistinguishable.

Chapter 1

HOW TO BEGIN

Where to start

Find your own
beginning

A book can have only one beginning but campaigns can have many different beginnings. First you need to find your own beginning, and that depends on where you are at:

- If you know your issue but you don't know exactly what you want to achieve, begin by defining your objective (see Chapter 4, 'ambition box')
- If you need to campaign because you are faced with a known specific problem, and that tells you your objective but you don't know how to get that changed, then begin with the campaign motivation sequence (this chapter)
- If you have a concern but don't know how the issue works – the forces and processes behind the problem – then start with issue mapping and gathering intelligence (Chapter 3)
- If you already run a campaign and feel a need to change strategy or tactics, try looking at factors such as resources and assets (Chapter 8)
- If you have an organization which thinks it might like to campaign but is not sure, then step back and examine the bigger picture (Chapter 11), and try locating your approach in the ambition box.

See also the campaign planning star in Chapter 4, which illustrates factors needed in generating a campaign plan and proposition.

What communication is

The two words 'information' and 'communication' are often used interchangeably, but they signify quite different things. Information is giving out; communication is getting through.

Sidney J. Harris, American journalist and author

Successful communication needs to be two-way

Good communication isn't noticed. It's like good design: we only notice bad design. The London Underground map is often cited as a classic. We don't notice it because it fits its purpose so well (use it to *walk* around London, and you find it bears little resemblance to 'reality').

Forget old saws such as 'getting your message across'. Campaigners who focus on 'sending messages' will never succeed: they will persuade no-one but themselves. Successful communication needs to be two-way: more telephone than megaphone, with the active involvement of both parties.

Real communication, it has been said,[1] is rare and involves 'the transferring of an idea from the mind of the sender to the mind of the receiver'.

If someone does not want to receive your message, they won't. Would-be communicators therefore need to understand the motivations of their audience.

All too often, communication is treated as a technical, one-way process beautifully designed to reflect the views of the sender, unsullied by the need to be effective with the receiver.

'Delivering messages', 'sending information', 'targeting advertising': it becomes like targeting missiles – fire and forget – except that forgetting is the last thing that should be happening. Campaigners should spend at least as much time listening to the public and the

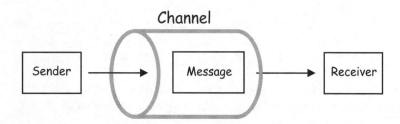

Figure 1.1 *Basic model of communications*

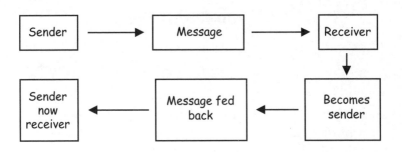

Figure 1.2 *Communication model incorporating feedback*

target, allies and opponents they seek to influence as they spend in working on communications back in the office.

The word 'audience' wrongly implies that receivers are passive. A dialogue is usually best, and if that's impossible, repetition may succeed in 'reaching' the audience.

A popular basic model of communications is illustrated in Figure 1.1.

We all know that serious misunderstandings can occur even in one-to-one communication. Introduce a third party – such as a newspaper or radio station and its journalists – and volume may increase but noise gets into the channel because of journalists' interpretations, or pollution by the thousands of other messages to which we are exposed each day.[2]

To improve communication, obtain feedback, whether volunteered or obtained through qualitative research.

Des Wilson, founder of Shelter, says: 'Remember, the bigger the audience, the simpler the message'.[3] So with public media, messages need to become simpler, compared to the complexities you can deal with in conversations at home or in the office.

Figure 1.3 *Example of a fire safety notice*

If you find a fire

The short words are best, and the old words are the best of all.
Sir Winston Churchill

Design communications to get a result

Motivational communication follows some well-established sequences, developed and refined by generations of salespeople. A useful version for campaigns is:

awareness > alignment > engagement > action.

Take the example of a fire safety notice that you might find in a hotel.

These notices keep it simple. They look something like the example shown in Figure 1.3.

At first sight, constructing this message seems easy but, in fact, it is carefully designed. It instructs to raise the alarm first – this is in the best interests of the hotel residents. It doesn't say 'call the fire brigade' – which might be in the best financial interests of the hotel owner, but which could mean searching for a phone in smoke-filled corridors. It puts lives over property. Then it says to go to the place of safety – and only then call the fire brigade.

So it's communication with a *purpose* (here = save lives). You need to know *why* you are trying to communicate, what the objective is in terms of an *action*, what you want someone to *do*, before you can communicate effectively.

Also, the sign is very simple and it instructs rather than offering a discussion, which would not be appropriate in an emergency. It is unambiguous. Lastly, it follows the sequence shown in Table 1.1:

Awareness establishes the subject. Alignment establishes that it is relevant to everyone. Engagement is an appeal to join in – and requires a commonly available mechanism (see Chapter 2). The action is what is needed. Omit or reorder any of these steps and problems result.

Table 1.1 *Sequence followed by fire safety notice*

If you find a fire	Awareness
We are all in danger	Alignment
Lets go this way	Engagement
We are leaving	Action

IF YOU FIND A FIRE

1. Network with your neighbours
2. Explain the issues and the processes of ignition, fuel effects, oxidation and ion plasmas, and address the social and economic justice dimensions
3. Educate decision-makers regarding the establishment of an adequately resourced fire brigade and fire prevention culture, ask your neighbours to join in

Figure 1.4 *Alternative fire safety notice*

If all our communication was so simple, we'd all be more effective. Yet all too often our communication is not like this but more like the alternative fire sign shown in Figure 1.4.

This addresses the same subject: it, too, is about fire. It's 'on message'. But it is not very clear and would probably lead to people frying in their rooms. It is a message about an issue, not communication designed to get a result in terms of a specific action. It invites 'education' and 'networking': things that involve reflection and discussion, and are open to interpretation.

This can occur when:

• an internal agenda is transmitted to the outside world – easily done if exhausted by getting it through the system;
• a policy or plan is transmitted as a 'message';
• everyone has a say and the message mentions every important issue;
• there is an attempt to educate rather than to motivate.

Campaign sequence

Roll your campaign out like an unfolding story

Many of the best campaigns are planned as a simple chronology of events. Often there are only one or two fixed dates and the rest is a chain of objectives that need to be reached, like climbing from one level to another or stepping from one stone to the next, with no firm way of predicting just when that will occur.

Plan *backwards* from the call to action. That should be either a fixed date (such as an event) or a date that can be estimated sufficiently well to have all the necessary communications, assets and capabilities in place when it arrives. The possible start date is then generated by adding together the critical time periods needed for each stage before the call to action opportunity.

Campaigns usually need to start with awareness. Awareness of the problem, preferably made more compelling by showing the victim.[4]

The campaign sequence[5] illustrated in Figure 1.5 shows how to plan using the basic formula of the fire notice: awareness > alignment > engagement > action. Each part needs to fit to the next like a jigsaw – the 'enemy' needs to be the particular one that fits with that victim, the solution really does have to solve the specific problem, and so on.

So in this classic communication path, the story begins when we see the problem – we see 'victims'. These might be human or physical, or animal or even plants. Fish dying from pollution, or a building damaged by acid rain, for example, or someone suffering torture. This is the awareness-building phase.

Next we see what or who is responsible, the 'enemy' or causal agent that is to blame – with no cause, a problem is not an issue. This is followed by a period of reinforcement by repetition or 'demonization': former UK Prime Minister Margaret Thatcher was an expert at this; she demonized striking miners, for example. This phase ought to last until the problem is established in the mind of our audience. By this time the public state of mind is one of concern.

If the 'bad news' just continues, the audience gets fed up and withdraws or switches off – the problem is just another tragedy. Concern with no solution will lead to withdrawal; with no constructive outlet it will create frustration, most probably towards the messenger. You can't hold people's emotional attention in that way for long.

If an 'answer' is supplied by revealing a solution, the campaign can progress because we get angry. It's no longer a tragedy but an *avoidable*

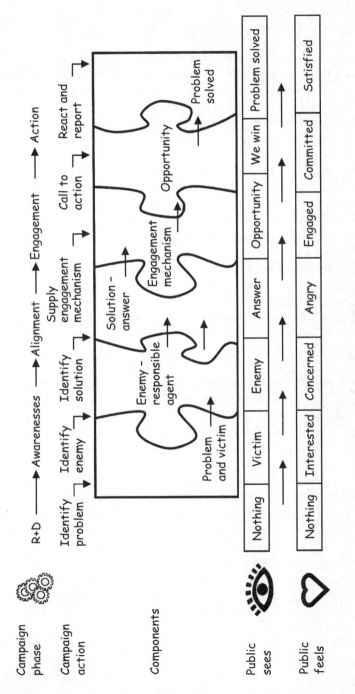

Figure 1.5 *Motivation sequence campaign model*

	Nothing	Victim	Enemy	Answer	Opportunity	We win	Problem solved
Public sees	Nothing	Victim	Enemy	Answer	Opportunity	We win	Problem solved
Public feels	Nothing	Interested	Concerned	Angry	Engaged	Committed	Satisfied

Campaign phase: R+D → Awarenesses → Alignment → Engagement → Action

Campaign action: Identify problem | Identify enemy | Identify solution | Supply engagement mechanism | Call to action | React and report

Components: Problem and victim | Enemy – responsible agent | Solution – answer | Engagement mechanism | Opportunity | Problem solved

7

Box 1.1 It doesn't have to be like this

In the 1990 European Election, the UK Green Party won a record-breaking percentage of the vote in the UK. Its election broadcast of that year was perhaps the Greens' only really great piece of communication.[6] A series of children appeared and did 'pieces to camera'. Each illustrated the simple point that the environment was polluted, and by implication, didn't need to be and wouldn't be under the Greens. 'This is a glass of water,' said one child. An adult hand poured in a white powder from above. 'Add some nitrates, and some fertilizer,' said the boy. 'Now it's tap water – and I have to drink it.' Each sequence ended with the caption: 'It doesn't have to be like this'. Victim = child, enemy = anonymous industry figure, solution = vote Green, opportunity = election.

Similarly, seen by hundreds of millions on TV, a woman who had given birth in a flood-bound tree was rescued, along with her baby, by a helicopter winchman in Mozambique in 2000. A tragedy was clearly averted – it didn't need to happen. The incident was compelling, motivating because change was possible.[7]

problem: 'it doesn't have to be like this'. In journalistic terms you have the elements of a scandal (Chapter 7).

Alignment gets everyone looking in the same direction, agreeing what the problem is, who suffers, who's to blame and what the solution is. Skip any of this part and the audience won't see what you are doing as relevant to them.

An unaligned audience can be misread as not 'caring' about the problem if they don't engage after a call to action. In contrast, very strong alignment will result in spontaneous attempts to take action. For example, in 1995 during French nuclear tests at Moruroa, protests were organized outside French embassies all over the world, but soon thousands of people were taking action against any sort of French target they could reach. Art students in genteel English Bournemouth painted a mushroom cloud into the background of a Renault poster advertisement, while from Holland a group of Dutchmen cycled off to conquer Mont Blanc.

For the campaign to call for action it must have a suitable engagement mechanism ready; and when the timing is just right, give a clear call. In a public advocacy campaign this might be a call to lobby a politician to pressure the government, visit a shop to lobby the manager about a brand or contact a company about corporate behaviour. For a fund-raising group, if the campaign is at all successful, this may be when it goes back to its supporters or stakeholders to explain the success, and ask for further help. If campaigners become too obsessed with the media, they may neglect engagement mechanisms, and the campaign generates publicity but no effective pressure.

In this way, the campaign rolls out like a story, told from the beginning, with each step revealing something new. It does *not* start by communicating the whole route – if so, there won't be any change because there won't be engagement, there will be no build-up and focus of pressure.

Unlike a play or a film, which progresses irrespective of audience interest, a campaign must not press on until the present stage is successfully completed. It has to gather support for each step – 'take people with you'. Sometimes this is a long, slow process. An over-ambitious project may try to take too many people along too far, too fast. An overcautious one may do the opposite.

Communicate by doing: Make events happen

Think in terms
of doing things

Events work as communication: they are the stuff of politics, the essential nutrients of news. Asked what was the most difficult thing about running the country, British Prime Minister Harold MacMillan famously replied, 'Events my dear boy, events.'

Creating events is the best way to be proactive and, as a rule, the winner in any persuasion struggle will be she or he who takes the initiative and sets the agenda. If your time is spent reacting to the events of others, you are unlikely to win. Pundits comment on change, campaigners make it happen.

Hope, injustice or anxiety may be the fuel but events should be the engine of campaigns. With luck, your campaign may register a big enough wave to blow your opponents off course. You stand most chance of doing that with a significant event, not a continuous effort.

The best campaigns communicate themselves because they involve doing, not advocacy. Deeds speak louder than words. We remember events and outcomes, not opinions. As one ex-director of Friends of the Earth[8] is fond of saying: 'Nobody remembers what David and Goliath were fighting about – everyone knows who won.' News is about doing: we don't come across a crowd and ask 'what are people thinking ?' We ask, 'What's happening?' Yet so many campaigners try to convey information, facts and even data, not actions and events.

Events help make media work far easier. I have often found myself trying to sell a story to a journalist and getting them interested, only to find that I can't answer the obvious question: 'So, what are you doing?' or 'What will happen?' because the campaign hadn't yet been planned as a series of events. Events can be news, your opinion isn't, and nor is an issue.

To make an event occur, we need to think in terms of doing things, activities that take us from point to point along a critical path. For people schooled in issues and facts, this can be a difficult transition, as they tend to produce arguments instead. Bear in mind the remark of political philosopher Macaulay: 'Argument is constructed in one way and government in entirely another' (and, he might now say, so is business). Your campaign planning should be based on events, not production of arguments.

Campaigning is not education

Education leads to confusion. Campaigning leads to action

Campaigning involves stimulating action, best achieved by narrowing the focus and eliminating distractions and reducing options, as in advertising (Figure 1.6). Typically, it starts (the left column) with a problem and moves a target audience through the stages of awareness (and alignment, not shown here), concern and so on, to action.

In contrast, education expands awareness of options and complexity (right-hand column). It typically takes a problem and shows that it is not so simple as you may have first thought.

The educational model is great for education but not for campaigning. It reaches understanding but not action. Using it to try and decide or stimulate action is likely to lead to confusion and frustration.

Attend meetings of university professors discussing a practicality to see this in practice. In one university I know, a discussion over what to do with a gap left by a 1940s World War II bomb, subsequently occupied by a car park, remained unresolved until the 1980s.

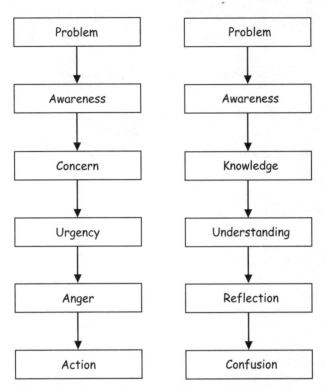

Figure 1.6 *Comparing a campaign model (left) with an education model (right)*

Contesting professors tend to make things complex, and dazzle each other with clever re-framing, find angles nobody had thought of, or make reference to additional bodies of information that must be taken into account. Perpetual questioning is how knowledge advances. The same discussion in a bank or a double-glazing company would probably be over in minutes. Questioning fundamentals and reflecting on things is not how business, politics or war advances.

On the other hand, listen to the professors discussing the meaning of life or public motivations, or what music is, and you will probably leave impressed, turning over new insights in your mind, maybe seeing your whole existence in a new way. Ask the bankers and the sales directors to hold the same discussion (or even 'what business is') and you will quickly find it bottoms out in cliché, leaden tautologies and the sort of wisdom you can find in a fortune cookie (Figure 1.7).

Beware campaigners who want to educate others to see the issue in the right way before accepting their support. To be driven by

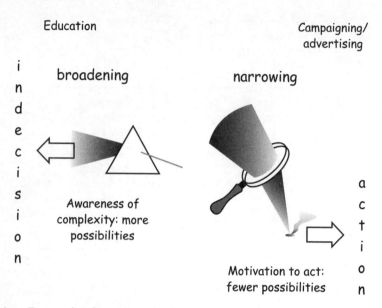

Note: Too much information stimulates interesting discussion but leads to indecision, while action is quicker when fewer and fewer possibilities are discussed but increasingly reinforced.

Figure 1.7 *Educating and campaigning work in opposing directions*

principle is an admirable thing. but to campaign by trying to make others adopt your principles is not likely to be effective. As Gerd Leipold has written: 'Campaign organizations have to be opportunistic, not in terms of their beliefs and values but in terms of reaching audiences.'[9]

CAMP CAT essential communication components

Essential communication components

Discussion of what will be an 'effective' communication can easily become circular. Try to avoid the pivotal word 'message'. If a discussion starts by asking: 'What messages do we want to use?', it is quite likely to lead to a one-way process rather than two-way communication.

For communication to have the right effect, at least seven key components need to work together: CAMP CAT.

- Channel – **how** the message gets there
- Action – **what** we want to happen (and what the audience is asked to do)
- Messenger – who **delivers** the message
- Programme – **why** we're doing it (essential to know this to assess effectiveness)
- Context – **where** and when the message arrives (including what else is going on)
- Audience – **who** we are communicating with
- Trigger – what will **motivate** the audience to act.

The actual message is, like a binary warhead: the call-to-action (effectively 'do this'), plus the trigger or motivator (effectively 'why you should'). They may be communicated by an example or argument, or visually, but not often as an instruction or admonishment.

The programme is internal. The audience and the action should be determined by the critical path of the campaign (Chapter 4). Qualitative research (Chapter 3) should determine the trigger, context, messenger and channel. Campaigners have to accept that they will not always be the best messenger: in the words of Ayerman and Jamison's classic study of Greenpeace, they need to be users of research: 'intelligencers'. There's no point going on the radio or TV to make your point for the sake of publicity: it's having an effect that counts.[10]

Some campaigners enjoy sending messages so much that they scarcely ever stop to try and find out what message was received by the assumed target audience. The messengers themselves can then become 'noise in the channel'. You see the campaigner on TV. You get the message – that she or he is campaigning – but what about? Quite probably, we don't remember.[11]

Timing (part of context) can alter the effect. Anti-smoking radio commercials were found to be more effective on Sunday mornings, when many listeners regretted the amount they had smoked the night before, than on Saturday evening; an equally relevant time when people were just about to go for a night out.[12]

Remember the chickens

In most campaigning, it's best to abide by the marketing dictum 'Start from where your audience is', and find a way to lead to the action you want people to take, or the conclusion you need them to reach, by starting from something they are already interested in, or concerned about. Campaigners who project their concerns and perspectives onto others – trying to 'sell', adding arguments and pointing to benefits, rather than researching audience perceptions, tend to fail.

Start from where your audience is

Research is essential to find out how others perceive your proposition, and how they talk about it. For example, not long ago, there was a successful aid agency development project in part of East Africa.[13] Following its success, the agency wanted to explain this idea to villagers elsewhere. So it sent a crew to make a short film explaining the project, and equipped a vehicle as a mobile cinema to show it.

The film was made and toured to the target villages. Afterwards, a survey found that what villagers most remembered about the film was 'the chickens'. The agency was puzzled: chickens had nothing to do with the project at all.

Eventually the agency looked at the film. A cut-away shot showed an agency Land Rover speeding past a hut, and as it did so, a large group of chickens flew across the screen. Unfortunately, in the target village area, chickens were a sign of wealth, and this therefore was by far the most interesting feature of the film. The villagers had been shown wealth on the scale of *Dynasty* or *Dallas*, only measured in chickens. Because it did not understand the language of the area (or the priorities of the villagers), the agency had no idea of what its film really showed.

I once helped win a debate before a live audience because our opponent – a wealthy English farmer – illustrated his case against planning controls by attacking suburbs, apparently unaware that the audience came mostly from the London suburbs.[14]

The exception to this rule is if you want to change minds. In this case it's important not to trigger familiar frames (Chapter 10). Contrary to popular assumption, good campaigning rarely involves changing minds. More often, it works through new applications of existing beliefs, perceptions and motivations.

Potential audiences may not be obvious. They may be 'sleeping', and you need to work out who they are and have them woken up in the appropriate manner. So 'starting from where the audience is' could mean for instance, in a campaign about genetically modified (GM) food, getting chefs to talk about food quality, taste and goodness, in order to engage with people interested in food, rather than trying to reach them by talking about agricultural policy via news coverage.

Framing

Choice of frame determines the outcome of a debate

All our communication, particularly condensed 'snapshots' such as news or advertising, is dominated by hidden mental short cuts that we use to make sense of the world, and of new information. These are 'frames', an idea attributed by the Frameworks Institute to Walter Lippman 'a grandfather of public affairs'.[15]

When confronted by something unknown we reach for established patterns (also called 'pattern matching') or experiences to say: 'Aha: it's a one-of-those.'

This largely unconscious and silent process is profoundly powerful because each frame comes with its logic, rationale and explanation as to who or what is responsible, and what a built-in solution looks like. The choice of frame determines the outcome of a debate because it sets the terms of resolution – how something will be decided.

Words can trigger frames, but most often and most powerfully, images trigger frames. Effective campaigns trigger the 'right' frame – the one that reinforces the impression or conclusion you want – and are planned to do so again, and again, and again.

The Institute gives examples from international relations to US elections and dental care at www.frameworksinstitute.org. Its Global Interdependence Study showed how Americans use the frames of neighbours and families to understand international affairs, with quite different results from Europeans, because it has different embedded assumptions. Americans also tend to see 'climate' as made by God or Nature, and hence the idea of human-made climate change (a frame) as inherently implausible, whereas reducing carbon dioxide (CO_2) pollution (a different frame) sounds more feasible to them.

The cognitive cultural models that are sparked by the frame allow us to forget certain information and to invent other details, because the frame is now in effect. For example, if people believe that kids are in trouble, they will be drawn to facts in a news story that reinforce this notion, and will disregard those that deny it. If the facts don't fit the frame, it's the facts that are rejected, not the frame...

If the messenger in a TV news story is a teacher, for example, the viewer is likely to assume that this is about education or about a problem that should be solved by schools. If the visuals show people sitting around doing little, the viewer may decide this is about laziness, regardless of what the narrator is saying about unemployment statistics among rural peasants in a certain country.

The Frameworks Institute

So who you put up as a spokesperson can easily trigger a particular frame, as may your organization's very presence.

Triggering the frame is more important than defining a particular message or argument. Once a frame is established – for example in an interview or other communication episode – attempts to argue against it are doomed.

Frame a 'new issue', carefully. Hair-shirt climate campaigners so successfully embedded the idea that climate change is a huge, intractable problem with painful 'solutions' that contrary information is discounted. So when American climatologist Stephen Schneider, and Swedish energy economist Christian Azar, showed the total cost of 'fixing' global warming meant only a two year delay in a fivefold increase in wealth over a hundred years, the response was negligible.[16] They were boxed in by conventional wisdom – their facts did not fit the frame.

Rhetoricians and therapists[17] trigger frames with words to redirect conversation. The outcome frame evaluates things in terms of outcomes. The ecology frame in terms of fit with what's going on around us. The evidence frame tests detail – how will we know when we have succeeded? The 'as if' frame supposes that something has happened, or not happened, in order to test how we feel about it.

Strategy

A pattern or plan that integrates an organization's major goals, policies and action sequences into a cohesive whole. It helps marshal and allocate an organization's resources into a unique and viable posture based on its relative internal competencies and shortcomings, anticipating changes in the environment and contingent moves by intelligent opponents.

James Brian Quinn[18]

Change the prevailing forces to win

Strategy means changing the prevailing forces so that you can win. Strategy is your route map for change: more than a conventional navigation, one that doesn't just traverse the terrain of society but reshapes it. Your communications strategy and engagement tactics need to take supporters on a journey, too.

Military planners quickly learned that the big choices, the 'first cut' among options, are those that determine much of what follows. Once a campaign starts, major changes are usually not an option. Prussian General Helmuth von Moltke said: 'A mistake in the original concentration of the armies is very difficult to rectify in the course of the campaign'.

Making strategy is followed by making plans, and that is followed by campaigning. Expect chaotic, unpredictable turns of events. The expression 'cry chaos and let loose the dogs of war' is well founded.

Rick Le Coyte, formerly a Greenpeace strategist, says:

If strategy involves having goals and plans to reach them, but remaining flexible about the extent that they are fixed and how exactly they are to be achieved, it means that the strategy, especially for a pressure group, is like an odyssey of ancient mythology. There is some big, over-riding purpose to the whole venture and on the way there are some tasks to perform. However, do not be surprised if the intervention of various gods, Cyclops and other mortals causes some surprises and distractions en route.

Strategies differ according to your view of how change can come about. Since 1988, hundreds of organizations have run climate campaigns, and though many focused on the United Nations Framework Convention on Climate Change (UNFCCC), they vary widely. For example:[19]

- Bottom-up city campaigns (for example, www.iclei.org) led by setting CO_2 emission limits
- Lobbying for stronger commitments under the UNFCCC – for example, the Kyoto Protocol and its ratification[20]
- Promoting solar power (various, including Greenpeace in Crete) instead of oil for electricity generation
- Energy efficiency campaigns – policy-, lifestyle-, product- or household-level
- Transport campaigns, such as for new US fuel efficiency standards (see, for example, www.cleancarcampaign.org)
- Opposing development of gas reserves (The Netherlands, Norway)
- Promoting 'zero-carbon' (or negative) products – for example, biofuels, wind[21] or solar energy
- Promoting tree planting or carbon-offsets (eg www.idealswork.com 'carbon-free' shipping, and www.futureforests.com)
- Opposing development of oil-sand deposits (Australia, Canada)
- Opposing the dumping of CO_2 into the ocean (see Coalition Against CO_2 Dumping, www.kahea.org) or underground reservoirs
- Opposing production of hydrofluorocarbons (HFCs) and other potent industrial greenhouse gases (e.g. www.mipiggs.org)
- Opposing new oil development on the grounds of 'carbon logic',[22] see for example the Greenpeace Atlantic Frontier campaign (e.g. www.gpuk.org/atlantic/) and the Arctic (http://archive. greenpeace.org/~climate/arctic99/indexb.html).

These are not tactical differences but incompatible strategic choices. Incompatible because they require so much effort and resources that any one organization could not run both at once, or because they will impede each other, or because they compete for attention, which, like goodwill and political capital, is in short and limited supply.

Similarly, when *New Scientist* magazine gave seven leading forest conservationists a notional US$10 million to spend on protecting tropical forests, they came up with wildly varying answers – ranging from changing the global economy to educating future leaders and short-term site protection.[23]

To achieve a significant objective it is often necessary to fight shorter-term tactical battles, sometimes with different targets. In the 1980s, for example, while at Friends of the Earth, I campaigned against habitat destruction by intensive farming in the UK countryside. The prevailing 'Dan Archer'[24] myth was, however, so strong that the media and public rejected the idea that farming could be to blame (rather than, say, building development). To overcome the power of the farming lobby we first had to weaken it. So we paused to run a campaign against straw-burning, because this was widely seen as unacceptable, and by achieving a ban we set a psychological precedent, and began the process of dismantling the public facade of industrial farming.

Aims and objectives

Objectives are steps towards the ultimate aim

Terms such as aims, objectives and goals are used in many ways. I find it most useful to refer to 'aims' as long-term end points.

Aims can be fulfilled, objectives achieved. Objectives are the waypoints that can be actually planned for.

To achieve any one objective, you will normally need to achieve intermediate or sub-objectives. All can be 'campaigns': the processes of campaign planning are almost the same, from the smallest to the largest scales.

At one extreme, once a mission-level campaign is achieved, the organization itself may be no longer needed;[25] at the other, individual campaign projects or 'pushes' may be just weeks or months.

The aim is what we ultimately want. The strategic objective of the campaign is the big difference we are planning to make in order to (help) achieve that. The objective of the current campaign is what we're trying to do now, or first. The project-level campaign objective is one of the things we need to do in order to get there.

Possible campaign aims and objectives

Table 1.2 *Possible campaign aims and objectives*

Aim	World peace	Protect ancient forests	Save the climate
Long-term campaign objective	Nuclear disarmament	Stop destructive logging	End use of fossil fuels
Current campaign objective	Nuclear test ban treaty	Stop illegal logging in the Amazon	Stop further development of reserves
Project-level objective	Sign up country X to support it	Stop illegal mahogany exports	Stop new oil exploration
Sub-objective (project level)	Mobilize supporters of Y key politicians	Stop such exports into the US	Stop exploration at the UK Atlantic frontier

CHAPTER 2

COMMUNICATING WITH HUMANS

Stories

When a person listens to a story, both sides of the brain are working. The left brain is processing the words, while the right brain is actively filling in the gaps. This is the reason why it is so important to read to children, to allow their brains to imagine the story, rather than using television and films for all their learning'[1]

**People
remember stories**

Campaign communications need to roll out before an audience like a story, from the beginning.

Figures 2.1 and 2.2 show two ways of giving the same information.

We can immediately see what's happening in Figure 2.1 because it's a story. Figure 2.2 addresses the same subject – wolves, minors and near-death experiences – but in a quite different, less memorable way.

Figure 2.1 *A story involving a wolf, a little girl and a near-death experience*

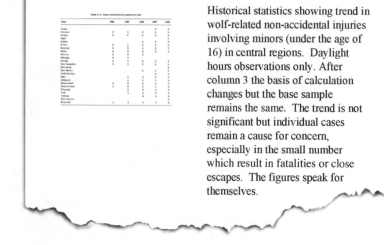

Report on Non Accidental Wolf Related Deaths

Historical statistics showing trend in wolf-related non-accidental injuries involving minors (under the age of 16) in central regions. Daylight hours observations only. After column 3 the basis of calculation changes but the base sample remains the same. The trend is not significant but individual cases remain a cause for concern, especially in the small number which result in fatalities or close escapes. The figures speak for themselves.

Figure 2.2 *Another way of displaying the information in Figure 2.1 – but less memorable*

Stories certainly pre-date writing, and probably art. Use stories wherever you can, because people remember them, and if possible use real people in stories, because we can identify with them. Save the academic report format for communicating with machines, or for professional seminars.

Stories are how we relate many important things in our lives, inside and outside organizations. They provide a free way for an idea to spread: as in urban myths, moral tales, or 'memes,[2] well beyond any paid-for communication.

Stories with human interest, based around a person, whether real or not, can move us from right-brain to left-brain communication, from facts and rationality to emotions and feelings. They take us there: 'it could be me'. Like pictures, stories don't need to argue, and you can't argue with them. Because *you* work out the meaning of a story yourself without having it thrust upon you, they can also more easily lead to that rare event, a change of mind. The deeper meaning can come to you long after you first hear a story.[3]

Using stories multiplies your options with the media: human stories are the stuff of feature pages, not news pages. That way you often get more space, and more readers, and your message is more likely to emerge intact, especially if it is embedded in the story structure.

Some say stories tap into fundamental psychology. Jan Stewart[4] points to four 'brain states': beta (awake and most active), alpha (awake but daydreaming), theta (almost asleep) and delta (sleeping). She says of stories:

> At the second attention level, as the brain searches for a deeper meaning … the right brain is often favoured as relationships and patterns are developed. Processing … is an unconscious process – that is, we are not aware that we are doing it. The second attention level is where the story is reformulated to have personal relevance. Sometimes the story stays at this level and causes unconscious behavioural change, or it can rise into the first attention level through an 'A-ha!' reaction.

> It is vital that the story, myth, legend or whatever is chosen, is selected carefully. Ideally, the story should be easily understood at the first attention level, but stimulate a search for a deeper meaning at some time in the future.

There are said to be a number of 'basic types' of story. These structures might help tell yours. Here are examples[5] applied to opera:

1   *Cinderella* – Unrecognized virtue recognized in the end. It's the same story as the Tortoise and the Hare or The Grasshopper and the Ant. Cinderella doesn't have to be a girl, nor does the story even have to be a love story. What is essential is that the good is at first despised, but recognized in the end. Further examples are *La Cenerentola*, *Cendrillon* and *The Magic Flute*

2   Achilles – The Fatal Flaw – this provides the groundwork for practically all classical tragedy, although it can be made into comedy, too – for example, *Samson et Dalila*, *Madame Butterfly*, *Falstaff*

3   Faust – The debt that must be paid, the fate that catches up with all of us sooner or later – other examples include La Bohème, *Rigoletto* and *La Traviata*

4   *Tristan and Isolde* – That standard triangular plot of two women and one man, or two men and one woman – also *The Marriage of Figaro*, *The Barber of Seville*, *Tosca* and *Lucia di Lammermoor*. *Carmen*, *L'elisir d'amore* (The Elixir of Love), *Pagliacci*, *Cavalleria Rusticana*

5   *Circe* – The spider and the fly – such as *Othello*, *Salome*

6   *Romeo and Juliet* – Boy meets girl, boy loses girl, boy either finds
     or does not find girl (it doesn't matter which) – *The Merry Widow*,
     L'italiana in Algeri, (The Italian Girl in Algiers), *La Bohème*, *Cosi
     fan tutte*, *Orpheus in the Underworld*
7   The gift taken away. This may take two forms: either the tragedy
     of the loss itself, or it may be about the search that follows the loss,
     such as in *Orfeo*, *Orpheus in the Underworld*, *Il Trovatore*
8   The hero who cannot be kept down. This is demonstrated in stories
     of perseverance and determination that result in either joy or
     destruction for the protagonist, as in *Turandot*, *Don Giovanni* and
     Aida.

The story often has a familiar pattern, 'grammar' or structure. Robert
McKee[6] identifies five stages: the inciting incident – which is the
primary cause of all that follows – the progressive complications, the
crisis, climax and resolution.

Campaigns are always full of stories but few campaigners have
made enough use of them, myself included. The biggest political
impact achieved by a pesticides campaign on which I worked with
Friends of the Earth resulted from the public response to crop-spraying
incidents, but not because we planned it that way. The campaign
presented policy arguments based on detailed desk research but we
were unexpectedly contacted by large numbers of the public with their
(often very distressing) stories. If we had appealed for the public to
come forward with their experiences from the start, and based the
campaign around those, we might have achieved more.[7]

Seeing is believing:
Communication preferences

*Of all of our inventions for mass communication, pictures still
speak the most universally understood language*

Walt Disney

If you need to
chose one
medium, then it
should be visual

Almost every campaign is best conducted
visually. Visuals give reach, accessibility and
impact; modern technology has created an
increasingly visual media world, and seeing,
generally, is believing, because most people
have an inbuilt preference for receiving
information visually.[8] For most people, a
picture is worth a thousand words.

When we understand, we often say: 'I see'.[9] Some people's inbuilt preference is for speech – 'we sang from the same hymn sheet' – or touch – 'we clicked'.

Visuals can reach our emotions, bypassing argument. They can reinforce or change views. Research any issue and you tend to find that people's views often track back to some event, recalled as a picture. 'It was when I saw X that I realized things were serious.'

A campaign should communicate in as many dimensions as possible, but if you needed to choose one medium, and without one-to-one knowledge of your intended audience, then it should be visuals. Once there's feel-touch-and-smell media, things may change.

Being visual often means escaping institutional preferences for text. Even if they accept the need for visual communication, many organizations communicate that with a written note!

However partial, TV is still enough of a window on the world for visuals to be used as a benchmark of truth. 'I just saw that – it's true.' All reporters tend to say 'we have seen' or 'we have been shown', when introducing an element of the story that they are positioning as true. If, on the other hand, a report begins with 'we are being told', then you are immediately suspicious that a 'claim' is being offered, something open to dispute and only a varnished version of the truth. The starting point is already some way below the 'truth'. So events that can be photographed or directly witnessed or participated in are important.

However, Gardner[10] argues that schools and culture focus on linguistic and logical mathematical intelligence (measured as intelligence quotient, IQ), to the detriment of other types of intelligence and ways of learning. Institutions tend to promote people who are good at text, speech or numbers, and their preferences tend to dominate internal communications. If this then dominates campaigns, however, the consequences can be disastrous.

Gardner proposes teaching based on multiple intelligences.[11] Campaigners could profitably do the same:[12]

- words (*linguistic intelligence* – offer speech or text);[13]
- numbers or logic (*logical-mathematical* – offer numbers, classifications);
- pictures (*visual-spatial* – offer visual aids, colour, art, visual organizers);
- music (*musical* – offer music or environmental sounds, or key points in a rhythm or melody);

- self-reflection (*intrapersonal* – self-discovery, self-analysis, setting your own goals – offer choices and evoke personal feelings or memories);
- a physical experience (*bodily-kinaesthetic* – 'hands-on' – involve the whole body);
- a social experience (*interpersonal* – for example a party or exhibition – offer peer or cross-age sharing or cooperative work);
- an experience in the natural world (*naturalist* – offer ways to relate the subject to environment or ecology).

Putting on a festival complete with opportunities for reading, logic workshops, model-making, quiet contemplation, and so on, may be impractical. Yet reliance on words and numbers is likely to be less effective than a more holistic approach.

Most successful NGO communication has hinged on visuals. Amnesty International's candle, symbolizing its role of bringing hope and light into dark places, the guide dog of Guide Dogs For The Blind, the Worldwide Fund for Nature's (WWF) 1961 launch with pictures of doomed rhinos and its panda logo, the Cousteau Foundation's ship Calypso, Greenpeace's actions at sea, the stylish advertisements of Médecins Sans Frontières (MSF),[14] invoking on the established dramatic format of the 'flying doctor'.

Face to face, our body language outweighs what we say. Although there are important cultural differences,[15] how we *look* generally says more than anything else. Psychologist Albert Mehrabian,[16] is said to have stated that when it comes to expressing feelings:[17]

- 55 per cent of the communication consists of body language;
- 38 per cent is through tone of voice;
- 7 per cent is through words.

Feelings are important in determining what we think of a person or proposal. Do we trust them? If not, we're unlikely to believe them. Emotional and psychological deficits easily overwhelm rational, scientific, economic or technical plus points. As the PR firm Burson-Marsteller states: 'You can't win an argument with someone who has more credibility than you do.'

Even if you don't bother to communicate in pictures, then visually dominated media, such as TV or even many newspapers, will do it for you and insert images themselves. These then dominate what is communicated and received – and may not be what you had hoped for. So make sure *your* pictures tell your story.

Engagement and agency:
What difference can I make?

The trouble with socialism is that it would take up too many evenings.

Oscar Wilde[18]

Campaign targets need to be big enough to matter and small enough to take on

---

Many campaigns fail because they simply never gather enough support. Campaigning is a 'follow me' or 'come with us' exercise. It invites others to give up some of their time, and make your agenda theirs. So why should anyone go out of their way to support or join your campaign?

Variations in campaign support are not just due to some people being better at it than others, or some causes being inherently 'sexier' or easier. If you hear a campaigner say that, it is likely that they haven't done the necessary design work to attract support.

In assessing a campaign proposition we all ask 'is it worth it?' We mostly assess the proposition intuitively: 'This is for me', or not.

The cause
Do we care about the cause? Is the campaign needed? (If the audience is already aligned, the answer should be 'yes'.)

The benefit
What will the results be if the campaign succeeds – generally or personally? Does it make a worthwhile difference? What agency does it give me: how does it increase my influence over the world around me? Does it make existing mechanisms work better, or provide new ones ?

The means
Are they attractive – or do they put me off?

The prospects
Does it stand a chance of success?

Three things – the objectives, resources and activities – 'triangulate' a campaign's perceived feasibility. If they are seen to match, the campaign can look attractive, workable and credible. If they do not, the campaign will be rejected, no matter how good the cause.

Figure 2.3 *The feasibility triangle*

The 'feasibility triangle' can be used to assess a campaign, project or an organization.

The 'feasibility triangle' is like a three-legged stool – if the legs don't match in length, it will topple over.

A lack of support may be put down to 'the fact that people don't care', or the idea that 'they are ignorant of the facts'. The press can take the rationalization a step further and call it 'compassion fatigue' or announce that something is 'no longer an issue – people don't care'. Just as likely, the project doesn't look credible.

Common feasibility problems
The objective is too big
The naive NGO failure, where the ultimate aim rather than an achievable objective is stated. For example, the Lower Snoring Campaign to Change World Trade (resources: four people and a dog). Many small groups 'taking on' big issues stay small and marginal, talking about change rather than achieving it.

Objectives too small
1990s research on the world views of UK Greenpeace supporters and others like them revealed a motivational 'black hole' that disconnected campaigns from potential support. People sympathetic to environmental issues often did not find them at all engaging.

Too small to be a public issue, e.g. recycling

Target size – campaign design must make 'problems' and 'solutions' this size to be motivating

Too big to change – for the UN, Greenpeace etc.

No

Size

Note: Campaign targets presented to individuals need to be bite-sized so that they are worthwhile and achievable

Figure 2.4 *The too-big-too-small problem*

Recycling was among a host of 'green' activities too small to be worth discussing in public: normal to do but not worth remarking upon. Others, such as global warming, were 'too large' for individuals to engage with: 'environment for environmentalists'. The answer to this is to break down big problems into smaller parts so that, for example, when Greenpeace and its supporters acted together, small efforts could add up to big results.[19]

Objective not visible
Public bodies often suffer from this when they fail to make the objective explicit, and simply announce activities or resources, leaving the audience to 'patch in' an assumed objective from rumour or what they may have heard or seen on TV. Frequently, the assumed objective is huge.

Too much time spent on the objective
Where campaigning is not the main activity of a voluntary organization, there is often too much focus on defining the objective, and too little on putting together activities and resources.

Figure 2.5 *Some of the doubts that can be raised if the objectives, activities and resources do not seem to fit*

Being vague

Companies tend to succumb to waffle outside their core business areas.

Poorly defined goals on 'difficult' issues sound good in a senior management team meeting, but look flimsy once they reach the annual report, and fall apart completely under public questioning.

Inadequate activities

Established NGOs can become too cautious to campaign effectively; too bureaucratic, with internal stakeholders defending their departmental interests or career paths, to take any serious risks. They may believe their own propaganda about being 'quietly effective' – if true, then of course there will be no need to campaign. Such groups set good objectives and have the resources, but they don't deploy them, don't invest in campaign tools, and don't involve top staff in campaigning.

Levels of engagement

Four stages
of 'doing'

Engagement often seems to fit a four-stage pattern:[20] Do nothing; do one thing; systematic change; and lastly, wholesale change.

Stage 1: Do nothing

People may not have heard of the problem, what causes it, or the solution. Or it may not be significant or interesting to them. There may be no trigger. It might be that they have yet to see it in the right context, or hear it from the right messenger.

Perhaps you need to use a different channel. If you are trying to move people from Stage 1 to Stage 2, then try using the CAMP CAT tool (see p12).

Because of circumstance or psychology, belief systems, social pressures or culture, some people will never be promoted from Stage 1.

Stage 2: Do one thing

Here we identify one thing we have done 'to make a difference'. People have bought the cause but not gone very far with it. In the UK, and probably many other countries, a large number of people are at this stage in relation to say, global environmental problems: 'I buy ozone-friendly products'. Media coverage is usually enough to recruit people to Stage 2.

With established issues, these are usually the best prospects to be 'promoted' to take more action, as they have already accepted that there is a problem/solution.

Campaigners sometimes dismiss just doing one thing as 'token', but this is a mistake. Token efforts are not a sign that people don't care: it's a sign that they do. It's a rational use of time and effort: a form of bet-hedging. By doing at least something, individuals make a small contribution to what they hope is a bigger effort.

Table 2.1 *Levels of personal engagement*

Stage	What people say
Do nothing	'I don't need to do anything'
One thing	'This is what I do about it'
Systematic	'I do a, b and c. I try to do d and e... I would like to do more but...'
Wholesale	'I have changed my life because of it'

Token efforts may also be debris from some tidal wave of public concern that once swept society. Although high, dry and isolated, token gestures remind society that the problem could come again, and may be touchstones for igniting popular perception and promoting an issue to the forefront of consciousness.

Token gestures provide handles, short cuts and communication footholds, sometimes becoming icons; symbols with more than their literal meaning.

A single action may also be a response to social pressure to conform, for example around a campaign issue that has become normalized.

Stage 3: Systematic engagement

For most of us, big life changes mean working alongside others doing the same thing. This is the beauty of campaigns: they enable people to act together. They provide examples, proofs that things work, a socially acceptable or impressive explanation for taking action, and the ways, means and support to 'step out of line' without undue costs.

People at this stage frequently feel that they are not doing enough, externalize and become advocates, and consciously search for the campaign in the media. As such, they are not indicative of interest in the cause in general, but will make good use of training opportunities or campaign resources.

Stage 4: Wholesale life change

Here people change their lives completely. They might:

- give up a job to join a campaign group full-time;
- embark on a new career;
- stop campaigning and start a business to achieve the same ends;
- adopt an 'alternative' lifestyle, such as becoming a traveller or building an 'eco-home'.[21]

I met one Dutch campaigner with a conviction that nuclear power posed a serious threat to future generations. Nothing unusual in that, except that he was a rather long-term thinker. He had formed this view at school, then enrolled at university and undertaken a degree in nuclear physics, just so he could understand the industry and find ways to convince politicians that it needed to be shut down.

Another colleague was a former chief inspector of police at Scotland Yard in London: for him, coming to Greenpeace meant that he could 'do something really useful' (which had been his original

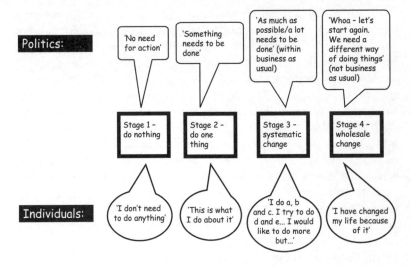

Figure 2.6 *Four-stage engagement*

motivation to join the Met), though it also meant reducing his salary by more than half.

Political institutions can show the same four-stage engagement with a campaign issue.

Engagement and shopping

Communicating with consumers

Campaigners use engagement mechanisms lifted more or less unaltered from centuries-old political campaigning: tracts, leaflets and their cyber-equivalents, polemics and speeches. This puts them at a disadvantage in a consumer context.

Discover how to best communicate in specific environments by talking to those in the business: practitioners, suppliers and trade journalists – check for them in your supporter base. They may well save you time, money and effort with free advice.

The engagement mechanism needs to match the timescale and dynamic of the process being targeted. A sustainable timber campaign might ask people to exercise buying power when moving home, a time when they may buy furniture or timber. It also needs to target the key actors – in most house-buying the critical decisions are mostly made by women, not men, for instance.

Each transaction has its own culture. In some cases it may be better to enlist the shop assistants rather than the consumers – purchases of white goods, for example, are often decided by a conversation with a sales person or engineer, who is treated as an expert.

Although shoppers may complain about supermarkets, they will be reluctant to change established habits. Context means getting both the time and place right. Potential supporters may be in supermarkets, making decisions about what products to buy – two essential factors – but that's not necessarily enough. Shoppers may be too busy. Parents of young children may be easier to reach with the same information while they are waiting to pick up the youngsters from school. Or perhaps you should go via their parents, who may have more time. Older shoppers might welcome a chat, especially if offered a cup of tea, as well. Young singles shopping in the evening might welcome an interview as a chance to meet others.

In 2000, Greenpeace UK adapted the technique known as 'accompanied shopping', in which a researcher shops with a consumer, for a genetically modified (GM) food campaign. Campaign director Jane Wildblood explains how it worked:

> Greenpeace trained a network of volunteers and provided them with a kit to run events at supermarkets, to inform and engage shoppers. They set up information points outside supermarkets on Saturdays over a period of months. These had an eye-catching backdrop in red (the big, vegetable-head logo of the campaign) and leaflets to take away, as well as knowledgeable people to talk to. They used the interaction outside the supermarket (that is, not interfering with the actual shopping) to recruit the really interested for 'supermarket tours giving information on GM and organic food, promoted as the safe solution to GM and other concerns'.

> These tours were scheduled throughout the day with the full backing of the supermarket managers (mostly![22]). This avoided haranguing or interfering with people when it would irritate them, but enabled high-quality engagement and visibility. The feedback mechanism was via a send-back coupon on the basic leaflet. These people were then entered on a database and sent further information and invitations to participate in campaign activity. At later stages, we gave people at supermarket entrances tear-off coupons to send into the local shop manager, MP and so on. Later still, a shopper's guide was created on the website…

Perception of change and significance

Choosing metrics to suit your campaign

Perception of change and significance often drives decision-making. *Relative* change may be the most effective thing to communicate – a rate of increase or decrease, for example. Or you may want to focus only on recruits or losses, not total amounts.

To win media attention, changes usually need to be abrupt and discontinuous. This can be achieved by using the right scale of focus, and looking for thresholds or discrete consequences of a trend.

Because of the dominance of economists and accountants in institutions, it's often said that 'what counts is what's measured'. Campaigners who supply some numbers will find it easier to get their case talked about. However, careless quantification can easily anchor debate in the wrong place.

A list of points or reasons is usually helpful, but reliance on statistics is not advisable. Though the press love them, the public generally does not trust statistics, at least in the UK.

He or she who chooses the measure, often determines the conclusion. 'Horse race' polls show which political candidate is ahead: a favourite news-making device of politicians and political commentators,[23] which also imply that things outside the focus can be disregarded.

The context affects whether something looks big or small, effective or ineffective. The old UK Central Electricity Generating Board used a demonstration of renewable energy to make it look small.[24] A solar panel that could illuminate one light bulb was placed outside a vast nuclear power station. On a bright day the bulb lit. The information panel explained words to the effect that: 'One day solar energy may have advanced to the point that we can use it to supply our energy needs. That day has not yet arrived, and for secure supplies of electricity, nuclear power is an essential part of a mix of reliable and proven energy sources.'

Altering perception of how to judge change may be the object of a campaign itself. Redefining progress[25] promotes a genuine progress indicator[26] in place of gross domestic product, because the latter fails to measure things such as depletion of nature, natural capital and ecological services. Here the gap between the two indicators may be the important thing to communicate.

Figure 2.7 *Gross production vs genuine progress, 1950 to 1999*

Bridging the engagement gap

Annual income twenty pounds, annual expenditure nineteen nineteen six, result happiness. Annual income twenty pounds, annual expenditure twenty pounds ought and six, result misery.
Mr Micawber, in Charles Dickens' David Copperfield[27]

_____
Making the
impossible
happen
_____

A campaign needs to be able to honestly say, and better, show, that 'without you, we will fail: with you we can succeed'. Support has to be needed.

Pick objectives you think are just possible with a reasonable degree of public engagement. Others will tend to view them as just about impossible. Engage enough support and you can bridge the gap and make the impossible possible. When a campaign bridges the gap, it succeeds. The longer the bridge, the more successful the campaign is seen to be.

This is what makes a campaign different from everyday life. It can make campaigning exciting, inspiring and motivating: the magic that helps to change the established order of things.

Without the gap, there's no need for anyone to support your campaign by joining in. It may amuse or please but it will not engage. People will not feel needed.

In campaigning, anything better than business as usual is achievement. It is the political equivalent of Mr Micawber's sixpence – result: happiness. Anything below is within expectations – result: misery. A campaigning organization is not necessarily expected to deliver huge change, but to change more than business as usual can. Normal politics is the art of the possible. Campaigning is the art of the impossible.

Alignment

Effective speakers begin by getting the attention of a group, and reminding everyone why they are there.

'Are you sitting comfortably? Then we'll begin'

Generations of British children were introduced to radio stories by the BBC[28] with the question 'Are you sitting comfortably? Then we'll begin'. The injunction to 'sit comfortably and listen', helps secure audience attention (awareness) by asking a question. It focuses your mind on your body and stops you thinking about whatever you were doing or were focused on before, and it aligns the audience – concerned with the same task. But the speaker doesn't need to explain all that. Indeed if she did, then it wouldn't work – you might even end up thinking about communications processes! Nor does the campaign need to explain it but the process still has to be followed.

In the process of trying to align an audience, use as few arguments as possible. Arguments come imprinted with age-old political meaning. Words are a fast lane to prejudices and preconceived ideas. Pictures are more reliable – they exist much more in the mind of the beholder, while words tend to remain the property of the source.

The more arguments you use, the more reasons you are giving that someone can disagree with. Resist the temptation to embellish a case with extra arguments: people only need one reason to disengage, adding arguments is likely to dilute strong ones with weaker ones while creating a wider range of options for disagreement. For alignment in the campaign sequence see Chapter 1 (problem–solution).

Human motivations

_____

Motivations and
appropriate
engagement
mechanisms
differ

_____

For campaigns about 'public goods' and
social causes, more useful than knowing
what 'social class' people are in (A, B, C, D,
E and so on) or what people buy and where
they live (see acorn-type databases, for
example, at www.upmystreet.com), it's
useful to understand motivation and
underlying human needs. Campaigns are,
after all, about persuasion and motivation,
not sales, taxes or profits.

One of the best-researched tools for this[29] is the Hierarchy of
Needs, coined by psychologist Abraham Maslow in 1962 .

Maslow proposed that people move through life stages, meeting
different needs at each stage. These needs affect how we see any issue
or treat any opportunity: they are overarching influences on our
behaviour, much deeper and more powerful than the whimsical notion
of an 'opinion'.

In the security- or sustenance-driven stages we need to meet the
needs of: safety, security and comfort, then belonging, love and
acceptance. If these needs are fully met, we may move on to meet the
needs of the esteem-driven or 'outer-directed' phase: here we want to
meet the needs for the esteem of others, recognition and approval,
then self-esteem and achievement. Once these are met, we can move
into the 'inner-directed' stage, where the needs to be met are: aesthetic,

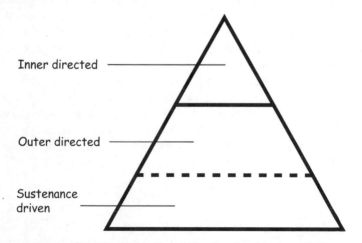

Figure 2.8 *The Hierarchy of Needs, after Maslow, 1962*

cognitive such as beauty, symmetry, to know, to understand and explore, and ultimately 'self-actualization' or 'meta-needs derived from integration and transcendence of all needs'.

Pat Dade, whose company Cultural Dynamics (www.cultdyn.co.uk) runs a rolling survey representative of the whole UK population, calls the three groups Settlers (security-driven), Prospectors (esteem-driven) and Pioneers (outer-directed). Dade's studies have tracked changes in the proportions of these groups in the UK and elsewhere over several decades, with significant implications for issues and politics (see Chapter 11). They also plot dozens of cultural attributes against the attitudes of the groups, producing a rich 'motivational landscape' (called value modes – see below). This shows, for example, that people with very different motivations may agree on the importance of one or another topic, but violently disagree about its relationship to other attributes.

Pioneers, Prospectors and Settlers react very differently to campaigns, campaign propositions and campaign mechanisms. To be 'sure' of gaining support across groups, in a mixed audience, or at least of being understood, campaigners need to communicate differently for each group (see 'ready reckoner', p43). To recruit support from each group, campaigners need to accept that motivations and appropriate engagement mechanisms differ.

Here are the 2002 top-line thumbnail sketches of the different groups as penned by Cultural Dynamics:[30]

- Pioneers – Eclectics: Self-starting, self-sustaining and self-contained, these highly individual, often solitary, people pursue their own higher purposes in life. They have a mature, down-to-earth acceptance of 'the way things are' but continually probe and refine their understanding of who they are and where they are going. They look inwards, not outwards. They are disinterested in social status, image and material acquisitions. Furthermore, they have a passion for acquiring a holistic, aesthetic perspective on life. They are endlessly inquisitive about the meaning of everything. They simply need to 'know' for the sake of 'knowing'
- Pioneers – Seekers. These aware, energetic and empathetic people continually develop an optimistic yet highly sophisticated understanding of themselves, others and the environments they share. Confident in, and invigorated by, this ongoing personal growth, they explore and extend the boundaries of their knowledge and experience with a natural enthusiasm. Their comfort with the self-sufficient way in which they think and act reflects an intuitive

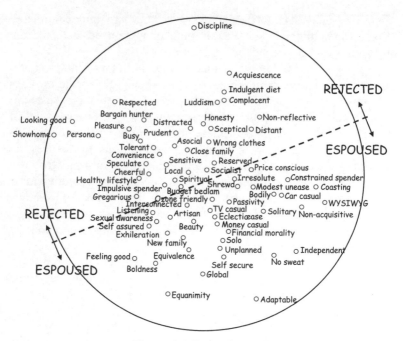

Figure 2.9 *Inner-directed*

understanding of the spiritual connectedness that exists among people. They therefore tend to be perceived as socially bold yet non-judgemental and wise

- Prospectors – Players: Life is a game to be played to the max – and to win – 'no surrender', 'whatever it takes', 'just do it'. Looking and feeling good, these socially skilled people both attract attention and offer it. Listening to others is a short cut to winning – because then they don't have to make the same mistakes. This flexible, instrumental morality enables them to question rules, push boundaries and switch allegiances with seamless ease. Shifting patterns in friendship and finance may follow in the wake of their energy and charm, but they thrive in the ambiguity and uncertainty that can paralyse others

- Prospectors – Optimists. Positive and ambitious, these are the tentative risk-takers. They are keen to chase the better things in life, but may be inconsistent in going about it. They hover between following safe, well-defined routes to success and more speculative, loosely defined ones. As a result, their optimism is supported by attempts at justifying their actions before they take them – typically by following the example of successful people that went before.

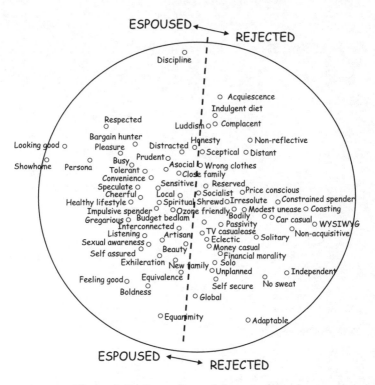

Figure 2.10 *Outer-directed (esteem driven)*

Similarly, with a basic need to gain respect and status through those around them, they may take risks but they are unlikely to engage in morally suspect ventures

- Settlers – Rationals. These people aim to enjoy life in a relaxed and organized way. The approval and respect of others, particularly close friends and family, are essential to achieving this. They need to do 'the right thing' – honesty and integrity are important to them. Because of their need for a calm and ordered life, they can be quite pedantic in interpreting and policing social rules in their dealings with others. Their real-world aspirations are tempered by a need for financial security, and a genuine need for material 'stuff'

- Settlers – Roots. In a world of constant, unpredictable change, these reserved, independent individuals adhere to the tried and tested. As responsible guardians of heritage for future generations, they take comfort from accepted rules yet question shifting pockets of 'authority'. However, this societal duty is but a symptom of their fundamental desire to provide identity, safety and certainty for

41

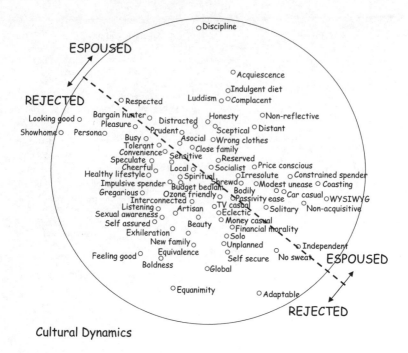

Cultural Dynamics

Figure 2.11 *Sustenance-driven*

themselves and others like them. Rules and routines simply make the struggle of daily life easier to manage.

Using Maslow-based value modes in campaign communications

Table 2.2 is a rule-of-thumb ready-reckoner to how value modes mapping and insights may help in constructing campaign propositions and running campaigns. To do so most effectively, campaigners should run issues across the map of attributes developed by Cultural Dynamics, and/or survey intended audiences to check their segmentation based on motivation.

Table 2.2 *A ready-reckoner for using Maslow-based value modes in campaign communications*

Segment of population	Dominant motivation	Action mode	Desire	Why they save dolphins in Seatown	I want a brand to …
Inner directed	Exploration	Do it yourself	Better questions	I feel I could be one myself – and for their own worth	Bring new possibilities
Outer directed	Status and esteem of others	Organize	Answers	Good for the town's image and economy (and my house price)	Make me look good
Security driven	Being safe and belonging	'Someone should do something about it'	Safeguard against external threat	So long as the dolphins keep coming back, Seatown will be Seatown	Make me secure

Segment of population	I like to meet	I connect through	I like to be associated with	I most respond to threats to	I
Inner directed	New, challenging and intriguing people	My own networks	Good causes that put my values into practice	Visions and causes	Am me
Outer directed	Desirable and important people	Big brands, systems and organizations	Success	What I've worked for	Am successful
Security driven	People like me and people I know	Club and family	Tradition	My way of life	Know my place

Chapter 3

CAMPAIGN RESEARCH AND DEVELOPMENT

Issue mapping

Unlocking hidden knowledge

Issue mapping helps define the ambition, the objective (Chapter 4), who the actors are and what interests are at stake. It can:

- illuminate the landscape of the issue;
- identify players, processes, forces and connections;
- show what you know and reveal what you do not know;
- stimulate thinking about how and where to intervene with a strategy.

Issue mapping puts information out on the table – or most often up on a flip chart. It pools and shares knowledge. It acknowledges that everyone will have something to contribute, enables people to be heard, and uncovers absences and gaps in intelligence. It begins to align people internally and can unlock hidden knowledge in your organization. Initially, at least, it is also quick, dirty and cheap. Mapping may show new strategy options, potential allies or points of influence.

To begin, look at all the main processes and attitudes you have identified and then simply ask for each, 'how?' or 'why?' Do we know how or why these decisions are made? Do we understand the reason country X or politician B or civil servant Z takes the view that they do – or seem to? If something is a 'closed book' to us, then have we tried to open it? Would a new technique help? If we cannot do it, is there someone who can? Try writing up issues, causes, effects, resources, needs or processes, just to get discussion flowing.

Box 3.1 THORP issue map

GOVERNMENT: THE DECISION MAKING SYSTEM
THE THORP PROBLEM

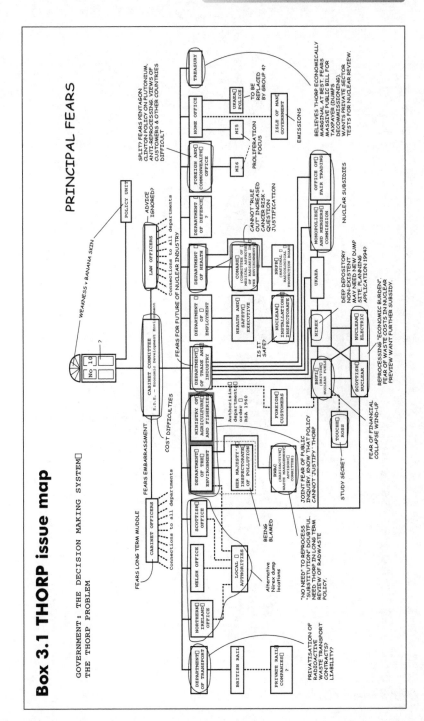

PRINCIPAL FEARS

Box 3.2 WWF homes issue map

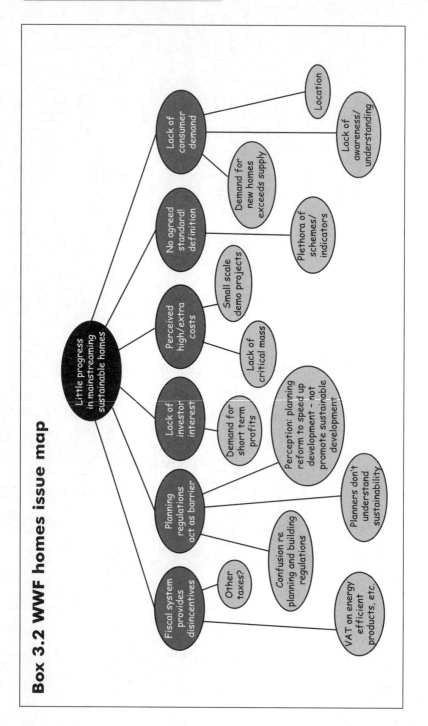

You can also map problems and solutions, and weigh up factors with force field analysis (Chapter 4). Following lines of industrial production or political accountability can be useful.

You can then identify possible areas of campaign intervention – the beginning of strategy-making – and later take one of these options, focus on a single link, and work out what would be needed to affect that (which is the critical path).

The relevant or most useful issue map will vary from topic to topic. In the case of the campaign against the opening of the Sellafield Thermal Oxide Reprocessing Plant (THORP), Greenpeace put a huge amount of effort into understanding the decision-making process (Box 3.1).

WWF-UK's 'Sustainable Homes Initiative' seeking one million sustainable houses in the UK, focused on characterizing the problem (See Box 3.2).[1] Paul King of WWF says:

> It is important to focus on a) what is the central problem or threat you are seeking to overcome and b) what are the root causes of this problem? By stating the central problem clearly you can ask the people interested in solving it, 'why does this problem exist?' In this way it is possible to break the central problem down, bit by bit, and to map all the sub-problems that contribute to it. These 'sub-problems' can then be further broken down in the same way, until you reach the root causes...

It is then relatively simple to turn each problem into a solution or 'desired future state' – that is, turning each negative into a positive. This will create your 'objectives tree'.

Gathering intelligence

Get to know the unknown

To help create and test a plan, gather intelligence about the players and forces at work – how change works:

- Who takes which decision?
- Who influences them?
- What formal and informal decision-making processes are at work?
- Who owns whom?
- Who owes whom what?
- Who are enemies and allies?
- How has change happened before?
- How it all works – what the main processes are
- Which are the critical steps?
- Where the players get their information from
- Networks, associations and get-togethers
- Fears and concerns – what worries them?

Good sources may include:

- academic studies;
- websites and publications (it is amazing how few people actually read publicly available information they profess to be interested in);
- your own experiences and those of colleagues;
- professional or trade networks you have connections with;
- supporters;
- people who work in the target institution or business;
- rival suppliers and customers of a target company;
- trade journalists or consultants (commission them to do a project, 'brain dump' or workshop);
- politicians with a track record in the area concerned;
- gossip and loose talk (not to mention the old standbys of journalists, such as dustbins[2]) – few organizations resist the temptation to treat a particular bar or café as the alternative canteen, and many people talk more freely about the office once they are outside it;
- staff at a former advertising or PR company that has lost the account;
- relevant conferences, exhibitions and meetings (a good reason to accept invitations to talk at the conferences of the 'opposition').

One short cut to finding Achille's heels, metaphorical jugulars and other important pinch points, is to talk to people who have lived with the target process for a long time. They are unlikely to be able to tell you how to run a campaign (though they may be very opinionated) but will often tell you something of significance that will give you an idea of how to do it. You need not ask for 'secrets', only for what in their world 'everybody knows already': how things work, and what changes them. Parting words[3] often say most: 'Of course, it's impossible, but what would really make a difference is...'

Rely on research: once battle lines are drawn it is tempting not to venture outside even to test the basic assumptions. An easy error to make is to assume that finding the 'right answer' means choosing between known options rather than findings new things out. The Antarctic policy example (Box 3.3) shows how wrong this can be: nobody realized there was, in effect, no political oversight.

This is probably what US Secretary of State for Defense at the time, Donald Rumsfeld meant to say when he famously said:

There are known knowns. These are things we know that we know. There are known unknowns. That is to say, there are things we know we don't know.
But, there are also unknown unknowns. These are things we don't know we don't know.

If the problem can be overcome with existing practices you do not need to campaign. So campaigns ought to innovate. As a result, expect to have to uncover something unknown, to find the best strategy.

The costliest and most arrogant form of research is to launch a campaign without doing any – that way you are allowing your prejudices free rein at the cost of your supporters.

Listen carefully to others: what leads people to take the actions they do? In constructing a campaign about chemicals, I once asked a businessman who was a major supplier to the industry what he thought the main concerns of his client companies would be. What would they see as a real threat? I had a vague idea that it might be things like government regulations or consumer behaviour. I was surprised when he said: 'Graduates – if they lose the supply of new graduates, then their business will fail.' Not knowing the sector, I failed to realize their business depended on the ability to innovate, and that relied on attracting and retaining bright young graduates. Suddenly we were no longer thinking of strategies involving politicians or voters or consumers, but chemistry students.

Beware of preconceptions. These can stop us really listening. Think how wrong people can be about your work and consider how wrong you probably are about theirs.

Common misconceptions include:

- Companies only ever do things for profit. Yes, generally, but I have come across companies that take environmental or social actions because they think it is morally the right thing to do (mostly privately owned companies), or because of reputation, or in the (often small) hope of long-term advantage. All 'against' the interests of the next results

- Politicians only do things for votes. Sometimes not; they may act because of deeply held beliefs; or internal party deals or to trade favours, or for ego, friendship or a place in the history books. The nearer to an election, and the smaller the majority, the more voter-sensitive they tend to become, unless they are not standing again, in which case they may back even electorally suicidal campaign propositions

- The government has 'a view'. It may express a single view, but inside most governments there are a number of often conflicting opinions on the same subject. Much of the time these are suppressed by the system and only fine nuances of difference can be seen from outside, but at times they are in free flux as policies are thought out or renewed, and those are the opportunities to lobby effectively from the inside.

Using issue maps

Choose an area to focus on

Figure 3.1 is an issue map for climate change. It's not in any way definitive – a lot of problems and opportunities are not shown. It illustrates the range of possible interventions, of which a dozen are shown. In reality, there are many more.

Some campaigns, such as the Multisectoral Initiative on Potent Industrial Greenhouse Gases (MIPIGG) and Future Forests, can be distinguished by the gases they are concerned with. Most are distinguished by how they engage with psychology and politics.

The Global Commons Institute punts its favoured *solution*, a single tool for terms of negotiation ('Contraction and Convergence') between nations. This, with WWF, Greenpeace and FoE lobbying, is designed

Box 3.3 Antarctica

In the early 1990s, UK environment groups were struggling to convince the UK government to change its policy over Antarctica. Two unknowns were: why did Britain have the policy it did, and why was that policy apparently immune to public opinion?[4]

Campaigners had promoted a World Park, rather than minerals development, since the 1970s. In the 1980s WWF, Greenpeace and the Cousteau Foundation persuaded many governments to support non-development of Antarctica, but the UK remained a hold-out. It was assumed that this simply reflected ministerial views.

Research at the Public Records Office confirmed what Prime Minister Mrs Thatcher had inadvertently hinted at during the Falklands War – that Britain wanted the minerals of Antarctica. Papers dating from the time of Winston Churchill showed prime-ministerial interest in hopes of gold, uranium and especially oil, and that exploration was deliberately disguised as purely 'scientific' study.

Also significantly, enquiries among diplomats revealed that one Foreign Office official, Dr John Heap, had maintained a firm grip on key aspects of Antarctic policy and its international presentation for decades, yet he was not a diplomat himself. One well-informed journalist said later: 'The situation with John Heap was remarkable – he was a law unto himself entirely'. In other words, it seemed Dr Heap was negotiating for the UK and effectively making policy, rather than Ministers making it.

Having discovered the underlying minerals rationale and the pivotal role of Dr Heap, NGOs were able to better target lobbying of ministers who, contrary to NGO assumptions, had not, in fact, given the issue much attention. When Margaret Thatcher resigned in 1990, Environment Minister Michael Heseltine was soon convinced to quickly reverse policy and back a 50-year mining moratorium.

to oil the wheels of the climate convention. The two World Resources Institute (WRI) initiatives operate outside the framework of the convention or its Kyoto Protocol – while Families Against Bush (FAB) Climate was a direct attempt to mobilize corporate pressure for the protocol.

Figure 3.1 *Issue map for climate change with interventions*

Note: See p207 for notes on Figure 3.1

The WRI corporate campaigns, like Greenpeace's campaigns for solar power, wind or wave energy, seek to drive progress *using* solutions. The impacts-related campaign of Clean-Air Cool-Planet is, in contrast, an awareness-raising, problem-driving strategy.

Organizations often try more than one intervention, sometimes at the same time. If you do, then be clear about which is the main 'bet' on which you wager most of your chances, resources and opportunities. The rest have to be tactical plays and 'hedges', not just in case the bet doesn't pay off, but so you are positioned for the next phase, cover exposed flanks or maintain essential contacts or roles that may be needed in the endgame.

A well-known campaign example based on mapping the *process* of an industry is the 'back-end strategy' pursued by Greenpeace and others against nuclear power. Opposition to nuclear power arises as much from its role in nuclear proliferation (creating waste from which bomb-making plutonium can be produced) as from the radiation dangers of reactors and waste. 'Reprocessing' was started in order to obtain plutonium to make bombs.

The nuclear industry is organized and sees itself as a 'cycle'. It likes to see this as an asset. Its critics tend to see it as a problem.

If 'Fast Breeder' reactors were used they could make more radioactive fuel in the form of plutonium than they started with, so generating a 'plutonium economy' but the cycle has been used to run logic in reverse. For example, to keep reprocessing going to 'handle' waste when in fact, it increases waste, and to create new types of 'fuel'[5] when there is no shortage of uranium, while justifying it as a way to get rid of plutonium, when plutonium is only produced in reactors – you get the idea.[6]

Instead of attacking nuclear electricity, which is exactly like any other electricity once it is 'downstream', anti-nuclear campaigns have focused on the 'back end': nuclear waste and its human and environmental costs. When householders and citizens have to live with waste, they rightly want to ask hard questions and have guarantees. When you disperse it into the sea or air,[7] the opportunity to ask useful questions is lost. Back-end strategy gets questions about risk asked now, before the risks are commissioned, rather than years – maybe hundreds or thousands of years – into the future. With dwindling options to dispose of nuclear waste, the industry has had to curb expansion and justify itself to the public in a way that it could always formerly avoid, as long as waste was dumped in the Atlantic Ocean.[8]

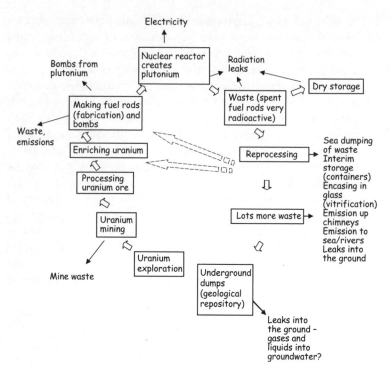

Figure 3.2 *Nuclear power issue map*

Quantitative research

Use quantitative research to evaluate a campaign

Quantitative market research, often called 'polling', tells you how many people say they think something. Popular with politicians and the news media, it makes it easy to tell stories that appear to have authority because they are quantified. This is often taken to be more 'objective' and 'scientific' than qualitative research, but this is largely false. Indeed, polling is sometimes argued to be an ideological rather than a 'scientific' instrument.[9] By determining what is discussed in the news through commissioning and releasing a poll, as well as deciding the questions, those who can afford to buy polling are able to frame what is important to society.

A more respectable use of quantitative research is a 'before-and-after' study to help evaluate a campaign or in communicating with key audiences – for instance, by showing how many other people think something.

Polling can be very persuasive in private lobbying, such as when you have data that relate to the customers of retailers that you want to influence. In 1987, for example, I was working for WWF International, and we were able to provide people close to the owners of the *Daily Mail* with unpublished MORI[10] survey results that showed 26 per cent of the newspaper's readers wanted more coverage of conservation issues. This figure was higher than that of any of its competitors, and this helped persuade the *Daily Mail* to start campaigning on the environment.[11]

Quantified data are useful in lobbying, because numbers can be passed around as a fixed 'fact' in conversation. Qualitative research is unlikely to make much of an impact in private lobbying unless the target is familiar with the methods, as its results sound like a matter of opinion.

Quantitative research is also useful for broad comparisons within an issue. For instance, Eurobarometer surveys commissioned by the European Commission, and global polls by Environics,[12] based in Canada, reveal something about levels of environmental concern. In each year since 1997, Environics International's *Environmental Monitor* has reported the views of randomly selected 'average citizens' from over 25 countries (it shows, for instance – and contrary to popular assumptions about motivation in the North – that concern is as high if not higher in most developing countries).

Qualitative research

Use qualitative research to understand why people think the way they do

This sets out to understand how and *why* people think the way they do. It can appear as 'soft' research, but you should resist the idea that qualitative research is less objective because it lacks numbers: quantification often lends a wholly spurious air of objectivity. Qualitative research may also inconveniently reveal that people don't think the way we'd like them to, and this may become a reason to resist doing it. Reject this idea!

At its simplest, qualitative research could mean conducting your own straw poll or, like Mass Observation of the 1950s, eavesdropping on the bus. Talking to colleagues, friends or relatives is, however, a very unreliable way of discerning motivations. Answers are heavily coloured by who is asking the question, and the respondents' relationship with the questioner.

Done well by experienced moderators, qualitative research is expensive but well worth it. Cheap qualitative research, however, tends to be useless or, worse, misleading. Before embarking on buying qualitative research it's a good idea to read up on the subject, look on the web[13] and take recommendations from people in your line of work.

Here's a list of why it's hard to understand motivation, from George Silverman and Eve Zukergood of Market Navigation:[14]

- People often do not understand why they are doing the things they are doing, and therefore can't tell you
- Even when they do understand why they are doing things, they don't want to tell you
- When they do tell you, they often don't tell you the truth, or the whole truth. Or, they tell you more than the truth
- It is more important for most people to preserve their view of themselves than tell you why they are doing what they are doing
- There is rarely a single reason why a given person does something. Any simple, single act of behaviour is usually the result of many complex forces from inside and outside the individual
- The same act of behaviour can be motivated by different things in different people. Members of the same group, performing the same task at the same time, may have vastly different motivations
- The same person will do the same thing at different times for different motivations
- Some motivations, even if you find them out, are often irrelevant to marketing, in that you can do little, if anything, about them. These may involve motivations based upon deep fears, pathology or illegal activities
- Yet motivations are extremely important for the marketer to understand, particularly those centring around fundamental beliefs, values, tastes and emotions.

'The best way' they say, 'to find out about motivation is by inferring the causes of behaviour from people's thoughts and actions. The worst way, often, is to ask them, "Why did you do it?"'

Take a product such as fish fingers. If you ask men why they buy fish fingers they may say that they are convenient, easy to cook, nutritious, covered in breadcrumbs, and so on. But the real reason,[15] which you need a deeper method of study to uncover, might be that it gives them social 'permission' to sit down with their kids to eat – in other words, to be a child again.

When my Greenpeace team was researching a campaign on ozone depletion in the 1990s, we found that, while people were quite prepared to accept that it was a serious problem and believed there might be evidence of a link to skin cancer, many were less willing to accept that commercial chemicals had to be banned as a result. Activists strongly agreed that ICI, a major British chemical company, was to blame,[16] but more typical public groups were reluctant to consider measures that might damage ICI, which was seen as a rare example of British industrial achievement.

Greenpeace tested different ways of talking about chemicals – about 'holes in the sky' or 'pepperpots' (lots of small holes), or edges of holes or expanding holes (all versions of reality). What finally turned out to motivate many of the younger women in the test groups was the threat to their holidays. The idea that ICI might be endangering their chance to sunbathe for two weeks was enough to blow away any concerns they might have for the profitability of the chemicals giant.

Research also showed that people were not surprised that solar electricity could power light bulbs (the standard demonstration used by campaigners), but believed that for 'hard work', such as washing clothes, other forms of electricity would be needed. So Greenpeace built a solar-powered kitchen containing a washing machine and cooker and toured it around shopping centres on the back of a truck.

Silverman and Zukergood emphasize the need for research within 'an atmosphere of psychological safety, about what [people] do – not why they do it – and how they feel about what they do'. Conventionally, the best way to do this is in a focus group[17] moderated by a psychologist. They noted: 'People get caught up in the spirit of the group' and when they discover others who are sympathetic, 'these other people quickly cease to be strangers, yet they aren't friends, family or co-workers. They begin to pour out information, opinions and feelings that they would not ordinarily share with most other people.'

Investigating conversation potential

Stimulate the need for action despite uncertainties

To reach 'cross-over', where new audiences discuss new ideas, and for campaign propositions to acquire the velocity to escape from old assumptions, campaigns need to become a lively 'conversation in society'. Doing that is hard if people are disinterested, and a potent new form of disinterest is the instant opinion. In a world where everyone begins to deconstruct messages – to ask who is behind it? how was it put together? how did it get here and why? – having an instant view about any proposition short-circuits most attempts to stimulate that conversation in society (witness the failures of politicians' attempts to launch 'big conversations' or stir up 'national debates').

This is bad news for campaigns. People have an increasing number of mental off-switches they can use to disengage with. Yet some things still bother them enough to form the conversation 'everyone is talking about', on the bus, at the rail station in phone-ins and, as qualitative researcher John Scott notes, in the queue at the chip shop.

So an important test for a campaign proposition (see Chapter 6) is whether or not it passes the chip shop queue test – does it stimulate that conversation? The magic ingredient, says Scott, is dilemmas: hard-to-resolve things that nag at us and we can't put down – hence they keep the conversation (read, campaign) going.

'Campaigns work,' he says,[18] 'according to the number of discussions they generate by two people who have nothing to do with it. In such moments people say things like "it's brilliant someone's doing that", or they pass on a factoid; they share something they didn't realize about the world. This is when campaigns achieve leverage: because things become currency. This effect is usually much bigger than a few people taking a lot of action.'

Rather than trying to test campaign propositions, Scott argues that campaigners would do better to use qualitative research to create an 'atlas of understanding' for an issue, and then look for and test out dilemmas. To do this he uses 'constructor groups', in which people are encouraged to effectively take on the role of researchers themselves by being given a brief and sent out to solve a communications problem, test it with friends and relations, amend and present it back.

'Get people to create something and sell it to you – that way you can challenge them, they challenge each other and you can better understand what they really think about something,' Scott says. 'As a result, they are confident enough to give you access to things that are not resolvable. Otherwise, they feel they must give you answers that add up.'

So don't try to shut down all uncertainty and ambiguity in campaign propositions, but stimulate the need for action despite paradoxes and ethical options that cannot be weighed or equated, even while uncertainties cannot be resolved. The UK government 'drink-driving' (anti-alcohol) campaigns are interesting, observes Scott, because 'they make people disapprove of each other'. They make it impossible to think 'the government's to blame': a thought that 'insulates people from dilemmas and irreconcilable things'.

He believes that one reason the Brent Spar issue resonated for so long is that it 'stimulated ongoing debate about whether Greenpeace should even have done it'. Something, as he points out, 'that you were unlikely to have ever discovered by research based on the campaign structure (the campaign plan)'. But, he suggests, if you had asked about dumping waste at sea and about corporate responsibility, then your atlas might have showed a potential for powerful ambivalences to collide. 'It's the gossip in the chip shop queue effect: the issue of whether the government is lying is actually more interesting to discuss than whether sea-dumping is a good idea.'

Using networks

A few years ago, statisticians worked out that we were 'just six handshakes' away from anyone in the world. Some say it's only four handshakes.[19] Studies of the internet and many other networks show the number of links needed tends to be even lower. This so-called 'small-world' effect may be bad news for disease transmission, but it helps explain how the public affairs industry works. Once you are in contact with a few people in an industry or political system, they are likely to be able to reach everyone else in it rather easily.

> Most of the connections you need are closer than you might think

Add human chemistry, and networks can deliver real punch. This is one reason why experienced international lobbyists go to such lengths to 'network' and press for changes in national policy positions even right down to the wire, hoping that personal pressure will win some shift in position at the last minute. Sometimes it works; most delegations have some scope for concessions, and many ministers can call on favours with their political bosses if they really need to get out of a situation they feel personally uncomfortable with. Many love the dramas of last-minute deals.

Supporters are often undervalued by NGOs. Chances are that most of the connections you need are closer at hand than you might think. Campaigns tend to be networks, with a disproportionate number of links to others. Many of the targets you may be after will tend to be in the minority of highly connected nodes that are over-influential in 'scale-free' networks.[20] Simply checking around your own network may uncover many useful links, and contacts of colleagues and supporters will reach into entirely new ones.

Families, too, are an important factor. Being lobbied by your sons or daughters is far more uncomfortable than being got at on a nine-to-five basis by professional pressure groups, PR agencies or political opponents. You may not know the chief executive officer (CEO) or brand manager or a minister, but do you know someone who does, or someone who might know someone who does? Use networks to their full advantage, but never 'hostage' private relationships and intrude unfairly.

Qualitative evidences

Ensure the audience sees the evidence

It is often more useful to show presence – or absence – from visual evidence rather than resorting to statistics. 'Evidences' are things people take as signs of something being true, or being the case. An egg frying on a pavement, for example – 'it's very hot'.

In one campaign, research[21] showed that segments of the UK public were aware of the depletion of the ozone layer and the link to ultraviolet light and skin cancer, but this information was beginning to lose its effect because it was 'not of their world', and nobody they knew was getting skin cancer. These would have been 'evidences' that warnings about the risks were indeed valid. Similarly, at that time the ice caps weren't seen to be melting; hence people were ambivalent about global warming. In another study, one person cited seeing Antarctic cod in a supermarket as evidence of globalization being real.

The important point is that these perceptions reflect the issue as constructed from existing perceptions, not from the viewpoint of campaigners or experts.

What's the expectation; what's understood as evidence that something is getting worse or could improve? How can you make sure that the relevant audience sees that evidence, maybe not just once but in a series of 'evidences'? Find out through research.

Choosing media and communication channels

Horses for courses

Different types of media are best used for different aspects of communication. Table 3.1 is based on my own experience.

Media such as advertising can reach a mass audience but carry only simple information. At the other extreme, face-to-face communication, such as at public events, can reach a relatively small audience but can handle greater complexity, while direct marketing and editorial are intermediate.[22]

The immediate impact (remember, of course, that this is not the same as long-term influence) of different media is probably something like this (in descending order):

- face-to-face (the 'sender' communicates with you directly);
- group (the sender communicates with a group directly);
- an event that just happens;
- a clearly organized public event/meeting;
- cinema or virtual reality;
- TV;
- photography (still pictures or large images/objects such as art installations);
- internet (with a degree of interactivity);
- internet (non-interactive);
- radio (but it can be extremely powerful as a form of one-on-one, especially when the content is an issue that requires reflection or is very personal. Radio is generally the most under-rated medium);
- print (not enough thought usually goes into using print – magazines that end up lying around in waiting rooms, for instance, have a valuable staying power if they contain interesting features).

Table 3.1 *Using different types of media for different aspects of communication*

Medium	Best uses	Less good for
Film/video (i.e. commissioned video) non-broadcast	Persuasion, emotions, feelings and stories, speaker support and group discussion	Information
Reportage (being reported by the media)	Endorsement	Engagement, recruitment
Newspaper reports	Establishing a campaign or project – matter of record, logging milestones, reaching political and corporate decision-makers	Persuasion
News websites	A record and archive (if maintained long term, e.g. BBC)	Social intrusion
TV news	Events, awareness, reaching status-conscious decision-makers, internal communication	Information, sensitive topics, reflection or messages that should be segmented
TV documentaries	Depth treatment, stories	Time-critical work
Local newspapers	How-to information for the home. Case studies and human interest stories which people can believe	Reaching young people (in most cases)
Advertisements, e.g. posters	Reinforcement, awareness	Information, persuasion
Advertisements in special interest magazines including women's, etc.	Reinforcement, awareness, cross-support to editorial or features, segmented messaging	Reaching wider audiences
Text – print	Information, reference, stories	Persuasion
Radio news	Breaking news (i.e. urgent)	A record
Radio general	Human interest, stories, reflection	Launches, events
Radio strand or specialist programmes	Segmented messaging and discussion of problems and opportunities	Reaching wider audiences

Table 3.1 *continued*

Medium	Best uses	Less good for
Radio advertising	Reinforcement (very cheap and can be targeted for certain audiences or localities by listenership)	Reaching 'decision-makers'
Human interaction, face-to-face (PR)	Persuasion, changing views	Large-scale recruitment
Events (to which people are invited or can attend)	Inspiration, integration (multimedia)	Reaching disinterested audiences
Tailored briefings by invitation or side meetings at conferences, etc.	Informing professionals and stakeholders, persuasion	Anything else (high cost)
Exhibitions and receptions	Introductions, making new contacts	Information
3-D	Reinforcement, events	Information
Entertainment activities, e.g. sports events, concerts	Awareness of an issue in new specific audience	Information, persuasion
Internet websites	Reference information, narrowcasting, network-building	Endorsement
E-mail (interactive)	Data, network updating, mobilizing existing contacts; networks	Persuasion, establishment, networking
Texting (interactive)	Updating, awareness	Information
Ambient	Awareness for groups that do not use other media, media-wary, or media-saturated	Networking, information
Stories, written or verbal	Changing minds	Information, pressure
Showbooks and laptop computer presentations	Small group persuasion, training, speaker support with small groups	Anything else

As well as media that can't be purchased, such as news or features, campaigns may want to use media that can be bought. Some may be glamorous and worth doing as a morale booster (a film with high production values, for example) to increase the 'presence' of the campaign. Few are as effective as face-to-face or edited communication (such as magazines and radio). This is why commercial PR (designed mostly to stimulate press coverage) has undergone a boom at the expense of advertising. The more 'paid for' a message is, and the less unsupported by surrounding and reinforcing free messages, the less it will be trusted.

'Ambient' means 'around you' and is an attempt to get messages out of obviously paid-for slots and onto the street or any other public space, bodies or any place that can be used. It works best while it's new.

Allies, decision-makers and opponents

Identify key audiences

Who's who, and what's what? Checking through the opponents, decision-makers and allies helps identify key audiences. A campaign might come down to wanting to know how to influence one individual, or even to influence one individual to influence another.

- Mapping individual contacts – a PR company favourite. Who knows who, and in what circumstances do they meet? Draw in your target person and then draw connections to those she or he knows, and who they know, and so on. Often you need to reach a series of 'audiences' to secure a chain of events
- Winners and losers – as it stands now, and as it will if your campaign succeeds – make a list; brainstorm; be prepared for strange bedfellows
- Where do costs and benefits fall and how might that be changed? For example, a well-known problem arises in energy efficiency if home-owners benefit from installing insulation (lower bills) but landlords have to pay for it
- Where is value added and profit made in a production chain?

- Don't assume beneficiaries will understand the campaign. They probably won't be expecting it – approach them directly or indirectly
- Potential allies may want to remain hidden. Possible exposure may shift them from complete inaction to giving a private help or useful intelligence
- Don't demand a lot at first – some will be quite happy to be counted as supporting you – for example in letter writing to newspapers – but are unlikely to do more. However, even that much may convert an invisible majority into a visible one
- Political, social or commercial competitors are potential allies. Credit-takers are another. Politicians who may finally put their imprint on the decision, even if they do little or nothing to force it to happen, and journalists who may 'discover' the issue with information you have fed to them, are also beneficiaries. Don't forget that there may also be people riding on their coat-tails, who may be even more ambitious for their success.

Chapter 4

CAMPAIGN PLANS

Generating a campaign plan

Finding a way to
make a
difference

Campaign planning should find what will make a strategic difference, and then find a way to make that happen. There are many ways to do it.[1] Here's one in six main steps:

1 Make a campaign concept: a vision of what you want to achieve, and how you'll do it
2 From the concept, make a critical path plan
3 Test it and revise it
4 Define the campaign proposition
5 Draw up the skeleton communications strategy
6 Before finally committing yourself to action, check that you or your organization is ready for the consequences of both success and failure.

The last stage is where the board or senior managers should give their final sign-off. They may also be involved right at the start in setting high-level priorities, but probably shouldn't be involved[2] in details along the way.

Figure 4.1 *Campaign planning star*

Making a campaign concept

Follow the
campaign
planning star

There's no escaping the need to consider a lot of factors together and come to a judgement. Campaigning can have method with 'scientific' inputs, but it's also an art, a craft. The 'planning star' (Figure 4.1) gathers inputs from five main points:

- Ambition: what we want to achieve in terms of change (both to the problem directly, and in terms of changing potentials, or the context, to increase the possibility of longer-term change). Analysing the significance of possible objectives
- Actors, obstacles and players: the who's who and what's what of the issue. Current situation analysis

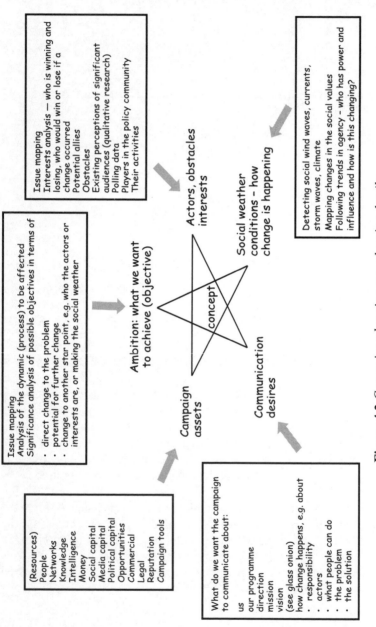

Issue mapping
Analysis of the dynamic (process) to be affected
Significance analysis of possible objectives in terms of

· direct change to the problem
· potential for further change
· change to another star point, e.g. who the actors or
  interests are, or making the social weather

Issue mapping
Interests analysis — who is winning and
losing, who would win or lose if a
change occurred
Potential allies
Obstacles
Existing perceptions of significant
audiences (qualitative research)
Polling data
Players in the policy community
Their activities

Detecting social wind waves, currents,
storm waves, climate
Mapping changes in the social values
Following trends in agency – who has power and
influence and how is this changing?

Ambition: what we want
to achieve (objective)

concept

Actors, obstacles
interests

Social weather
conditions – how
change is happening

Campaign
assets

Communication
desires

(Resources)
People
Networks
Knowledge
Intelligence
Money
Social capital
Media capital
Political capital
Opportunities
Commercial
Legal
Reputation
Campaign tools

What do we want the campaign
to communicate about:

us
our programme
direction
mission
vision
(see glass onion)
how change happens, e.g. about
· responsibility
· actors
· what people can do
· the problem
· the solution

Figure 4.2 *Campaign planning star, showing details*

- Social weather conditions: how things change in our society today, and how we think they're going to change in future, the means of change and agency. Reading the tea leaves
- Communication desires: what we want to communicate as an individual or, more likely, as an organization. This may exist quite independently of the need to achieve the immediate objective
- Campaign assets: the tools for the job. Social, material, financial, intellectual and other resources, including intelligence capacities and special campaigning tools.

The decision to start a campaign can be driven from any one of these points. A change in who's involved in an issue, or a new resource becoming available, is just as legitimate in determining that now is the moment to campaign, as is a study of objectives or the issue.

Each organization will have its own priorities and ways of making plans, and there's no way to convert these inputs into a numerical process so the right answer can be arrived at by calculation: it's always a question of judgement.

The concept needs to include a draft campaign proposition, any internal requirements or objectives, and an idea of key assumptions about why it ought to work. Most organizations need something like this in order to give a go-ahead to a campaign idea.

Making a critical path

Converting a
concept into a
series of events

A critical path is a series of steps in which achieving one is necessary in order to move onto the next one, as with a series of dominoes set up to fall over, one onto another (Figure 4.3). It is best planned backwards from the chosen objective. Each step is essential for achieving the end objective and is then a sub-objective.

The critical path converts a concept into a do-able mechanism, a series of events linked by campaign activities. These in turn roll out as a story visible in the outside world.

There are two key parts to this: first, using your existing knowledge, work out a path that would, if achieved, arrive at your chosen objective. This also generates a skeletal communications strategy as a series of activities and events. Second, go out and test this critical path plan by doing some more research, to see if it looks viable.

Figure 4.3 *A critical path is like a set of dominoes set up to fall –*
only when the first domino has fallen will it make the others fall,
one after another

Such planning[3] hinges on knowing the causal relationship between
each component: *how* one leads to another, or *why* one has to happen
before another. It's not just a 'time line' or 'plan' of things that
someone has decided ought to happen on particular dates. Critical-
path planning can be used at the 'mission' level (or 'aim'), the
'campaign' level and the 'project' level. Here's a hypothetical anti-
smoking campaign (Figure 4.4).

In this campaign, suppose that research – intelligence gathering –
revealed that while a council decision was needed to deliver the desired
final objective, politicians would only act if they felt the organization
was ready. So an intermediate objective became informal, self-declared
bans. To get those, the support of managers was key. But managers in
turn were unlikely to act without both an informal signal of staff
opinion, and formal pressure from the trade union. So achieving these
became prior requirements. Finally, because the union was most likely
to act if it began to look out of step with popular concerns, organizing
an opinion poll became Step (objective) 1.

Simply going straight for the final objective would have resulted in
failure – maybe sustained failure. Note also that planning required
working backwards from the final objective and figuring out what the
preceding objectives had to be.

Figure 4.4 *A hypothetical anti-smoking campaign*

Moving down a level, each step would require micro-campaigning, identifying likely champions, working out who could be brought on side, and who to ignore, and so on. The campaign sequence (awareness > alignment > engagement > action) would be needed at each. Moving up a level, achieving the ban in Ambridge would help in a bigger critical path (not shown here) of council decisions across the UK.

So the project-level objective, a ban in Ambridge Council offices, might be followed by projects to secure bans in other government offices. Then this might be followed (E–Z) by a series of other campaigns to stop smoking in all other offices, and wider public places.

The case of the Brent Spar

The Brent Spar campaign, detailed in *The Turning of the Spar*,[4] was a real strategy with critical paths at all the above three levels. It came some decades into a long-running Greenpeace campaign[5] against ocean dumping. More recently, Greenpeace has focused on space junk, sea-disposal of the Mir space station, and carbon dioxide emissions, but it began with sea-dumping of nuclear waste.[6]

The focus on stopping the dumping of radioactive waste at sea was not because this was the worst or biggest part of marine pollution. You can't sensibly compare, say, nutrients, persistent organic pollutants (POPs), sewage or radiation. The topic was selected because it could be done, and because it was the least acceptable, most awful[7] treatment of the sea, and particularly reckless.

Greenpeace eventually got nuclear waste dumping ended, and moved to stop the dumping of industrial wastes at sea, securing a ban by the Oslo Commission in 1990[8] and worldwide under the London Convention in 1993. After that, it stopped the less obvious problem of incineration (such as toxic solvents) at sea, and won a prohibition on the dumping of nuclear submarines in 1989, and sewage sludge dumping in European waters in the 1990s,[9] while POPs were progressively restricted. These fell under the Oslo and Paris Commission regulating the disposal of wastes in the North East Atlantic (OSPAR) convention. Greenpeace political director Remi Parmentier[10] saw it as the progressive elimination of the philosophy of 'out of sight, out of mind'. At the largest political scale, Greenpeace sought to use the North East Atlantic, and OSPAR to set a precedent for how the seas ought to be treated worldwide.

In 1994, campaigners were told that the oil industry was about to test-drive a loophole that oil lobbyists had secured within OSPAR, which allowed sea disposal of obsolete offshore installations. This was despite the 1958 Geneva Convention 'Law of the Sea', which said that any offshore installations being abandoned should be entirely removed, and a political commitment to do so made when the North Sea fields were first developed.

As the oldest installation in the oldest field in the North Sea,[11] the Spar was a test case for the legal and industrial processes that would be used to dump much of the rest of the oil industry's major waste problem.

So at the next scale down, stopping governments and the oil industry from taking the Brent Spar on a test-drive through the loophole became the objective of the campaign. Greenpeace determined that if political lobbying failed, it would use non-violent direct action to try and force the issue.

Industry sources said Shell planned to tow the Spar from its mid-sea moorings near the border of Norwegian–UK waters, to a deep-water Atlantic dump site west of Scotland, in the summer of 1995. The 'weather window' would open around May and close again by October. Accordingly, the Greenpeace strategy was to occupy the Spar, on the assumption that if people were on it, then it could not be sunk.

Greenpeace had been invited to participate in preparatory meetings for a North Sea Ministers Conference.[12] There it raised the

Notes: At the highest strategy level, oil installations were the third of three campaigns, starting in the 1970s with radioactive waste dumping. The political strategy framework for the campaign to stop dumping of oil installations was the 'OSPAR' convention. The long term aim of the entire sequence of campaigns was to help achieve clean seas

Figure 4.5 *Evolution of Greenpeace anti-dumping strategy*

anomaly of the oil industry exemption, and the Brent Spar.[13] In autumn 1994 it published a detailed policy paper by Simon Reddy, *No Grounds for Dumping*, making a call for oil installations not to be dumped. Greenpeace expected it to be ignored, and it was.

At international meetings, the Spar case met no interest from any government. As late as March 1995, at an OSPAR meeting, UK civil servant Alan Simcock announced that he did not feel the need to answer questions from Greenpeace as it wasn't a nation state. In February 1995, Greenpeace objected to the granting of the dumping licence, again expecting to be ignored by the UK government, which it was. Inside Shell, the head of public affairs circulated a self-congratulatory memo on how a potentially difficult exercise had been successfully negotiated. Later she recovered all but one of the memos and presumably shredded them.

At the end of April 1995, Greenpeace occupied the Spar,[14] under the bemused gaze of oil workers on nearby platforms.

Figure 4.6 *Original critical path project plan for Brent Spar*

Greenpeace's favoured alternative was to scrap the Spar at the Norwegian fjord where it had been assembled. That had been the original plan[15] of Shell/Esso, the owners, and that was what eventually happened.

The Greenpeace plan was to use the occupied Spar as a platform for pirate radio, with which to broadcast to Europe about environmental issues during the North Sea Ministers Conference in Esjberg. By making the source dramatic, they hoped to make the message much more interesting. The radio station never came about, but the dramatization worked better than anyone expected.

The occupation escalated into a major physical, legal and political confrontation, culminating in the removal of dozens of protestors over a period of several days. Then Shell blew the anchor chains and tried to start towing the Spar towards its dumping ground, just as the North Sea Ministers Conference was about to begin. By this time, German church groups had spontaneously started a boycott of Shell petrol, soon supported by many newspapers, radio stations and millions of consumers all over Europe. Many governments called on Shell to change its plans.

Greenpeace re-boarded the Spar, were removed and re-boarded it. From 30 April to 20 June the campaign involved more or less continuous, very visual direct actions, backed up by political lobbying, media furore and consumer boycott. One UK newspaper described it as the 'mother of all environmental battles'.

In terms of a critical path, the Spar campaign was planned as a series of events, working around three key points in time: when towing could begin, when it had to end by, and in between, the political meeting of North Sea ministers.

Skeleton campaign communications strategy from critical paths

Activities drive events

The event that takes place at each objective (how that objective is finally achieved) is the switch from the pre-campaign to the post-campaign condition, like flicking a switch from off to on. This is what can be photographed (see photo test, this chapter) and experienced. It automatically generates a communications strategy.

The stage-by-stage changes from 'off' to 'on' or wrong to right are objectives that, as they are achieved, can be communicated, preferably visually.

The *activities* that drive this process – which might be petitioning, direct action, public speaking, voting, buying, selling or a host of other things – can also be filmed, photographed, experienced or described.

Figure 4.7 *Stage-by-stage objectives towards a communications strategy*

Figure 4.8 *Outputs to which you should apply the CAMP CAT grid*

So the two communications outputs that a critical path-based campaign generates are *state-changes* in the target, the sub-objectives or waypoints (for example, when a pen is put to paper, a prisoner is released, a waste pipe is blocked), and the *campaigning activities* that the campaigners or their supporters do in order to make that happen. These are all events: activity (event) > objective being achieved (event) activity (event) > objective being achieved (event), and so on.

For each of these outputs you need to apply the CAMP CAT factors (see Chapter 1). This creates a communications planning grid (Figure 4.9).

Start at the top with the images created by doing the activities and achieving the objectives.

Then decide who (which audiences) they need to be shown to, based on what effect you want to have.

Start here
– decide
this first

Change to objective												
Campaign activity												
Audience												
Message												
Medium												

Decide
this last

Figure 4.9 *Communications planning grid generated by critical path*

Figure 4.10 *The campaign communicates an image of activity, followed by image of change, followed by image of activity, et seq*

Knowing that, you can decide what meaning to give the 'message' – what action you say it calls for, what motivation or trigger needs to accompany it.

Having decided, that will, in turn, help tell you which channels, context and media to use (choice of TV, video, radio, exhibition, face-to-face, direct-mail, newspapers, and so on). This has to be the final step, not the first one.

Never start by saying 'let's have a video', or 'so we need a press release', or commissioning a report, and then trying to construct the campaign to make use of it. This is a classic 'communications amateur' error, and can be very expensive – and you may need a warehouse to store the unusable results.

Testing a critical path

Let in the cold light of reality

You can't discover *exactly* what will happen if you do run a campaign, but you can find pitfalls to avoid, and research almost always uncovers some hitherto unknown opportunities.

For a significant campaign, this stage can take quite a while. It's a process of research and revision – which can go on as long as you have time, patience and resources – although generally, the 80:20 rule will apply. The bulk of useful insights (80 per cent) will be gathered in the first few (20 per cent) trawls of research or testing.

It's effort well spent, because it's your prototype-testing, research and development phase. Pennies spent here will save you pounds later on. It's also where you let the cold light of reality in on the ideas from the hothouse, and check external perceptions against internal assumptions.

Most of the research usually consists of checking assumptions, using the sorts of tools and processes described in this book, to 'ground-truth' the plan.

Finding the red thread: Achieving simplicity

Understanding complexity to get to a winning strategy

In Germany, campaigners speak of 'finding the red thread', the vital line that runs through an issue. Defining this and discarding other possibilities is one of the hardest and most pivotal steps in organizing a campaign concept. It is about achieving simplicity, not simplification.

Simplification would take the whole issue and try to reduce it to a simple explanation – but as such, it would be a misrepresentation, a deception or self-deception or a bland précis. Simplicity is achieved by understanding the complexity, identifying the key part that can be changed to strategic advantage, and making a campaign that deals *only* with that single, pure element.

A common difficulty is knowing far too much about the subject you wish to campaign on. Any campaign organization will rapidly accumulate a huge store of knowledge. It will probably find it very hard to sort out which bits are relevant, and, which of those illuminate a potential battle-winning strategy.

The best way to make the choice easier is to produce concepts, then test them as critical paths for feasibility, so eliminating possibilities. Another is to ensure that most of the inputs to a campaign discussion are about how to change the issue, and not the issue itself.

Is an objective real? Using the photo test

If you can't photograph the objective, it probably isn't much use

If you can't photograph the objective, or at least *imagine* photographing it – a fly-on-the-wall test – it's probably not much use, and quite likely not real.

The photo test avoids ambiguity. A good campaign objective often involves something happening, or no longer happening – stopping or starting. For example:

- A political agreement – the objective should not just be to 'get the agreement'; it needs to be the relevant act. This might be a vote – the moment when enough people put up their hands in a parliament
- A corporate decision – similar to the above, except it might be a board decision, or a decision by a brand manger. Who knows? You really need to know, if only to make sure you are pushing or pulling at the right part of the organization.
- Public awareness. Of what? Rarely an objective worth having in itself. As you can't see inside people's heads, this sort of objective needs to employ a proxy; such as a before-and-after survey, or an action that from research you know people will take once they are 'aware'; or some sort of self-declaration by those who do become aware. In which case, one of those, not awareness itself, becomes the objective
- Stopping a process. A negative or absence can be converted into a positive that can be photographed – whaling ships staying in port, for example
- A solution. Can you photograph it being put in place? Can it be inserted into the problem, like a plug in a plug hole, or by direct substitution? Examples are renewable energy being plugged in, or Forest Stewardship Council (FSC)-certified doors being installed at the UK Cabinet Office, in place of forest-damaging ones, in a Greenpeace action in 2002.

The photo test focuses the mind and forces you to cut away vague concepts:

- It can be communicated in pictures
- It leads you to discover exactly what the delivery mechanism is for a change – how it comes about, who does it
- It can be inspiring, because it shows that the objective is real, concrete, achievable and understandable
- It helps resolve internal debate and progress planning
- It can be detected, and so evaluated. It is often said that it's important to have 'quantifiable' objectives, but this is not as important as being *detectable*.

The ambition box

For a strategic effect, it is a target's significance – not size or difficulty – that counts

Picking the right objective means considering:

- your ambition for changing the overall problem;
- resources and activities;
- organizational strategy – on a revolutionary–managerialist spectrum.

These translate into three dimensions, creating the 'ambition box' of possible objectives:

- Size – how much of the overall problem does it represent (immediate yield)?
- Toughness – how hard do you have to try to achieve it?
- Significance – what consequential effect results from achieving the objective (longer-term yield)?

For a government agency or an organization charged with doing something about a problem in the most cost-effective way, the rational place to start is with the low-hanging fruit. For a campaign organization, the targets are likely to be tougher. After all, the low-hanging fruit has probably already been picked by someone else.

If you want a strategic effect, it is no use picking a target simply because it is 'relevant' or 'connected' to the problem. It might be a brick at the top of the wall. Pull it out, or if it's tough, chisel it out, and

Figure 4.11 *Immediate target in terms of hardness and size*

the result is maybe not much. If, however, it is the keystone brick in an arch, then it may bring the whole thing down. This quality is not to do with the immediate 'toughness' or size of the target, but its *significance*, another dimension making up the 3-D 'objectives box'.

For example, in the Florida Everglades, the alligator acts as a 'keystone species' by creating dry-season ponds, which also allow a host

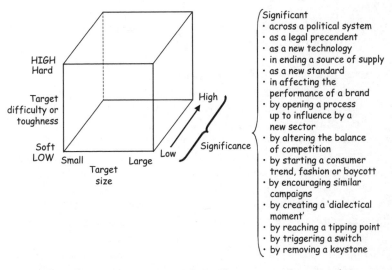

Figure 4.12 *Target in terms of significance, toughness and size*

of other species to survive. In *The Tipping Point*, Malcolm Gladwell gives numerous examples of how specific social dynamics can lead the spread of ideas to have big effects.[16]

Campaign groups may deliberately pick 'hard nuts' in order to draw attention to a problem. Exxon, for example, is unlikely to succumb to pressure from www.stopesso.com but is likely to remain deserving as a climate campaign target with huge political resonance. Greenpeace's tryst with the PVC industry, eminently logical (PVC being a linchpin of chemical pollution), has proved a war of attrition because of communication problems – a less-resonant tough nut.

The Californian car market has proved itself to be a political-industrial keystone of great significance, from catalytic converters in the 1970s to electric vehicles in the 2000s. Eron Shosteck, spokesman for the Alliance of Automobile Manufacturers, said in 2002: 'You can't make one car for California and another car for Washington, DC.'

In the Brent Spar campaign the target was known to be:

- of strategic importance to the oil *industry* – as an industrial test case for a waste disposal option (sea dumping) for all North Sea 'brownfielding';
- a *political* precedent (within OSPAR) regulating the disposal of wastes in the North East Atlantic;
- a *legal* precedent within the same framework.

Quite unexpectedly, it also became of strategic significance:

- as a symbol and trigger for change within Shell, including its view of its future as an energy company, rather than simply an oil company;
- as a touchstone and jumping-off point for a lot of corporate thinking about corporate social responsibility (CSR) – some, such as Stephen Colegreave, business development director at McCann-Erickson, say it is where the notion came from;[17]
- as a demonstration of what 'new politics' might achieve – consumers, businesses and NGOs negotiating an outcome, independent of government.

Disputes over which is the 'right' objective can often be resolved if the three dimensions are teased out and discussed separately.

Force field analysis

Looking for less obvious places to make a difference

This is a fancy name for identifying and weighing up the factors acting for and against the change you want to achieve, at any stage of planning. It involves identifying each component of change and then assessing the factors acting for and against it. Usually, it's possible to assign scores to most factors just from a discussion among colleagues – for example low, medium or high intensity.

Force field analysis[18] is a useful way to hit upon less-obvious factors that may provide the most fruitful avenues for change. The media will tend to focus on the points in your issue at which there are powerful forces opposing each other. These will generate a lot of sound, fury and heat, but may also involve a stalemate. Doing the obvious and adding your weight here may not be very cost-effective. If you can find a factor where there are few or no forces in opposing what you want, and only a small force already acting *for* what you want, then this may be where you can make a significant difference.

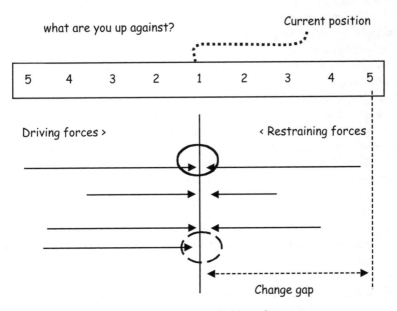

Figure 4.13 *Force field analysis*

In Figure 4.13, above the point circled by the hatched line, rather than the more obvious solid circle, is the best place to intervene and add extra force. The objective is to bridge the 'change gap'. Each set of arrows represents a line of conflict or point of dispute within the issue.

As well as finding the best place to add weight to 'pro' factors, force field analysis can help spot opportunities to reduce the impact of opposition.

Choosing an antagonist

To pick an opponent, examine the chain of responsibility

How a campaign opens is all-important. Who is it against? All campaigns have an opponent; the antagonist to you as the protagonist in your story.

Like a tennis player, you may serve for the first point. Where you place the ball will play a part in determining what happens next. Unlike tennis, the campaign game may be joined by any number of other players, including the spectators. It's more like the original versions of football, played between villages, in which the whole community could participate if it felt like it.

The campaigning dialogue is with society, your opponent, your supporters and, sometimes, between them all. The starting conditions help determine the future route of the 'conversations' just as surely as if you stood on a watershed and dropped a toy boat into one headwater or another.

So try to think several steps ahead: use 'what if' scenarios. 'If I communicate this, then what will the reaction be?' Then 'what will I do next – and what will be the response to that?' And so on, as far ahead as you can envisage. Then try another sequence and another.

To pick an opponent, examine the chain of responsibility – from who or what you think is ultimately responsible, to who is immediately responsible. Decide where in that chain to start. Consider:

* how the buck-passing will work;
* public motivation – how do people feel about blaming a potential target (demonology)?
* likely response – can you ignite a conversation?
* are some ostensible opponents actually closet supporters, who'd welcome pressure?

84

Companies, encouraged by their PR companies and some journalists, tend to assume that the main factor in deciding a target is demonology – how big and bad the reputation is. Effective campaign planners, in fact, spend much more time thinking through the dynamics – the buck-passing and interests at play.

To make these choices is very hard if you haven't worked out a critical path. Tip: this is the part of campaign planning that politicians tend to be very good at, so involve them if they are available. For a more detailed example, see 'The grim tale of mud' at www.campaignstrategy.org.

Check for consequences

Avoid
unpleasant
surprises

Do you really want to do this? Before lighting the blue touchpaper, get everyone to buy in to the plan. Success can have consequences as well as failure. There may be a backlash, or expectations will be created. You need to know what you'll do next, and what to do with enthusiastic supporters or allies. Have you thought through the effects on losers?

Of course, your decision-makers should have given an in-principle 'OK' long before this, but it's good to make sure that any unpleasant surprises generated by the campaign arise on the outside, not within your organization.

Chapter 5

ORGANIZING CAMPAIGN COMMUNICATIONS

Visual language

Magic bullet communications that slip under our conscious radar

Few campaigners are unaware of the general importance of visual communication, yet often it is not used effectively. Frequently, it's an afterthought. Using visual language often involves taking existing icons, symbols, objects or styles with an established meaning, and constructing a message from them. It doesn't just mean arranging for things to be filmed or photographed.

The classic example is the launch of a report. Many times, organizations hold a press conference or even a photo-call, when all there is to film or photograph is the report itself, and the proud authors. A campaigner waving a report looks only as if they are trying to sell it or swat a fly. 'Tarting up' the image with a few props, or a corporate backdrop is usually an expensive waste of money unless the important audience is the organization's own senior managers.

Even the viewpoint may have meaning. A film director told me for example, that if he wanted someone to be believed, he shot the discussion with them on the right of the screen, and if he wanted them to be doubted, he arranged it so they were on the left. Apparently, in many Christian religious stories and in many traditional plays, the left is the 'sinister' side: bad characters apparently tend to enter stage left; good ones occupy the right-hand side. Other things are more obvious – the way the camera may be used to suggest nervousness or lying, by close-ups of fidgeting fingers, for example.

Figure 5.1 *Boy throwing stone at a tank: David and Goliath*

Visual language is *independent* of written or spoken words. It is *not* a visualization of words or slogans. When that happens, the result is usually an unhappy one. In 2003, for example, the excellent organization Common Ground[1] wanted to celebrate and encourage care of trees. Its thought was 'every tree counts', and campaigners visualized this with a group of trees in London's Shaftsbury Avenue, decorated in numbers. What did it say visually – an odd piece of art, perhaps? A Christmas tree, on the other hand, says 'Christmas'. The intention behind 'every tree counts' might have been better expressed with some sort of caring for trees – hugging even the smallest or ugliest tree, perhaps.

Belgian Amnesty International leaves thousands of empty shoes on the pavement outside a government building. In Argentina, the 'Mothers of the Disappeared' hold up framed photographs of loved ones whose whereabouts are unknown. Former US President Bill Clinton stands on the lawn of the White House with an Israeli and Palestinian leader, and as they shake hands, doves are released. Teddy bears hang on the wire of a nuclear military base. Flags are raised, half-raised or burned. Emperors wear purple, protestors don white suits, pilots and admirals have navy blue and gold stripes on their jackets, Greenpeace ventures out in a small inflatable to confront a vast ship.

Figure 5.2 *David and Goliath*

All of these show effective use of visual language. It's not simply a question of producing images, but of using visual cues, norms, traditions, cultural references and icons to give added value to communications. These are 'magic-bullet' communications because they slip in under our conscious radar.

Figures 5.1 to 5.3 are three David-and-Goliath images which chime subconsciously. Figure 5.3 says 'Greenpeace', and is immediately recognizable as something small and good versus something big and bad: David and Goliath again.

The Brent Spar image is elemental, reduced to uncluttered essentials. The Spar, a vast lump of industrial junk (bad). Greenpeace, small good thing. The sea, the waiting victim, metaphor for all nature. The fire hoses are the hand of Shell reaching out to try and stop Greenpeace. The absence of any headland, another ship or other

Source: Photograph by David Sims

Figure 5.3 *Greenpeace at Brent Spar: David and Goliath at sea*

geographic reference renders the image placeless, timeless, undiluted. You can apply the same principle in any interview or event: eliminate everything that muddies or clutters the visual message; say only one thing.

Constructing visual echoes

'I have to have those pictures'

One trick of effective visual language is to make people respond to an image without considering whether they have seen it before. Find something powerful and then create a visual echo of it.

In spring 1995, Greenpeace 'invaded' the Sellafield nuclear plant, and blocked various parts to try and stop the separation of plutonium. The action was timed to coincide with talks about to be held in New York on the Nuclear Non-Proliferation Treaty. Greenpeace was concerned to make the Sellafield 'invasion' look interesting, and like an *invading* swarm of people rather than just another white-suit protest.

Figure 5.4 *Representation of Greenpeace Sellafield 'invasion', 1994*

Sarah Wise, one of the organizers of the campaign, had just seen the Japanese film *Ran*. This featured a battle with hundreds of warriors carrying orange banners streaming across the screen. It enjoyed cult status with TV professionals because of its cinematography.

If they could make the Greenpeace action look like that, she reasoned, TV news editors might say 'I have to have those pictures', rather than waiting (it was on Easter Bank Holiday Monday at 0600 hours) for the skeleton staff in the newsroom to find time to haul some energy or nuclear journalist out of bed to pronounce on whether the story was newsworthy, and trying to describe the footage to them over the phone. So Greenpeace put hundreds of its local group activists in orange boiler suits and gave them pole banners, echoing the troops in *Ran*.

Wise says: 'It worked so well because the sky was indigo blue in the film, and the scenery was a dark green – not unlike the hills around Sellafield. We considered using smoke bombs to ensure the dark-sky effect, but decided they would be a choking hazard. As it was, the morning was dark and rain-filled, just like in the movie.' The film ran extensively on TV.

Caution: watch out for inadvertent echoes. Google for images on the Web, and you may find a PR event in WWF-UK's (quite successful) wildlife-trade campaign, with a man holding a skull. It is a striking image, but for theatrical rather than ecological reasons, because it echoes a famous scene from Shakespeare's *Hamlet*. It says theatre, not save animals.

Figure 5.5 *Still from 'Ran', redrawn*

Be multidimensional

> The critical path needs to pass through as many dimensions of communication as possible

A campaign has more chance of success if it communicates in many dimensions. Ideally, each of the points on a critical path should register in each dimension.

In terms of argument and the research needed for it, this means being able to *make a case* in each. In terms of perception, the campaign should be *visible* in each dimension. Ask yourself what the picture would be, what you would be doing at each point (the photo test).

For example, there might be scientific, technical, political, economic and emotional dimensions, and maybe ethical, moral, historical, cultural or others (Figure 5.6).

Atlantic Frontier

The Greenpeace Atlantic Frontier campaign[2] was deliberately designed to communicate in a number of dimensions:

- Scientific/logical – it opposed development of more fossil fuel resources, intervening at the point of political responsibility (licensing development), based on the 'carbon logic',[3] which shows that burning available oil, coal and gas in the atmosphere will cause catastrophic climate change (so don't develop new reserves)
- Political – it drew a line in the sand at the Atlantic Frontier oil field of West Scotland, and at specific development blocks within that.

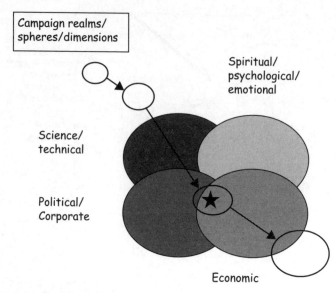

Campaign realms/ spheres/dimensions

Spiritual/ psychological/ emotional

Science/ technical

Political/ Corporate

Economic

Note: see the Atlantic Frontier example

Figure 5.6 *Critical path passing through multiple dimensions*

It contrasted UK climate rhetoric with fossil fuel in practice. It planned to make the contrast between Tony Blair's oil policy at home with his climate rhetoric at the UN[4]

- Ethical-political – it challenged the UK's right to take the oil beneath the Atlantic based on its claim to the remote islet of Rockall – and, likewise, that of Iceland, Ireland and Denmark, by occupying the rock for a record time. It called for establishment of a world park

- Ethical-emotional – it communicated (with surveys and information) the wildlife of St Kilda, and the Rockall Trough, known as a 'motorway' for migrating whales. It also raised the case against destructive deep-sea fishing to support the world park set-aside case

- Legal-ethical – it challenged[5] oil development in court on grounds of damage to ancient cold-water corals and other species (resulting in a successful ruling to greatly extend application of the European Union Habitats Directive)

- Economic-political – it argued for conversion of oil fabrication yards to wave- and wind-power manufacturing (with some success). It also challenged BP over its internal allocation of funds to renewables as opposed to new oil, for example with shareholder actions.

The campaign was also designed[6] to take place in a national theatre of great romance, mystery and physical security and drama – an inspirational setting of epic scale – making it more natural to raise fundamental questions about the future direction of society. This context (see CAMP CAT, Chapter 1) also helped increase the possibility of making some sort of progress, because the immediate target was a 'tough nut' (see p80), on the grounds that if you wanted to initiate a campaign to stop littering, then the easiest place to start might be a cathedral.

Thinking in pictures

Tips for communicating visually

You can control things to change visuals. An invisible process can be made visible. Changing the colour or clothes or equipment, or the size of something might suddenly make the 'point' of the picture more obvious. For example, a magazine carried a photograph of a large 'fossil fish' from an exhibition at the London Natural History Museum. Not a memorable picture – until the photographer took the scientist-curator onto the roof and got him to hold up the fish nose to nose – then it was an arresting picture, made that way by changing the context.

Tips for communicating visually:

- Decide the most important thing (one thing only) that you want to communicate
- Work out how to make a picture show that one thing (without words) – do a story-board, step by step
- Invest in visual communication. For example, building a 3D realization of what you want to say, or organizing a day-long event that says it, may cost thousands of pounds, but it may save you from having to produce a printed report of equal cost, and be more effective
- Think about what message the context sends. An office interview says 'bureaucrat'. If your work or project is about people, be with people. If it is about a community, be there to be interviewed. If there is a victim, show the victim. If a solution, show the solution.

Check with the campaign motivational sequence. If it's an engagement opportunity, be hands-on, demonstrate it

- Itemize success. Map out processes stage by stage until you can identify the moment or step where success occurs. Which ones can you photograph?

- If you have trouble brainstorming but have a friendly or commissioned advertising agency, then get their creatives to take part

- Research what the target audience think success (or a problem, or whatever is relevant) would look like. Then think how to play that back in communication when success occurs, so that it gets noticed

- Remember that TV needs movement. Only huge stories are covered by a reporter standing outside a closed door.

Check and test intended and unintended 'take-out'. A demonstration, for example, is a visual manifestation of support for a cause, but what does it say about that level? Do you engender the thought that: 'there's a lot more than we expected, and there's a lot more still at home' or, conversely: 'there's less than we expected, is this all there is?'[7]

Icons

Things become icons when they gain meaning beyond their literal meaning. A white dove is more than just a white dove. Coke is more than a brown, fizzy drink: it's America. Friends of the Earth's bottle dump became an environmental icon – despite the campaign's failure to encourage reuse of bottles.

Beyond literal meaning

Images can be used to prompt thoughts and anticipation. 'The Earth seen from space', an image from Apollo 11, deeply affected a generation for whom it was a revelation. *Spaceship Earth*, by the environmentalist Barbara Ward, was in press around that time.[8] The National Aeronautics and Space Administration (NASA)'s images took a metaphor and made it real (Figure 5.7).

Astronauts then added to its power by creating environmental parables, becoming witnesses – almost disciples – to environmental concern, deeply affected by what they had seen humankind doing to the planet, as viewed from space.

Note: This image is now often used to denote 'what comes next is environmental'
Source: With permission from NASA

Figure 5.7 *The Earth viewed from Apollo 11*

NASA and other space-related agencies developed an environmental subtext to their mission. Was this not helped by the fact that astronauts looked down upon the earth like angels and flew silently above it in white suits with gold visors (Figure 5.8)?[9] Astronauts and cosmonauts acquired an unusual status as bringers of honest environmental wisdom, as privileged, disinterested witnesses bearing testimony to the condition of Planet Earth. Their role echoed a religious frame of belief and authority.

95

Source: © Corbis

Figure 5.8 *An angel?*

While it's not difficult to construct events that draw on the power of established visual language, overuse creates a cliché: 'We've seen this before'. White-suited protestors, for example, have lost all the wit and chill that they once had. White, paper suits were once only associated with 'ultra-clean high-tech' and high-hazard environments. Their transfer to another environment had some shock value. Friends of the Earth produced a striking anti-nuclear poster in which cricketers wore such suits and gas masks, instead of cricketing whites, playing on the expression: 'It's not cricket' (meaning, it's not fair).

The unconscious visual impact of 9/11, an horrific event that had people looking at the images again and again, is explored in a brilliant essay: *September 11, 2001, The Power of the Images* by Professor George Lakoff:[10]

The images we see and recall interact with our system of metaphors. The results can be powerful. There are a number of metaphors for buildings.

Children's drawings often depict houses and buildings as people, with the door as a mouth or nose and the windows as eyes. For many people, this metaphor interacted with the image of a plane going into South Tower of the World Trade Center, producing, via visual metaphor, the unconscious, but powerful image of a bullet going through someone's head, the flame pouring from the other side representing blood spurting out.

This, in turn, echoed the famous Vietnam war image of a Vietcong suspect being executed by being shot through the head. Tall buildings also represent power, control, sexuality.

Problem phase and solution phase

All campaigns need to exist in two modes: problem-driving, and solution-driving. Change tends to be alternately driven by the problem and the solution. This is how the media helps us all make sense of change, and lack of change. In a problem-driven phase, lack of change is explained by 'if enough people care'. In a solution- or feasibility-driven phase, change is halted if 'it's not economic' or 'no solution exists', or 'it's not possible'.

> Don't lead
> people up the
> garden path

Overall change can be thought of as the resolution of two forces in the public consciousness: perceived urgency and perceived feasibility. Campaigners need to think about which phase their campaign is in now, or will be in next.

The conversation with society (or here, typically, with politicians in the news media) that this leads to, is something like Figure 5.9.

Psychologically and physiologically we are hard-wired to pay attention to problems first, with fright, flight and fear. 'Look at how they sell pain-relief headache pills,' a colleague pointed out some years ago. 'It's 80 per cent problem, 20 per cent solution'. Fire (see Chapter 1) is news: urgent life-threatening problems get our attention.

At a deep level, the most urgent, most important news is always the bad news, the immediate problems. For security-driven people this is usually the only important news (see Chapter 1) and studies for the BBC for example, show that they dominate regular news watchers, looking out for the next bad thing.

The public relations industry has become adept at using this to sell 'solutions' by wrapping them in a problem. PR director Ed Gyde[11] says: 'We call these "negative-positive stories". Say you have a drugs

Figure 5.9 *Change as a resolution of two forces, and the dialogue that often results*

information leaflet to promote to local parents. In itself that's not news: it is boring. But if you survey parents and find that 70 per cent of them are worried that they don't have enough information about drugs their children may use – then that's local news. Suddenly your leaflet, a "solution", is newsworthy.'

Problems alone soon become demotivating (see communications sequence, Chapter 1). So any campaign design needs to paint the issue in characters of light and darkness, of solution and problem.

If we engage people with a problem and then abandon them without a solution, we've 'led them up the garden path' – and next time they won't come. While working with Media Natura[12] I saw one study after another in which we interviewed people who had ended their subscriptions to campaigning NGOs or who were aware of the 'issues' and the problems, but who were 'turned off'. Usually, their decision to leave or not to connect wasn't because they disagreed with the cause, or, as was often assumed, due to dissatisfaction with the efforts of the group, but because they wanted to 'stop the flow of bad news' and felt they 'couldn't do enough to help'.

Without an opportunity to take action, sympathetic people feel guilty, overwhelmed by the tragedy of the situation. In the end they have to disengage for their own protection. This is a good reason to start campaign planning with an opportunity to take action and work back from it.

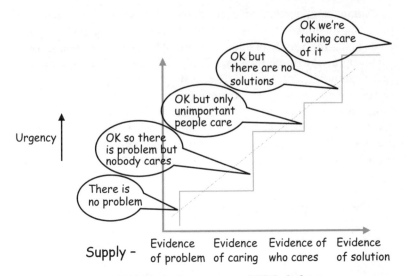

Figure 5.10 *Typical government/NGO dialogue*

For others, the lack of a feasible alternative is the watertight excuse they need not to take part. For those who don't want to *appear* unsympathetic or uncaring, the fact that 'nothing can be done' is the most comfortable excuse, maintaining self-esteem while providing a moral hand-wash.

The speech bubbles in Figure 5.10 show what politicians say. Between each horizontal 'step' the campaign reverts to 'problem-driving'. How the problem is framed changes at each step. Surmounting each step will be a project or a campaign in itself. This process is 'scale free' – it can apply from the level of the conversation between two individuals up to a wholesale revolution in national consciousness or behaviour. The role of the campaign has to change from supplying evidence of the problem to caring, to who cares, to the solution. It's no use sticking with showing how many people care, if the 'debate' moves on to *who* cares, or beyond that, to solutions. After these steps, the issue becomes one of enforcement and delivery.

Lastly, present only one problem at a time. Too many injustices at one time are indigestible. They can induce a state of denial, a mental and moral retreat not because of the impossibility of taking action on them.[13] In fund-raising, the usual rule is only to offer one action, at several different levels: typically three ways of doing the same thing. Too many options can induce indecision.

Some campaigners love to point to linkages, but too many problems all linked together are hard to take in: 'What am I supposed to do?' It's the woolly blanket problem. 'There's a problem in there somewhere – I can see the shape of it, or I thought I could – but now there's another, and two more, and they're moving about, and as it twists and turns and gets more complicated, it gets snagged on one thing and then another until the original thing I was fixed on is lost, somewhere in a huge woolly bundle of smothering evidence and other problems.' In the end, all it says is: 'There's definitely a problem in here somewhere, but it's surrounded by complications.'

Solutions in environmental campaigns

Showing that it can be done

Originally, environmental campaigns were all about pressing for problems to be recognized. Once politicians accepted these, however, people wanted solutions to be delivered.[14] The conventional campaign format was to promote policy formulae: lists for an enlightened government. But by the 1990s, government was in full-tilt mode away from 'doing things' and business was stepping into the breach. Moreover, solutions and 'progress' had for centuries been provided by business, coupled to science and technology: progress and technology were synonymous. So Greenpeace, led by its German section, set out to take the technological initiative; changing campaigns from 'they said there was no problem' to 'they said it couldn't be done'.

Chlorine-free paper

Christoph Thies, toxics campaigner, knew a small Swedish pulp manufacturer, Aspa Bruk, had made the first totally chlorine-free (TCF) paper (bleached without chlorine, so with none of the dioxins and other toxins associated with that). Aspa Bruk was followed by larger producer Sodra-Cell. German printers and publishers resisted using new sorts of paper, and paper-makers were even less keen on making it.

Eventually, Greenpeace found a supplier willing to try. Together they produced *Der Plagiat* (the plagiary), a spoof of the leading magazine *Der Spiegel*, using TCF (*Der Spiegel* had pointedly refused to countenance TCF, citing technical impossibility). Greenpeace delivered a giant roll of printing paper to *Der Spiegel*'s offices as a 'gift', and somehow managed to obtain the magazine's mailing list. Campaigners then mailed the magazine's readers with evidence that what the management had been saying – that TCF was unavailable and of low quality – was unfounded.

Confronted by this evidence, and criticism from its readers, *Der Spiegel* changed over to being printed on TCF paper in the autumn of 1992. Other German periodicals followed suit.[15]

Greenfreeze solution

In 2000,[16] UK Prime Minister Tony Blair said:

> ... *eight years ago, Greenpeace began research on greenfreeze refrigeration technology to reduce the destruction of the ozone layer. It is now a highly successful example of green organization and industry working together for the benefit of the ozone layer. Coca Cola and Unilever have just announced they will move towards such alternative refrigerants such as greenfreeze by 2005.*

'Greenfreeze' is the name given to non-fluorocarbon refrigeration technology – used in fridges, chillers and air conditioning. It's energy-efficient, used by all major European refrigeration manufacturers, and is in large-scale production in countries such as China. It avoids 'fluorocarbons' such as chloroflurocarbons (CFCs), hydrofluoro-carbons (HFCs) or hydrochlorofluorocarbons (HCFCs).

Yet if it had been left to governments and business, all those millions of fridges would have been using (and leaking) CFCs and their descendants, HCFCs and HFCs.

In the early 1990s, the government parties to the Montreal Protocol were accepting chemical industry claims that the only way to get rid of CFCs was to replace them with another of their products, HCFCs (still damaging to the ozone layer but less so), and then yet another; HFCs (not damaging to ozone but with a very bad impact on climate).

Two technologists approached Greenpeace to propose using an 'old' alternative technology based on the more-or-less benign and cheap 'natural' hydrocarbons such as propane. Next, Greenpeace rescued an ailing East German fridge company, secured finance and marketing, generated thousands of orders from the public, and 'greenfreeze' technologies were born.

After a long struggle in the market and in the secretive world of industrial product standards, most nations have now taken up the 'greenfreeze' technology in domestic refrigeration.[17]

Notes: (top) Greenfreeze production line, Germany; (bottom) Greenfreeze
– ozone friendly refrigeration containing no freons or CFCs.
Source: (top) © Greenpeace/Ali Paczensky; (bottom) © Greenpeace/Robert
Visser

Figure 5.11 *Greenfreeze is highly efficient, is now used by all major*
European refrigeration manufacturers, and is in production on a
large scale in countries such as China

These principles can be applied to almost any campaign. There are times when change, and making the case for change, is best achieved through proving the feasibility of solutions.

The division bell

Timing the moment of reckoning

The call to action is the point at which you 'cash in your chips' and see whether or not you can win this round or battle. It acts like a division bell, the sound that signals the call to vote in the old-fashioned UK Parliament.

At this point, your campaign tries to force a taking of sides for the reckoning. It's therefore important that you go at the right moment. Too late and your support may have dissipated. People may burn out from the commitment, lose interest or be depressed by the problem and turn off.

More often, campaigners call the division too soon. Force a division among the audience too early and you are unlikely to have accumulated enough committed support to win. So try to show your audience a story using the sequence (Chapter 1) and let them make their discoveries, reflect and get angry – don't try to force them along by telling them what to think.

Make campaigns from 'doing'

Showing what
you are doing
allows supporters
to be there too

For events, news and visual language we need doing, not arguments or talking. Ask 'what's the verb?', what's the 'doing' bit in this campaign?

Many classic direct-action tactics come from this approach: asking what the problem is, then how can it be reversed. 'Return to sender', for example, involves taking waste or other immorally dumped material and returning it.

In 1992, Greenpeace campaigners discovered 2000 tonnes of German chemical pesticide wastes, all with deficient paperwork. For months, the German government resisted calls from Greenpeace and Romania to take them back. Then, in February 1993, a letter from the German government announced it would accept the poison barrels. On 11 March 1993, the returns began, and Environment Minister Claus Toepfer apologized to the Romanian population. In May, all the still-discoverable German poison barrels – 450 tonnes – were returned by a 1.3km-long train to Germany.

The first campaign with a 'return-to-sender' objective that I am aware of was by Friends of the Earth in its historic 1971 bottles action.

Of course, Greenpeace did not invent non-violent direct action (NVDA). Before the Phyllis Cormack[18] sailed to the Aleutian Islands, the Quakers had sailed, to 'bear witness' against nuclear testing. They, too, were confronted by the military, only few knew about it. The Quaker *Golden Rule* was impounded near Bikini Atoll in Hawaii in 1958 – that gave Jim Bohlen the idea to take a ship to Amchitka, and that led to the formation of Greenpeace.[19] The difference with Greenpeace was the pictures[20] which gave supporters a way of 'being there', too. Actions are one way of composing campaigns by 'doing' (see Box 5.1).

Box 5.1 Why we do actions: Their importance for Greenpeace

An extract from a memo I wrote for incoming campaigners in Greenpeace

Fundamentals
Founding proposition – Greenpeace started with action
Founding principles – non-violent direct action (NVDA), bearing witness, Quaker inspiration (see below)
Action motivates and communicates
Action demands decisiveness and honesty of purpose
Action is just a stunt if it is just for an image, action has to be real:
• stopping the problem;
• inserting the solution;
• challenging what is wrong;
• voicing the public conscience.

Communication and action strategy
Our communication strategy[21]
1st   action
2nd   image
3rd   information
Action-led
Creates image which communicates
Supported and explained with information

Not
1st   information
2nd   image
3rd   action
Where stunts are used to create images in order to draw attention to a campaign or issue pursued through information

Campaign benefits/properties of actions
Convert diffuse (grey) issues to acute ones (black/white)
So converts unclear to clear responsibility
So converts not urgent to urgent political problems
Represented by pictures of an event
Not an argument – an action is done
Cannot be questioned or interrogated
Not communicated in ideological terms
Represented by anonymous individuals
Supporters can 'be there': supporters share through anonymity

Box 5.1 continued

Not individual named heroes
Converts public support to public action
Enables people to connect values and actions
Makes Greenpeace a bargaining rather than influencing group
'argument is constructed in one way: politics in quite another'
Politics is about events. News is about events. Actions are events
Issues may be defined as ideas but are changed by events

Greenpeace campaign strategies and action
Greenpeace campaigns in three realms:
• political (government/industry);
• emotional/values;
• technical/scientific.

Actions must be done at the point of intersection of all three
This is often uncomfortable
Campaigns are planned as a process of changing power along a critical pathway
Actions and other campaign work help progress along these long-term pathways
Successful actions in themselves cause change that leads directly, in the long term, to major change: the 'inevitable consequence'

Hearts and minds

Both sides of the brain are important in real-world decision-making

To succeed you usually need to win hearts as well as minds. The usual failure is not winning hearts. Many campaigns about the ethics of public goods are disabled by a common strategy of the public affairs industry, which is to invoke the 'rational-not-emotional' frame, and so avoid the 'ethical-or-unethical' frame.

This trick works because journalists, public debaters, politicians and even campaigners frequently equate 'emotional' and 'ethical'. Those in power – usually governments or corporations – will often respond to any criticism by labelling it 'emotional', and then try to confine debate to the emotional-or-rational frame,[22] which is usually accepted without question by the media and many professional politicians. This enables them to avoid having to justify their actions in ethical terms – a frame in which they are far more likely to lose a debate.

Campaigners have three issues to deal with. First, how to avoid the trap above. Do so by explicitly raising an *ethical* challenge – for example, in terms of responsibility. Call out the opponent in those terms.

Second, how to avoid opponents or third parties suggesting that your 'rational case' rests on emotional power. Separate communication events in the different dimensions and make sure you get your rationalistic case out first, early in the campaign, in a non-emotive context – for example, scientific, economic, legal. Make sure that it evokes a response. Get it on the record. Then work through your ethical challenge, and after that, move on to trigger emotion. This won't stop opponents trying to imply your case is 'only emotional' but it will prevent that becoming a winning strategy.

Third, how to introduce emotion. It all depends on the circumstance, but it may be best done through images rather than words, and through human interest – the struggle or plight of individuals. If your campaign intervenes to help others who are less powerful, and they convey emotion, that may help most. Remember that the public will sense natural justice or injustices.

Finally, don't forget that, although the left side of the brain is said to be the seat of language and processes in a logical and sequential order, and the right side is said to work more visually, and processes intuitively, holistically, and randomly,[23] in the real world, the right side is just as important in making decisions. Its significance is widely denied, even when your opponents concede.

Faced with a successful campaign, conventional Anglo politicians/businesses generally accede on 'rational' or quasi-scientific or other 'professional' or 'objective' grounds that do not threaten their self-image or intrude on their personal ethics. Here, for example, is Heinz Rothermund, one of Shell's most intelligent board directors, on the subject of the Atlantic Frontier campaign (see emphasized section):

> *The specific attack, by Greenpeace in particular, on oil and gas developments in the Atlantic margin,* accompanied by the usual exaggerated claims about last wilderness and environmental devastation, with emotional references to whales and endangered species, *also raises a key question: 'In how far is it sensible to explore for and develop new hydrocarbon reserves, given that the atmosphere may not be able to cope with the greenhouse gases that will emanate from the utilization of the hydrocarbon reserves discovered already'.*[24]

Note how Rothermund divides the description of the campaign into the 'emotional' (assumed to be synonymous with 'exaggerated') which can be discounted, and the 'rational' part, which is (this time) worth a response.[25]

Chapter 6

CONSTRUCTING CAMPAIGN PROPOSITIONS

Constructing RASPB propositions

The proposition sums up what the campaign is about. A helpful starting point is the popular radio news format of PSB – Problem, Solution, Benefit.[1]

> The proposition is about how the campaign works and the role of the supporter

'Well, good morning Mrs Campaigner for X, welcome to Wake Up With Borset. Now, you're concerned about X and are holding a press conference later this morning – tell us, what's the problem?'

... first answer

'So what's the solution?'

... second answer

'Well, that's all very well Mrs Campaigner, but how will it benefit the people of Borsetshire?'

... third answer

'Well, thanks for coming in... Now here's Sophie with the traffic'

If your campaign proposition can meet this format, you're off to a head start. The proposition usually needs to include RASPBerry:

- Responsible party (the enemy – who's to blame);
- Action – the action you want people (who?) to take;
- Solution;
- Problem;
- Benefit.

For example:

> *Illegal loggers are felling valuable timber and wrecking this ancient forest*
>
> (Problem)

> *Effective policing and certification of timber has stopped this elsewhere*
>
> (Solution)

> *Wildlife and communities benefit from sustainable management*
> (Benefit)

> *The government of X is to blame because it's not enforcing the law*
> (Responsible party)

> *We want people to call their MP/Senator to lobby the government*
> (Action)

A real campaign should be more excitingly worded!

So this is *your* 'government lobbying campaign to save ancient forest from illegal logging' or 'the campaign against illegal logging to help communities in ancient forest'.

You may be able to then reduce this proposition to a much simpler rallying call.

The campaign 'proposition' contains the implicit promise that if you do certain things, then others will follow – such as 'sign the online petition to call on Pharmaceutical International to supply river-blindness drugs at cost in Africa'.

The 'proposition' isn't just about the cause or even the objective – it is also about how the campaign works, and what role the supporter has.

It normally helps to have the problem and the solution well up at the front of your communication, and to be able to start either from the general or from the particular – with both the big picture and the specific example readily available. Some people will like to start from one place, others insist on another, depending on their communication preferences. Relevant preferences for constructing propositions include the following.[2]

Away from/towards

The towards person stays focused on his/her own goals and is motivated by achievement. The away person focuses on problems to be avoided rather than goals to be achieved.

Internal/external

The internal person has internal standards and decides for him/herself. The external person takes standards from outside and needs direction and instruction to come from others.

Small chunk/big chunk

Big-chunk people are most comfortable dealing with large chunks of information. They do not pay attention to details. Small-chunk people pay attention to details and need small chunks to make sense of a larger picture.

Match/mismatch

People who match will mostly notice points of similarity in a comparison. People who mismatch will notice differences when making a comparison.

We all have these preferences to different degrees. Campaign planners need to ask themselves if they are simply designing a campaign that fits *their* preferences. This is a good reason to do research, and test out what works. To do that you need to know *who* you want to convince. A focus on 'problems to be avoided rather than goals to be achieved' (towards/away – the half-full/half-empty axis) obviously has immediate relevance to campaigning on problems or solutions, or how those are spoken of.

What's unlikely to ring any bells with anyone is a bland process description, as in 'our campaign addresses legal and other issues around certain forests and the political measures needed to encourage conditions of sustainability'.

Agency New Oceans[3] says:

Remember the old argument in business, education and parenting: whether to use the carrot or the stick approach? In other words, is it better to offer people incentives or threats? The answer of course is: it all depends who you want to motivate. 'Towards' people are energized by goals and rewards. 'Away' people are motivated to avoid problems and punishment.

Knowing what motivates a target group or institution would be very useful. If you don't know that, you can at least consciously hedge your bets.

Many 'campaigns of transition' utilize standard-setting as their intervention: WWF's Forest Stewardship Council, for example. The Internal-External filter describes *where* people find their standards. If people have an internal reference, says Oceans, they 'instinctively know if they have done a good job'. On the other hand, 'people with an external reference need someone else to tell them. Successful entrepreneurs are extremely internally referenced – they know when they have made a good or a bad decision. Many people in organizations are externally referenced and need a management structure to give them feedback on the standard of their work.'

So if you are campaigning to introduce a standard with an entrepreneur, you might want to start with his or her work as the benchmark, but for a large institution, you might better use evidence of good practice by others.

The self-validating proposition

'Now you come to mention it, that is exactly what I found'

We most trust information from sources we know most – hence, the power of introductions from friends. Most of all, we trust ourselves – and are most easily convinced when we draw our own conclusions. Drawing on our own experience, we think we can hold a conversation in our own heads, which nobody can spin, argue with or interfere in.

No campaigner should try to 'sell' a proposition or message that will be negated or gainsaid by the experience of the audience. This may seem blindingly obvious advice, but it's often not followed. Politicians trying to warn children from using illegal drugs, for example, may tell them that a particular drug 'kills' or 'can be fatal' and should therefore be avoided. But if young people see others using it and they don't see anyone dying, then the experience will undermine the message, and by association, this can undermine everything else on that subject that comes from the same source.

There's one type of proposition that I call 'self-righting' or 'self-validating'. Like a lifeboat with built-in buoyancy, it stays upright no matter which way you start it off. You can look at it starting from either end, and it will always appear validated. Here, two or more pieces of 'evidence' have a link that can be discovered to be true. They are like the buoyancy tanks. Many are in the form: 'X is true because all As are B', in which the A–B relationship is true, but the connection to X may not be.

For example:

All environmental campaigners are just after publicity: (because) all campaigns involve publicity – they're always trying to get on the news, the only time you ever see them is when they're doing some sort of stunt (and so on).

Test:

Do all campaigns involve publicity? *'They appear to do so.'*

Are they always trying to get on the news? *'Seems like it to me.'*

Is the only time you ever see them is when they're doing some sort of stunt? *'Yes, every time they're on TV.'*

So it's true, then? *'Guess so.'*

If you examine this proposition by starting *either* from who campaigners are, *or* what's on the news, it seems valid. It works because the audience either draws on his or her very limited existing experience (mainly gleaned from the 'news' anyway) or they check it out by watching the news. The person who wants to use this approach to mislead will be careful to pitch it so that the evidence likely to be to hand, will validate the proposition. The fact that the audience actually adds it up from their own first-hand experience adds to its veracity: *'Now you come to mention it, that's exactly what I found.'*

Mrs Thatcher's appeal to the simple homilies of home economics – the money in your handbag, that you can't spend if you haven't got it, seemed instantly verifiable by anyone with a handbag. She used it to dismiss ideas of government spending and borrowing, thereby obscuring the fact that countries are quite *unlike* individuals with handbags because, for one thing, they have future generations that reap the benefits of investment made with borrowed money, for instance in public infrastructure. Thatcher was a brilliant communicator who exploited the difference between popular and elite understanding, which, in the case of routine media debate of economics, was an unbridgeable crevasse. So she successfully marginalized her critics, who were left stranded and inaudible on the elite side, waving detailed reports and text books, not handbags.

Saying 'go test it yourself, next time you are…' can be much more powerful than trying to lead a person through a version of your own experience.

More subtle versions of this in spin and propaganda work by use of association and loose ends, laid out like bait. Over a period of time it can be given the *form* of a discovery, the search for truth, and by suggestion, implies that it is the truth.

The net effect can be that the audience falls back on things that it already feels to be true, and judges any new information with those things. By giving cues and prompts, the orchestrators can ensure the 'right' things get used as evidence and so the 'right' conclusions are drawn.

A similar technique is to ask 'how good' something was or 'how much' of it there was, so implying that the thing you are measuring is relevant or really 'the issue'. This works on the basis that attention fertilizes belief. Simply discussing a possibility a lot makes it seem more likely.

A variation is the search for the 'smoking gun'. If expanded to become a mainstream quest, it implies that the connection must exist, simply because of the psychology of group belief or action. Most of us don't like to feel that we're wrong by being out of step.

This is similar to framing (see Chapter 1). The selection of the initial frame largely determines conclusions. For example:

'These new car technologies are unproven – they may be good for the environment but they can be expensive – don't we all pay quite enough for petrol already? Who here wants to pay more?'

Triggering a cost framework rapidly leads to the established thought: 'Yes, I pay too much already.' Anything new is equated with 'maybe more expensive' and so rejected unless it is proven cheaper. Then arguing with cost is a dead end. The choice of frame is all important.

Any attempt to argue against the frame will fail. Respond for example: 'Yes, it will initially be slightly more expensive, but…' and you've just confirmed it's 'too expensive'.

Rationalists and people who are unused to being in a confrontational situation may tend to try and find middle ground by agreeing with part of a proposition and then arguing their case. This ploy is usually doomed.

In the car-engine case, by choosing an element such as cost, which they know can lead an audience to a rapid rejection, the critics successfully invoke a fatal frame for the public view of the proposal.

If instead one had started with:

'These engines can bring harmful emissions below the level known to trigger childhood asthma,'

then the benefit and test would be in a quite different frame. Do you know any children with asthma? Is it true that these emissions are that low (yes). Is it true that this level exists (yes). Well, we must have that then. Is there a price increase – yes, but it's only very small and there won't be by the time it's commercialized. OK, then.

A self-validating proposition can then be used to further dismiss critics with a vested interest. For example:

Interviewer: *'But Mrs Campaigner, some people are saying that these new engines are much more expensive …'*

Mrs Campaigner: *'They are saying that and if you check you will find that those people represent the car industry who are making significant profits from the current grossly polluting engines, whose emissions as we all know cause asthma.'*

Or she might have added:

'As anyone who's seen the prices of new cars will know, there's a lot of money being made somewhere.'

Have you seen the prices? – Gosh, yes, now you come to mention it.

Make the issue an 'either/or'

A yes/no, 'binary', presence/absence, black/white, either/or type of proposition is more compelling than a matter of degree, such as a how-much or a bit-less. It is more useful and robust, invulnerable to differing perceptions of 'how much is enough'. Monitoring, evaluation and accountability are easier. It allows for 'closure': a supporter can see there can be a clear end point.

To reduce a campaign proposition to an elemental level, map out your issue in all its complexity. Like an aerial photograph of a great city, from high up it looks grey. Zoom in to any part, however, and eventually it resolves itself into black and white. At this point, the difference between the two parts is absolute, incapable of further reduction.

Find the 'point of irreducibility' where the two adjacent bits of the issue are differentiated by a single simple difference: one is what you want, and is right, the other is not what you want, and is wrong. Here's your objective.

For example, the UK campaigns against the sale of school playing fields for development can be boiled down to 'for-sale' or 'not-for-sale' propositions. Somewhere, in an office or in a school, there will be an individual whose pen will or won't be poised to sign the order to sell. It can be photographed; you can go there.

Advantages of irreducible propositions

Propositions and objectives around elemental, irreducible differences have five advantages:

1   They pass what communicator John Wyatt[4] calls the 'dinner party test'. You can pass these propositions around and they come back to you the same as they set out. They cannot be unpicked or unravelled, and as such, they travel without losing their meaning. They can 'go viral' without mutating in the process

2   They are also news-proof. News polarizes, reduces, clarifies, crystallizes, sensationalizes. Remember the old news dictum: first simplify, then exaggerate. Put grey stuff into the news machine and

it comes out black and white. Put a qualified, gradualist or multi-component campaign proposition into news and it will be converted into a black-and-white something (probably a something-else). So don't do it. Only put yes/no, present/absent, black/white, 0/1-type campaign propositions into the news system. They can't be simplified, and are hard to exaggerate

3   They set up a moral line of absolute right and wrong. This, in turn, can plumb the depths and heights of emotional and spiritual engagement, which is hard – if not impossible – with a 'matter of degree'. Take transport, a subject that many people feel strongly about and which is notoriously a tangle of issues, perceptions and motivations. If, for some reason, it is morally wrong to allow traffic down a street, we may block its path with our bodies – a classic non-violent direct action. If, however, we want a one-third reduction in traffic, then blocking every third car fails all the tests of natural justice

4   They are unambiguous. Creative ambiguity may help align more people initially, but a campaign is a journey, and if it becomes apparent that you meant one thing and followers thought you meant another, it's a recipe for defections

5   They make it easy to apply the reversibility test. If a proposition is sound, it gets you what you really want when the objective is achieved. If you will still not be satisfied when the objective is achieved, the campaign will irritate sympathizers and disappoint supporters. Trust and support are quickly lost. So try reversing the problem statement – does it become the solution? If not, rethink it until it does.

Focus on the unacceptable

Focus on the small part that is unacceptable to most

Some campaigns only need to re-awaken interest. Most have to mobilize new and additional support, and need a target that motivates a large enough number of people. Focus on a small part of the problem that is unacceptable to a large part of the population, rather than a large part of the problem that is unacceptable to a tiny part of the population.

The Campaign for Lead-free Air (CLEAR) against lead in petrol visibly focused on the most motivating part of the problem – lead's impact on the brains of children – by conducting a survey of street dust, targeting primary school playgrounds by busy roads, using a clearly labelled white van.

German and Austrian traffic pollution campaigners achieved a similar result by taking air samples at children's nose-height, instead of the usual sampling points employed by local authorities, which were typically high up on buildings.

Convert the diffuse to the acute

Make hard-to-evaluate problems tangible

Political reflexes are stimulated by acute problems, not diffuse ones. The former threaten careers, reputations and interests. The latter can be more safely ignored, not because they are not serious problems, but because watchdogs such as voters, the media and campaigners have a hard time showing that they are there and needing attention now. In this way, 'soft disasters' creep up on us undetected or ignored by political systems.

So, for example, climate change is accepted as the single greatest problem facing humanity, but safeguarding jobs at a car plant, or responding to a fuel-price protest, is often a greater political priority. On the other hand, the ozone hole over Antarctica was an acute political problem – almost all the ozone had disappeared in one place – while moderate ozone depletion across a much larger areas was not.

Events, physics, ecology, nature or human affairs can all convert the diffuse to the acute or vice versa, but so can campaigners. In 2002, for example, the Dutch section of Greenpeace vacuumed homes to convert the hard-to-see, hard-to-evaluate problem of chemical toxins in household dust into a campaign tool that could be used in engaging celebrities and the public. By concentrating the dust, it became possible to analyse its contents, and work out which household products – such as paints, TV sets, carpets, plastics – had contributed which chemicals.[5] Being able to collect such evidence paved the way to strategies to confront those responsible. What 'vacuum cleaner' opportunities does your issue offer?

Other ways to convert a diffuse to an acute problem can include bringing victims together, closing the distance between the commissioning of a problem and its consequences, or altering timings.

Beware of slogans!

Slogans are
often a substitute
for thought

A slogan is not the same as a proposition. It doesn't usually propose much; it just expresses an attitude. Memorable and short is good, but they often say more about the source than they do to persuade the audience. Being handy and familiar, slogans are often a substitute for thought about how to communicate effectively If you hear the word 'slogan', reach for the CAMP CAT checklist (Chapter 1).

As slogans are fixed, they can easily turn into liabilities when context changes. Before the 2003 Iraq War, some UK organizations banded together as the Stop the War coalition. Before the war started, the majority of people in the UK opposed it. After it started, however, the majority supported it, or so it appeared from the way polls were conducted and reported. The media often represented this as a 'change of mind' by the public. It was implied that those who had spoken against the war,[6] were 'wrong' now that they were out of step.

They had trouble dealing with these questions because the literal meaning of the slogan 'Stop the War' meant one thing *before* any war started (don't start it, stop it from starting), and another (don't finish it, or don't win it), once it was underway. Yet the statement itself had remained the same. 'Stop the War' was insensitive to this difference.

Many people took the view that the war was wrong and should not start, but once it had begun, the least-bad option available was to continue and win it. Their view could not, however, be differentiated within the 'Stop the War' formula. Consequently, the groups also failed to take control of the agenda on issues such as the nature of the peace, because they were stuck with 'unfinished business'.

The gross factor

Does your campaign include something gross? Something that reaches you in the heart or the guts and makes you feel sick, angry or revolted? If not, what motivates you to work on the 'issue'? Try redrafting your plan to include it.

Good campaigning means getting your emotional hands dirty

If your critical path intersects with something gross – a huge injustice, an intolerable act of selfishness, a stomach-turning consequence, an event that moves you to tears – it will have power that any amount of argument or design can never bring.

Good campaigning means getting your emotional hands dirty. Polite hand-washing classes may enjoy 'expert' status in policy circles, and discuss a problem knowledgeably while allowing it to continue, but effective campaigns can't run on reasonableness. When you are retired, or on your deathbed, they should be things that you feel glad you did, not ashamed that you left aside to maintain credibility with experts who stress facts but whose real motivation is to not rock the boat.

In this case of the Brent Spar, the gross factor was supplied by the world's biggest piece of litter, by one of the world's biggest corporations, in the backyard of one of the world's richest countries.

After the campaign, I developed the 'Brent Spar Scale' (Figure 6.1) to try and explain how the public seemed to see things.

Corporate and government issue specialists often live in a world where 'good practices' are defined between themselves or policy benchmarks and professional consensus. They may regard these norms as more objective and superior to opinions of outsiders. They may be concerned to meet internal performance targets. This objectified world view focuses on the bottom levels of the Brent Spar Scale.

Many bosses and managers used to (and some still) resort to the 'bottom line' of legality as the first response to external challenge. 'We're going about our business, and this is legal.' If that failed, their focus slid up to relative performance – are we better or worse than others? – and output failures (was there something we failed to deliver?). Yet the things that count for more – complacency, incompetence, deceit, and grossness – they tended to dismiss as 'soft' issues. Institutions doing this are continually frustrated by the 'wrong' perceptions of the public.

Figure 6.1 *The Brent Spar Scale*

The public doesn't know about things like best practice. If we are not involved in a 'professional' world, we assess the actions of organizations as we see and judge individuals. We say: 'Switzerland did this', or 'Shell thinks... ', or 'Greenpeace has said... '.

Second worst behind gross acts come deceitful acts. Exxon did this when it tried to fix climate science by evicting Bob Watson from his job at the Intergovernmental Panel on Climate Change (IPCC), and Pfizer when it continued to sell hip-replacement joints it knew to be faulty.[7] After that comes uncaring complacency, as Dow[8] appeared to be over Bhopal, and that is less forgivable than being incompetent. Just being legal is not impressive – decades of commercial lobbying have ensured that most laws to protect the public interest are as weak as possible.

So with the Spar, Greenpeace said it was gross, and Shell said it was legal. Arguably, both were correct. Greenpeace won, however, because the public felt Shell was in the wrong.

Elimination and sacrifice

A big outcome grabs the attention much more than a small one. The technology that, at a stroke, can eliminate a whole factory's worth of pollution, is dramatic.

To eliminate a problem is stronger than mere mitigation

Stopping all the traffic in a city has an audacious 'make-another-world-possible' appeal. Hence the initial adrenaline-spiked attraction of the group Reclaim the Streets. To leave your car at home on 'Car-Free Day', however, when you know that everyone else in the street will probably drive as normal, is less attractive because it seems futile.

In the words of eco-philosopher Theodore Roszak:

> ... *prudence is such a lacklustre virtue. It does not match the exhilaration of the heroic exploits to which the myth of limitless progress summons us. If ecological wisdom cannot be made as engaging as the reshaping of continents, the harvesting of the seas, the exploration of space, if it cannot compete with the material gratifications of industrial growth, it will run a poor second to those who appeal to stronger emotions.*[9]

Propositions to *eliminate* a problem are stronger than those that merely mitigate it.

Campaigns that promise entry to a new world where anything is possible may inspire support, despite considerable sacrifice or discomfort. Those that leave all the underlying causes and constraints in place simply offer major re-adjustments, rather than fundamental re-alignments: benefits that may only prove temporary. Why sacrifice anything for that?

Inspiration and drama

Does your
campaign
excite you?

Campaigners can take to heart the admonishments of Theodore Roszak. Once your attention is captured, it's a lot more fun to run a campaign composed of positive, exciting, 'doing' things rather than one that makes people feel guilty and just asks them to do less. Roszak quotes *Earth Island Journal*,[9] which stated: 'It is not enough to find "50 simple things you can do to save the Earth". We need <u>50 difficult</u> things.' The list begins:

1   dismantle your car;
2   become a total vegetarian;
3   grow your own vegetables;
4   have your power lines disconnected;
5   don't have children...

Says Roszak:

> ... *habitual reliance on gloom, apocalyptic panic, and the psychology of shame takes a heavy toll in public confidence. In part, the problem arises from the way the environment movement has come to be organized. The pattern resembles the telethon disease-of-the-month approach...*

> *Like all political activists busy with their mission, environmentalists often work from poor and short-sighted ideas about human motivation; they overlook the unreason, the perversity, the sick desire that lie at the core of the psyche. Their strategy is to shock and shame. But it is one thing to have the Good clearly in view; it is another to find ways to make people want the Good...*

> *Are dread and desperation the only motivations we have to play on? What are we connecting with in people that is generous, joyous, freely given – perhaps heroic?*

Benny Haerlin is a former German MEP and, most recently, anti-GM campaigner. I asked him why the Brent Spar campaign attracted such public attention. He pointed out something that, in retrospect was obvious: 'It was a drama. There was a struggle and the outcome was unknown, right up until the very last moment. It lasted for weeks, and many people thought it was over many times. It was not until the very last second that we knew the outcome.'

Drama holds our attention. We want to know the outcome of the struggle. Drama could arise through a parliamentary vote if enough hangs on it, or a protestor in hiding, such as the English anti-roads tunneller 'Swampy'.

Yet so many campaigns are quite unlike that. Many seem unambitious, or simply an extended form of complaint: unexciting, uninspiring. Does your campaign excite you? If not, stop it and rework it until it does. Select your campaign from among the things that excite you, not the ones that you feel you ought to be seen to work on. Plan for drama by embarking on adventures where you do not know the outcome yourself. As a friend once said to me: 'Have a nice adventure.'

Chapter 7

WORKING WITH NEWS MEDIA

Using the media

_____

How to deal with
the media
machine

_____

It's natural for campaigners and journalists to develop a close relationship. Too much focus on news though, is a bad thing. News can report conflict beautifully, but it isn't a very good tool to help *promote* change.

Nevertheless, almost every campaign is likely to involve substantial media work, so it pays to discover how to deal with the media machine. The news media[1] presents a version of reality. From within, it is a machine and a community. Once you learn how to gain access, it can be entrancing, flattering and addictive[2] so be careful.

Friends of the Earth (FoE)[3] answers the question 'Why do press work?' in this way:

- Profile – making sure people know you exist, what kind of organization you are and what you do
- Specific publicity – the fastest and most effective way to reach a wide audience
- Leverage – targets (for example, local authorities, industries) are more likely to get a move on and change their ways if they know that the debate is visible and very public.

To which I would add third-party endorsement. Being reported by someone else implies that someone has evaluated and tested a version of events, and found it true enough to be worth passing on.

FoE's 20 ways to get into the news (with my comments):

1   Launch a campaign (make sure there are activities to report, as well as objectives)
2   Hold a public meeting (see www.campaignstrategy.org)
3   Mark an anniversary (this can be the anniversary of a related event, even a setback)
4   Hold an AGM (only likely to excite core followers, unless dramatized, for example with a vote)
5   Announce formation of a new group (if true!)
6   Welcome new proposals (in media-speak this is 'giving reaction')
7   Condemn new proposals (as above)
8   Call for a public inquiry
9   Give evidence to a public inquiry
10 Lobby someone else's meeting
11 Publish findings of a survey or opinion poll – public (these can be very simple and cheap – they don't have to be the best possible, only better than anything else around that day)
12 The same for trade/industry
13 Involve a local celebrity
14 Invite a local dignitary to an event – they don't have to accept for this to be press-worthy. (the media then goes to them for 'reaction' – often it's best to leave a story as an open invitation for the media to complete it – an unfinished story has more 'legs')
15 Send a letter to someone important (be sure to hand-deliver or courier it, or confirm a fax: if the press will want a reaction from them, they must have it!)
16 Present a petition
17 Quiz election candidates (council, parliamentary or EC)
18 Hold a vigil (looks much better at night)
19 Direct action (follow the principles of non-violence)
20 Stunts/dressing up/build a display (use visual language – see Chapter 5).

Eleven things to know about the media

**Understanding
the messenger**

1 Create your own events and public conversations (such as using face-to-face approaches, e-mail, internet) and then get the media to cover that – create the reality, don't let the media become the reality – they will turn on you

2 News is not the only media – features pages/programmes and magazines are often better read and remembered – news polarizes but features don't. Only use news for irreducible either/or stories; use other media channels for more complex stories

3 News media needs events and people – provide both

4 Local media are (in the UK) more trusted than national media – it's more important to correct inaccuracies in local media

5 News has the absolution of time. Each day begins anew. A good letter or the story of your own event is better than a small comment embedded in a story framed by an opponent

6 Find out about timing and markets (listeners, readers, viewers) for each outlet – they determine what's covered. Even news is in the entertainment business

7 Invest in contacts – get to know journalists and help them

8 News is about a change to something already understood. Don't use it to explain something completely new. For that, first carry it to the social mainstream and then into local or specialist press

9 Find out which media your audience consume and target those. First though, check you can't go direct – which may be more effective

10 Don't count publicity as success – plan, and look for effect

11 Don't waste time arguing with the media unless it becomes unavoidable. Don't 'have a pissing match with a skunk'.

Pure opposition … is the force behind much radio and television journalism. Broadcasters change the subject whenever they are proved wrong. They show irresponsibility in its purest form because they are not required to defend the stands they take. What works well for the BBC, however, is fatal for the politically committed, [who] are meant to understand the world and show how their principles could improve it.

Nick Cohen[4]

'News values'

News is history in its first and best form, its vivid and fascinating form, and … history is the pale and tranquil reflection of it.

Mark Twain

Factors that make a story valuable

News in the end is what we think it is and say it is. News is what people talk about – gossip, scandal and events that matter, shock or surprise.

Key factors making something newsworthy are 'news values'. For years, I thought these were a set of values in the sense of moral principles, but no: they are factors that make a story valuable – that is, useful – to news outlets. They develop sales and egos, not ethics. In 1965, Johan Galtung and Marie Holmboe Ruge compiled a much-quoted list of 'news values' based on coverage of international events:

- Frequency: Timing and how it fits news schedules and deadlines. 'On this basis,' says media researcher Mick Underwood,[5] 'motorway pile-ups, murders, plane crashes will qualify, as they are all of short duration and therefore nearly always fit into the schedule. Such events are also unambiguous, their meaning is quickly arrived at.' Trends and complex processes are generally ruled out unless they can be told through one-off events such as trade figures – hence the importance of indices such as the FTSE500 as a way of covering things deemed important but difficult
- Threshold: Is it big enough to count?
- Clarity: Underwood says: 'The mass media generally tend to go for closure, unlike literature, where the ambiguity of meaning of events is exploited and explored'. He cites[6] a US survey that revealed that 'the most regular reason why stories don't appear is that they are too complicated'. So only ever ask news to cover things that are unambiguous. An action, or a criticism, or a call for a resignation, can be the 'news', while the reasons for it may contain too many unknowns or ambiguities to be reported
- Meaningfulness: Will readers or viewers see it as relevant to them? The media reflect popular culture
- Consonance: Does the event match the media's expectations? An early warning sign can be unexpected media wanting to come to cover your event or taking an unusual interest: they will probably be using it for some other news purpose. Find out what it is!

- Unexpectedness: Classically, 'man bites dog' is news, vice versa is not. Hence, skateboarding ducks are news. Unexpected success can be news – a positive story!
- Continuity: This is a question of convenience. It's why the media loves anniversaries as 'pegs'. Don't let its 'no brainer' nature put you off. Campaigners often try to be too clever. PR agencies, on the other hand, go for the easiest option. It enables TV to pull out some old footage – no cost involved. TV news budgets have plummeted, and cost is a major reason why news coverage is increasingly spasmodic, cheap and shallow. The BBC has a website devoted to anniversaries of events 'on this day'
- News context and competition: Is it a heavy news day or not? Is there a lot of news? If so, of course your story stands less chance
- Important or elite nations: 'People like us' get most coverage in our media – similar nations, for instance. Local media often demand that someone 'local' features in the story. The adage 'every name mentioned is a copy sold' is true – only it ought to be 'every name mentioned is probably several copies sold' once relatives are taken into account. 'Aberdeen Man Lost At Sea' was allegedly the headline in the *Aberdeen Journal* in 1912, on the occasion of the sinking of the Titanic, which also killed 2223 other people (not from Aberdeen)
- Reference to elite persons: Anything done by the most powerful people is news. The US President having a cold, for instance. Campaigners can add important people to make an issue media-friendly. In May 2003, Christian Aid published a report on oil wealth, which, it argued, often caused inequality, conflict and poverty rather than sustainable forms of development. Not an easy sell to the mainstream news media, but Christian Aid also sent actor and sympathetic supporter Joseph Fiennes (of the movie *Shakespeare in Love*), to Angola. Fiennes came back to give a first-hand report of what he saw, which was covered along with a Christian Aid spokesman in a studio discussion on BBC Radio 4's *Today* programme[7]
- Personalization: Politics is often presented as a tussle between two party leaders. Campaigns can do this – for example by focusing on the personal responsibility of a World Trade Organization (WTO) official over globalization
- Negativity: most news is bad. Fiske[8] refers to a US journalist arriving in the war-torn Belgian Congo, running up to a group of white women waiting for a plane to leave, and shouting out: 'Has anyone here been raped and speaks English?'

Then there are other professed news values – educational value for instance, and some which just seem self-evident, such as stories involving money or sex.

Press releases

Making a journalist's job easier

A press release is simply a written statement that aims to entice the media into covering an issue you want to communicate. FoE quotes journalist and politician Denis McShane in his book *Using the Media*,[9] describing it as:

a partially digested helping of news which can then be made into the real thing by the journalists in the newsroom.

- One side of A4, double-spaced, is ideal
- Use descriptive, not clever, headings, with an active verb
- No jargon or professional speak
- Check that a 14-year-old understands it
- Keep a hard-copy archive and one online, if you have a website
- Use e-mail – most journalists now write from their desk
- Allow three days for hard-copy material to be opened and reach them
- If justified, use an 'embargo' – which means it should not be used before a particular time and date. It allows journalists time to investigate and prepare. Embargoes are, however, informal and rely on neither side abusing the system. Don't try to embargo news that has already broken in order to control it or break an embargo you have set
- Make a follow-up phone call, to find out if it has been received, who is handling it, and whether you can help at all
- To simply notify an upcoming event, make it a Press *Notice*
- If it's immediate reaction write 'For Immediate Release' with time, place and date.

The first paragraph is the most important part of a press release and should contain the most interesting point of the issue, using the four Ws: Who? What? Where? and When? – Why? and How? can follow. For example:

Ambridge group launches drive to save hedges

In a year-long project starting today, the Ambridge Tree Team plans to save hedges in three ways:

- *Mapping all the ancient hedges in Borsetshire with a metre-by-metre field survey*
- *Running 'Project Hedge', a new grant scheme to help with management costs*
- *Hedgeline – communities whistle-blowing if valuable hedges are being cut down, with a free-phone number and website.*

The project follows last year's council survey showing a 20 per cent increase in the rate of loss of hedges in the county. 'It's time to stop the rot', said Cindy Thaxter, project coordinator.

If there are a lot of points, use bullets. Helpful background information should go under 'Notes to editors' after 24/7 phone and e-mail contacts at the end of a release. Where the actual press release finishes, write 'Ends'.

Press conferences

Meet a lot of characters in one place

Press conferences appear on TV, so they look important. They can be useful, but backfire badly if used without real justification. Meeting people is key – if it's just you and a pack that could be posted, then don't bother.

Checklist[10]

- Define the story and your key messages
- Decide who are the best/appropriate people to speak (ideally no more than three)
- Identify key media and send them an invitation
- Decide on a time that suits key media you want to reach (10.30am or 11.30am is usually good). To catch the breakfast broadcast media you will need to have a breakfast briefing at 7.30am/8.00am – a high-risk time!
- Remind news desks by phone the day before (expect a high drop-out, even so)
- Brief all speakers, and any other people who might be interviewed (case histories) beforehand. Have bullet points for each speaker

- Rehearse the conference the day before: key points and the possible problem questions, rehearsing answers – time well spent
- Check the room, ensure all equipment works and provide simple visual backdrops that add to the story
- Provide coffee and tea on tap and take the names of all journalists attending
- Issue journalists with a press pack on arrival – including the press release (with pre-formatted quotes from the speakers) and any other useful background material (research synopsis, background information about your agency and what it has achieved, facts and figures, and so on)
- Start and end on time
- Ask the chairman to welcome and introduce speakers, and briefly review the issue
- Each speaker should have a different role and subject area. They should talk for a maximum of five minutes, clearly and concisely
- Have a balance of 'experts' and 'real people'
- Chairman should invite questions
- Remember all that is said is 'on the record' – but remember that there is no such thing as 'off the record'
- Offer interviews afterwards – usually for radio and TV. But stick to the key messages laid out in the conference
- Send the press release out by fax or e-mail to journalists who didn't attend.
- Evaluate the media coverage gained.

Disadvantages of a press conference include journalists getting ideas and 'hunting in a pack', and speakers who start arguing or contradicting each other. Preparation and control are key. Advantages are that it can help journalists enlarge a story from a news piece into a longer feature with visuals, because they can meet a lot of different characters in one place.

The environment should reinforce the content and tone of what is said.

The interview suitcase

**Don't forget
your trousers**

Only do interviews or media appearances if you have something to say – something that you *want* to say. Have some communication points – write them down – and pack your 'suitcase', including:

- A headline: the *main* thing you want to say. Whatever happens, say this! It's your 'jacket'
- Three reasons supporting the headline (for example: 'Save this forest for its beauty, its genetic resources and because it safeguards a clean water supply for 10,000 people'). Journalists won't just accept your headline point, they'll ask 'W' 'why?'. These are the 'shirts' or proofs
- One fact to go with each reason[11] – preferably a number. Many news stories have one number. This is the 'skirt' or 'trousers'
- Lastly, anecdotes, the 'socks and underwear': an anecdote converts a view into a story and brings an interview to life – 'Let me tell you about a little girl I met only the other day, whose life has been so improved by... ' Have one in mind that you will try to bring in if you get the chance. Few interviewers will cut off a short story in mid-flow, but all will feel entitled to cut short a list of 'points'. To begin with an anecdote is high risk, as people will weigh up all the issues in their head against your example, and one example is unlikely to be generally applicable. It's best to start with the big picture and introduce examples later.

Bridging

**Know your
A-B-C**

In any interview, the journalist will have his or her agenda and you yours (communication points). A struggle ensues as to what gets recorded. You can't trick the press into reporting what you want, so seek the best in the relationship.

Remember, their task is to sell newspapers, keep viewers watching and stop listeners switching to another station. Journalists need you to fill their airtime or column inches, so cooperate by being as interesting as possible.

Ed Gyde says:

In the 'battle of agendas', you need to follow very different rules from a conversation with a friend whom you might meet in the pub or in the office. An interview is not like a normal chat – it may look like one, but it's run on quite different lines. 'Bridging' is the way you can get back from the journalist's agenda to your communication points. Used properly, it is very useful and wholly legitimate. Used badly, it's annoying to all concerned. It follows the sequence A-B-C. A stands for acknowledge; B stands for bridge; C for your communication points.

Don't ignore questions, but don't be led by them unless they lead to your communication points. Instead, acknowledge them, and bridge away to what you want to say. This needs practising – preferably with a media trainer – as it's not a natural way to talk, but it sounds fine in a media interview.

The reason you need to do this is that very few, if any, questions will either be open – 'So tell us all about it' – or appropriate to your communication points. If you are asked nine questions and only one naturally leads to your points, and you answer them directly, the other eight answers will dominate and the audience won't remember your points at all. If you manage to repeat them nine times, they probably will get at least one of them. Bridges are verbal invitations to yourself to make your points.

Some bridges:

- 'That's an issue, but *what the public are most concerned about* is… '
- 'Some say that, but *what our research shows* is'
- 'Yes that debate will run and run, and *today we are focused on*'
- 'An important point and *I'd like to answer it in three ways, if I may…* ' (high risk, as it requires style and confidence, but used to great effect by elder statesman who, of course, never do answer)
- 'I agree that needs answering and *I will in a moment, if I may*, but first I would just like to say… ' (using politesse to take control of the interview agenda)
- 'That is an issue but *the important thing to focus on…* ' (very popular but patently judgemental and thus rather obvious)
- 'Well I think *the three main things to focus on* are' (double bridge, only viable if the question wasn't very clear)
- 'Let me *be absolutely clear*' (not a bridge at all, a smokescreen favourite of UK Prime Minister Tony Blair, which everyone takes as 'I'm not answering that')

- 'But what *we know works* in this field is… ' (useful, as long as you really do know)
- 'That's a possibility but what *we're calling for* is… ' (likewise)
- 'That's one view, but we need to look at *how this fits into the bigger picture*.'

Don't be like politicians and push past the question without acknowledging it, from A to C without B – that's rude.

The temptation may be to bridge everything and never to answer any question directly. That is a mistake. If you get questions that can be answered with a yes or no, do so, and add your key points. If it's reasonable, there's nothing wrong with saying: 'I don't know. but I'll find out and get back to you/the listeners' – in fact, come to think of it, that can also be a bridge.

Be prepared

Before agreeing to do an interview, find out who else is going to be there, who listens to the programme (is it drivers, teenagers, grannies?), and what the story is (why they want you). Make sure to know if it is live or recorded, and whether (especially TV) there's a studio audience. (Live is actually easier, though beginners find it more worrying. The thing is to have your points in your head, so they just come out naturally. Having 'time to think' in an interview doesn't help because you're likely to think of something new to say that isn't one of your key points!)

> Have your points in your head so they come out naturally

Be prepared: don't do interviews 'on the hoof'. Take time to think. Paint a picture with your words – particularly for radio. Media trainer Angela Coles lists five Ps:

- people (name or describe);
- pictures;
- passion;
- plain language;
- preparation.

She stresses PEP – point (make it), evidence (give it), point (repetition), and thinking about who your audience is, what language to use and what examples to give.

Stick to the points you've carefully prepared. Avoid last-minute brainwaves. As Alan Watson of Burson Marsteller says, 'the TV studio is no place for original thought'.

Finally, avoid unnecessary clarification. Don't focus on misconceptions, however annoying they may be – there isn't time to educate people in an interview. Make your points, not just once, but as many times as possible.

It's a scandal

Neglected alternatives can be highly newsworthy

Many news stories are driven by 'scandal'.[12] Obviously, a scandal revolving around a terrible problem is bigger than one that's only slight, but there's more to it than this. My scandal formula is:

$$\text{Scandal} = \text{awfulness} \times \frac{\text{what can be done about the problem?}}{\text{what is being done about it?}} \times \text{immoral profit}$$

'Awfulness' is often the first port of call for a news report. 'Just how bad is it?' Like most useful news story constructions, 'just how bad is it?' is a question that can be asked with an air of authority but without any knowledge of the subject matter.

Most scandals start with some sort of damage report. The 'immoral profit' factor is where the media go next, if there is the slightest hint that malpractice was involved. A favourite line of enquiry after a disaster is whether safety measures were compromised to save money. After the Potters Bar rail crash in the UK in 2002, where maintenance was seen to be at fault, there were accusations that 'insecure freelancers were cutting corners to meet the demands of cheese-paring managers'.[13]

Immoral profit is the reason, for instance, why deaths from illegal drugs are more scandalous than deaths from substances whose sale was legal. Paracetemol, for example, kills around 200 people each year in the UK through accidents or suicide. Few of those make headlines, whereas ecstasy deaths (27 in 2000[14]), cocaine (57) or amphetamines (19) are more likely to be reported.

Implicit in the media construction of a scandal is that it was *avoidable*. If there's no solution, if nothing can be done, then there is no scandal, only a tragedy. The world is full of problems, but there are far fewer clearly avoidable ones.

If alternatives are overlooked – or stronger still, neglected or *suppressed* – then a problem builds into a scandal. In this way, a solution-driven campaign can become highly newsworthy.

Check if:

• A solution to an accepted problem is being suppressed
• A solution to an accepted problem is being neglected
• If someone is doing something awful (check also, for grossness – see Chapter 6)
• If an immoral profit is being made from a problem continuing
• If an immoral profit is being made from a solution going unused
• If those responsible could do more.

Journalistically, scandals can be just awfulness x repression or secrecy:

$$\text{Scandal} = \text{awfulness} \times \frac{\text{what can be done about the problem?}}{\text{what is being done about it?}} \times \begin{array}{c} \text{immoral} \\ \text{profit} \end{array} \times \begin{array}{c} \text{suppression/} \\ \text{secrecy} \end{array}$$

Newspaper proprietor Lord Northcliffe once said: 'News is what somebody, somewhere, wants to suppress; everything else is advertising'.

Conflict makes news

**Your most
newsworthy
opportunity**

In May 1981, we were organizing the launch of the London Wildlife Group[15] with a conference. To help publicize this, I thought it would be a good idea to plant some primroses (wild ones rescued from a road development) on London's Primrose Hill, symbolizing an intent to return nature to the city. Equipped with primroses and photogenic local schoolchildren – even armed with the memories of an old lady who lived nearby and remembered picking primroses there as a child – I thought we had 'a package'. On 13 May, I embarked on a final 'ring-round', trying to interest news desks, and in particular, photo desks. Harassed photo editors answered with the question: 'You do know what's happened, don't you?' The Pope had just been shot. 'Yes, but there must still be *something* else going in the papers', I found myself saying plaintively, but without much hope.

Then we were rescued for the following Sunday newspapers by the inadvertent assistance of the government. The press were not very interested in planting wild flowers – until, that is, the Royal Parks unexpectedly refused us permission. Here was a story the press could handle – bureaucracy versus the little people trying to do the right thing. The official at the end of the phone even thought a primrose was a tree, and asked: 'How tall is it?' It got on the front page of the national newspaper *The Observer*.[16]

The primrose campaign taught me two things: first there was a conflict, along with the helpful ingredients of easy access for photographers and 'human interest'. Second, while newness is a news value, it was not entirely new. It was a formula that the newspaper had run many times before.

If you have a campaign it will be in conflict with someone somewhere. That is probably your most newsworthy opportunity.

Chapter 8

KEEPING A CAMPAIGN GOING

Staying on the side of the victims

Retaining
sympathy for
your campaign

A constant media reprise is that the 'real victims deserve our sympathy' (their case is implicitly right). Make sure that the most empathetic figure in the story is you, or on your side. Don't let the media fall out of love with your campaign through the natural tendency for it to dry out and become an elite dialogue.

- Causes start their lives as 'left-field', driven from the heart and over simple instances of injustice or abuse, expressed in everyday language
- As time goes by, progress brings calls for systematic evaluation, qualification, objectivity, dispassionate analysis. 'Expert' dialogue develops: this is harder to understand, less public
- Knowledge of problems and solutions progresses; the campaign pushes for further change; perhaps losers start to fight back. For example, polluting industries see costs rise and markets shrink as policies favour cleaner technologies. They are self-interested, yes; but what they now kick against is an abstraction, a bureaucratic policy, an esoteric issue and statistics, maybe about risks yet to arise or problems that seem far away.

Now flesh-and-blood 'victims' are appealing for 'fairness'. The woeful business person finds a sympathetic hearing in an economics report on TV, positioned against 'bleeding-heart liberals', 'rules' or 'the interests

HOW TO WIN CAMPAIGNS

of frogs'.[1] The campaign 'no longer deserves sympathy' and the media positions the campaigners as the ones to blame.

Avoid this roll-back in two ways: First, don't let it happen.

- Keep the victims' reality locked into the heart of the campaign, be they coral reefs succumbing to climate change, victims of chemical poisoning, cancer patients, or slum-dwellers thousands of miles away
- Make them the channels or messengers, or get as close as you can
- Keep experts on tap, not on top.

Second, lead renewed calls for progress with evidence of the victims in terms that make them the *most empathetic* characters in the story – not, say, the latest results of a computer model – unless a victim is also the messenger.

Left to drift, campaigns tend to dry out, become status conscious and accumulate experts – scientists, lobbyists, policy workers and others. It's cheap, too – expert chats have no need of costly mobilization, communications staffs, political theatre, legal, marketing, protest, action or other elements of the campaign army. Most experts like to talk to experts, not to the public. That is no way to run campaigns.

Fish and sympathy

A classic dried-out campaign problem is the annual crisis over fishing quotas in the European Union Common Fisheries Policy.

The problem starts because there's no news from the fish. As victims, fish don't take part in the media directly. Then it's generally a matter of degree – not an either/or problem (see Chapter 6). A bulging net can be visual evidence of either a 'good' or a 'bad' fishery: a victim problem, right away.

> The problem starts because there's no news from the fish

Pressure groups, and most of all governments, take advice on stock and fishing levels from fisheries scientists. The debate is elite, technical, inaccessible. Then officials set quotas – politics supplies the event – and fishing activity gets cut.

Now the 'issue' is the cuts, and fishermen, who are at least part of the problem, become 'the victims'. The media then reports *this* as the problem.

Politicians grandstand against their own conservation policy to play national interests. Campaigners see fishing in the news: talks are in 'crisis'. A 'solution' is urgently needed, but it's just political theatre. The media waits to see which Member State (in the case of the European Union fisheries policy debates) is going to come out on top. So the real players and victims are not fish, but politicians. Environment groups are largely irrelevant except for providing some pictures.[2]

The best campaign opportunity is outside such a forum and well before the endgame begins, in the stacking of odds and setting of terms. Politics then plays the cards that you have helped to mark. Make the fish the victims earlier on, and keep them there with visuals (for example, underwater visuals) and spokespeople, such as concerned field biologists and fishermen, throughout.

Not surprisingly, successful fisheries campaigns are almost as rare as hens' teeth. Witness the miniscule number of fisheries certified by the Marine Stewardship Council (MSC – see www.msc.org).

> *Severe cuts in white fish quotas will 'decimate' Scotland's fishing communities, it has been warned... In Brussels, an agreement was reached which will limit fishing vessels to 15 days at sea. There will also be a 45 per cent cut in cod quotas, a 50 per cent reduction in haddock catches, and 60 per cent cut in whiting catches.[3]*

> *For the World Wildlife Fund, Julie Cator also said that it falls far short of the cuts that environmentalists said were necessary to prevent the further decline of fish stocks. The deal came late on Friday after UK Prime Minister Tony Blair had made a telephone call to his Danish counterpart, Anders Fogh Rasmussen, in an attempt to end the deadlock...[4]*

BBC

Either/or campaigns to set aside no-take zones (in effect, nature reserves) or to stop fishing of one species altogether, are more winnable.

Who's to blame now ?

Who's responsible for not implementing the solution?

When starting a campaign, analyse who has the power to stop the problem; the capacity to cause change. The appropriate campaign target is usually the one with greatest direct culpability and capacity to act. Often, a major player will argue that the link from themselves to the problem is not clear. Multinational logging companies blame peasants for forest destruction. Chemical companies blame farmers for not following the instructions on pesticide packets. Oil companies blame car-owners for burning fossil fuels.

A favourite tactic of governments or corporations that don't want to act is to assign culpability to everyone, or to an abstract.

What are companies doing when they use methyl-bromide to fumigate cut flowers or vegetables, and in so doing, knock a massive whole in the ozone layer? They are 'meeting a need'. What's Irish businessman Kevin McHugh doing when he builds and launches the UK£50 million *Atlantic Dawn*, the world's largest trawler, able to fish as much from the waters of impoverished Mauritania as 7000 local artisan fishermen can in a year, and acquires permission to fish there?[5] He's meeting market demand. What's the answer to the problem of climate change? For us all to change our 'habits', or to 'end our love affair with the car'. Yes, it is true; to 'save the climate', we could all take to bicycles, buses and trains instead of cars. We could all go into our garden sheds and invent alternative technologies. We *could*, in theory, but we would find it rather difficult.

Campaigns become vulnerable to this dialogue when they are stuck in the problem-driving phase and need to shift to solution-driving.

Try turning the question upside down. Ask who's responsible for *not* implementing the solution, rather than just who's responsible for causing the problem. Whether it's through suppressing a solution or denying a problem, any party with the power to solve this is the problem-holder or problem-owner.

Fixing a campaign: Changing a strategy

A campaign can become tired or stuck, or both, or need a change. Here's one way to stimulate thinking on changing a strategy:

Techniques to try
when things
aren't working

The main areas in which it's usually worth thinking about change are resources, objective, and activities as perceived by supporters (including engagement opportunities).

The principal options for change are to become more (or less) popular, or more or less ambitious or to give greater agency. An example of popularization, cited by Gerd Leipold, is the involvement of Diana, the Princess of Wales in the campaign to ban landmines.[6] Change in effective resources could involve converting invisible or visible support. Change in the objective might be from one that is too

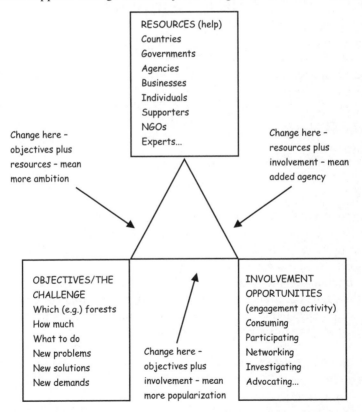

Figure 8.1 *Fixing a campaign that is drying up or becoming tired*

large or too small to stimulate engagement, to a 'bite-sized' objective. New forms of involvement might bring in whole new constituencies.

A useful technique can be to step up or down strategy levels. Consider if your campaign would do better if its proposition changed focus from one of those levels to another. (Example: climate change)

(Up)
* future of society;
* industrial future;
* energy future;
* fossil fuels future;
* oil company future;
* future of a site/technology;
* attribute of a site/component/brand.

(Down)

Stick to your route

Don't spend time on things that don't help achieve the objective

Once a campaign starts, chaos and enthusiasm can easily pull it off course. Any issue will offer multiple diversions and 'opportunities' that must be resisted if they take you away from your critical path.

Take the metaphorical campaign route through London using the 'Tube'. The London Underground is large and complex. It offers many possible journeys between its 272 stations – probably too many to even start thinking about.[7] A real issue would offer even more possibilities. The 'red thread' is your path, threaded through 'the issue map'. This is what everyone involved in the campaign has to stick to. Don't spend time in other parts of the 'issue' – they may be relevant, but that's unlikely to help achieve your objective.

Imagine a journey from, say, West Ruislip in north west London to Borough in central south London. That is the red thread through the map. You have plotted it one step at a time and there are a number of critical steps in this journey. They would include:

* find the station;
* go in;
* buy a ticket;
* board the (right) train;

- change at Bond Street onto the southbound Jubilee Line;
- change at London Bridge onto the southbound Northern Line;
- get off at Borough;
- go upstairs.

Fail at any of these stages and you won't arrive at the objective.

Other trains will come and go and fellow passengers may invite you to join them, say to discuss issues at Swiss Cottage. This could be interesting but, hopefully, you won't go. Journalists may board the train at Green Park and try to ask you about the controversy at Westminster – but London Bridge will still be your focus.

Other routes are possible to the same destination, but you've already researched this as the best. Stick to it. Transport issues extend beyond the Underground, but that is not relevant to this journey.

Organizing messages: A message hierarchy

Always steer the conversation back to your point of action

A 'message hierarchy' or ring can be a useful tool to help organize and prioritize conversations and reactive press work. However, it is not a replacement for making a communications strategy from a critical path. Brainstorm strategies – not messages alone (see also CAMP CAT, Chapter 1).

A message 'ring' and hierarchy can:

- Help people who deal with incoming queries, to get back to the issue you want most to talk about
- Acknowledge to allies that their issues are relevant, without losing focus
- Help in phone-ins, debates or other discussions where you need to show how your work is relevant to other issues, but where you still want to get back to your priority communication points.

It is an internal guide – not something that needs to be published. Construct it from your strategy messages, plus anything you think is likely to come up from the surrounding issue.

If you start from anywhere else, then before you can get there, journalists will have tried to define the issue by dividing it at that point, and you may never make it. Journalists will normally try to cast any issue in the starkest available terms, with the greatest contrast and

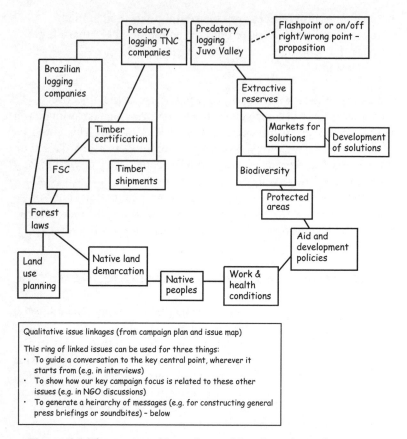

Figure 8.2 *The message hierarchy used in a hypothetical campaign*

drama. However unfounded, they will tend to play devil's advocate and can adopt wildly contradictory positions on the same subject in the course of one interview, or a series, or in a series of articles or even editorials.

Put your point of action, your central irreducible proposition, at the top. This is like the keystone, the summit to which you want to always steer the conversation back.

That is one reason why it's important to choose a proposition that really does draw the right/wrong line in exactly where you want to be, at the point of what is/what ought to be, the right-state/wrong-state.

Assets and resources

It may be
necessary to
change your
assets if you want
to achieve
change

A well-planned campaign should start with adequate resources to achieve the objective – if it succeeds in engaging the public. Time or success can enlarge the task so that the campaign, while better established, no longer has the right resources. Some campaigners respond to this by becoming shrill and trying to do more with what they have – a better move is often to analyse what's needed and find a way to expand the resources available.

So conduct a periodic inventory of the resources and assets available to your campaign, and think what can be done with them, but don't accept the status quo as inevitable.

US President Theodore Roosevelt once told Americans: 'Do what you can with what you have, where you are'. Good advice to those who can do nothing strategic, but not good advice to anyone who intends to run a campaign. Think more about what you can do *if* you *change* where you are, or change what you face, or change when things happen – or even, who 'you' are, and what your assets are. To plan solely for targets that are already within reach can lead to failure due to lack of imagination.

Roosevelt also said: 'A man who has never gone to school may steal from a freight car, but if he has a university education, he may steal from the whole railroad'. Transport campaigners note: before trying to change the system it may be necessary to change your assets.

A common failing of 'mature' NGOs is the failure to invest in logistical capacity. They may try, for example, to campaign on marine issues with no ships. Others fail to develop intelligence networks and end up talking to trade bodies or other front organizations instead of getting inside an industry or institution they want to change. Small groups grown larger tend not to invest in the necessary engagement mechanisms, such as direct-marketing capabilities. Intellectual ones used to communicating via publications are likely to need street capacity, such as touring buses, street theatre or other assets to create an intrusive visual presence necessary to set an agenda with events.

When publicity is good

It is easy to lose ground if you're not setting the pace

Publicity is a good thing when it moves you along your critical path, when it helps persuade or motivate your intended audience. Otherwise, it is bad because it will be wasting resources, taking up an opportunity that could be more usefully used for something else, and most probably, helping an opponent.

Publicity is good when it results from triggering or reinforcing a frame (see Chapter 1) that leads to your conclusion. It's a bad thing – pushing you backwards – when it supports someone else's framing! So taking part in debates initiated by others may be unavoidable, but it should be minimized and its effect outweighed by events created by you, at a time and place and with a visual message of your own choosing.

It's easy for a media-oriented campaign group to become very busy debating 'the issue' in the media while still being driven backwards, or at least being held stationary. This is especially the case if they are not investing much time and effort in creating events that set the pace or agenda (itself encouraged by under-investment in logistics and or working on too many issues at once), and if they don't have a campaign that is real outside the media.

Understanding 'support'

Many supporters won't be your members. Engage them too

The level of support can become a vexed question, but 'support' has many different meanings. In 1990–2003, research[8] showed around 10 per cent of the UK population were committed enough to environmental issues to be prepared to 'stand out' for it. A great majority considered themselves in some way 'environmentally aware' (ranging up to 90 per cent), only about 10 per cent were 'browns' and around 30 per cent were 'environmentally sensitive' or 'persuadable'. This last group generally did not want to be seen to join 'pressure-group activities' unless they were fashionable, but might join effective lobbying, or make significant lifestyle purchases.[9]

Figure 8.3 *Greenpeace supporter numbers*

How did this landscape of feelings towards the environment translate into other forms of support? By the end of the period, the National Trust had about 3,000,000 members (around 1 in 20) and the RSPB 1,000,000. More activist organizations had smaller engaged support bases.[10]

In the case of Greenpeace, around 6 in 10 people – 120 out of every 200 – said they 'supported' its aims. They tended to indicate similar agreement with the aims of other well-known environmental groups. This sensitivity was rarely mobilized unless they were confronted with a request that reinforced, rather than challenged, their lifestyle. Around 3 in 10 (60 in every 200) claimed to take some personal environmental action, such as shopping for green products. About 1 in 20 (10 in 200) said they would be prepared to take part in a Greenpeace campaign. Only 1 in 200, however, actually joined Greenpeace as subscribing supporters (see Figure 8.3).

Within the 1 in 200, a minority were 'dug in', fully expecting a pitched struggle with the forces of politics and big business who could be relied on to destroy much that was good about the planet. A majority had reached the same conclusions but more reluctantly. They still hoped that reason, democratic processes and decency would prevail, but believed that experience showed that vigorous campaigns were usually necessary.

This shows that the simple 'supporter' category is of limited use in communications. Many supportive people are outside the 'subscribing membership', and within it, there are significant differences. Campaign designers need to be aware of this – and to think about how to engage all those supportive people beyond the paying membership. The internet, for example, makes it almost free to maintain and service a list for an electronic newsletter.

Lastly, don't let critics talk down your support, especially in terms of legitimacy, and don't let enthusiasts run away with the idea that agreement automatically translates into activism.

Chapter 9

OLD MEDIA, NEW MEDIA

The changing news channels

<table>
<tr><td>

Not everyone
notices the news

</td><td>

Campaigners tend to be news watchers. So are politicians and journalists. But most people aren't, and only a few read the 'serious' newspapers. In 2001[1] only 16 per cent of UK people regarded themselves as 'regular current affairs watchers'.

</td></tr>
</table>

When this is overlooked in planning communication strategies, failure often follows – the rest of the population is better reached by using 'non-news', media. Overall, campaigners would do well to put less emphasis on national broadcast news or newspapers, and more on features, magazines, entertainment broadcasting, internet, texting and direct communications.

Conventional TV, radio and newspaper news remains important to the world of decision-makers – it's effectively their local media – but it's not a very good way to reach the 'public'. So to influence them and to influence events, it's generally better to use other channels to engage audiences, and then use the mainstream news media to alert politicians to the issue if you need to.

For decades, fewer and fewer people have watched mainstream broadcast news or read daily newspapers. A 2001 survey[2] by Ian Hargreaves and James Thomas showed that national newspaper readership had fallen to 31.6 million in the UK, or 68 per cent coverage of all adults. UK regional press readership increased to 39.4 million, 85 per cent coverage of all adults, of whom nearly half do not read a national daily newspaper.[3] UK local newspaper readership is going up, and local papers are more trusted by readers.

The Newspaper Association of America reports[4] adult readership of daily newspapers (at least once-weekly) fell from 80 per cent in 1964 to 55 per cent in 1997. In 1996, newspaper readership was falling in 10 of the 15 EU countries. In that year UK newspaper readership fell by 3.8 per cent, while Irish readership declined by 4.4 per cent.[5]

Sixty-five per cent of those in the Hargreaves-Thomas survey said their main source of news was TV, compared with 16 per cent for radio, 15 per cent for newspapers and 2 per cent for the internet.

The internet was the preferred news medium, however, among younger ethnic minority groups. Under-represented in 'mainstream' US news but over-represented in the military, black Americans have increasingly used the internet for news since the 2003 Iraq war. As of October 2001, ABC News[6] found that nearly half of Americans were receiving news over the internet, up by 11 points – perhaps 22 million individuals – since mid-1999. Of college graduates, over 60 per cent used the internet for news, a quarter of them doing so daily. Richer and younger people used it more.

The Iraq war also brought 'blogging' into the mainstream. Traffic to the web log site www.blogspot.com increased to 316,000 visitors in the week ending 23 March 2003. Eighty-six per cent of the audience traffic went to *Dear Raed*, a personal account of life in Baghdad.

Unmediated 'own news' use of the internet by campaigners includes www.webactive.com featuring the populist 'Hightower Radio Commentaries' and Counterspin, Radioactive, Working Assets Radio and a directory of 2000 cause-related sites.

The UK Independent Media Centre is at www.indymedia.org. It links to live, independent media web-radio sites, websites for climate, print, satellite, radio, video, and dozens of discussion groups and regional and local alternative news sites.

Web-only commercial magazines and news sites such as www.salon.com may more readily publish information that major political or corporate interests would prefer not to see the light of day. A growing number of independent web-based news networks challenge the old mainstream. One of the best is Anthony Barnett's www.opendemocracy.net.

Sites devoted to publishing what others would like to suppress, or to opposing censorship, include Information Clearing House, which is a remarkably comprehensive US-based site devoted to 'news that you won't find on CNN' (and quite often not on the BBC) www.informationclearinghouse.info (remarkable as it's the work of one person). See also Index On Censorship at www.indexonline.org and News Alternative at www.asia-stat.com.

Campaigners need to be aware of:

- Changes in news consumption, including the growth of web-based and other new media news sourcing
- The democratization of news-generation through blogging and other 'indymedia'
- The growth of participation-news, where the boundaries between journalist and audience break down
- An increase in 'news' outlets prepared to publish rumour or reports which authority would rather suppress, making verification easier and total suppression much more difficult (against this, mainstream media is increasingly dominated by corporate interests and ownership is more and more concentrated).

Taken together, the last three factors bode well for bringing things to public attention, but may not make it easier to bring them to *wide* public attention unless campaigners can break these stories into more mainstream media, and into large-scale networks.

Coding and how to avoid it

_____

Escaping the
news formula

_____

When hearing a story on the radio or watching a report on the TV, people often say: 'We've heard all this before.' Often, they haven't, but think they have because it *sounds* the same as previous stories. It has the same tune and the same phrases because of editing and formatting.

Studies by Jacquie Burgess[7] showed the format of environmental news created a weary sense of 'we've heard it all before' and then a feeling of powerlessness, cynicism and a distrust of news sources.

Coding is the construction of stories, especially news, according to a series of clichés or set formulae. Examples are equating environmentalists with protesting, no matter what they do; 'wrapping' disasters with a sign-off about exaggerated claims; or referring to any hazard as a 'scare'.

These codes not only make everything sound familiar but also, when added together, suggest that problems are either insoluble or certainly out of reach for ordinary people. Interview people who are actually members of pressure groups,[8] who have heard from the organization how campaigning can work, and you find that they are much more positive about the possibility of change than are otherwise similar non-members.

Messages run through the same channels tend to adopt the familiar cadences and tones of those channels. For example, steps in publicizing a report might be:

- Campaigner gets the idea
- Consultant researches and writes a report
- Project group discusses it and writes its own version for public consumption (recoding)
- Press office asks for a summary and bullet points (recoding)
- Press office writes press release, anticipates the principal target news outlet and their interests (for example, women's angles) and negotiates it with campaigner (recoding)
- Press conference – the campaign director presents it and gives own spin (recoding)
- Reporters take notes, get reaction from other parties, write story (recoding)
- Editor cuts down the story, changes the lead to fit in with another story and writes a headline (recoding)
- Newspaper publishes story
- Radio editor reads story
- Radio news carries its own version of the story (recoding)
- Listener hears it, thinks 'I've heard that before.'

Ways to avoid recoding:

- Communicate directly wherever possible
- Communicate in pictures – they are less susceptible to recoding: let the picture tell the story
- Create *events* that are reported or shown, not arguments, which are most vulnerable to re-framing.

Ambient media and networking

<table>
<tr><td>

Two
'unconventional'
communication
techniques

</td><td>

As people have increasingly 'switched off' to paid-for media, advertising has crept onto all sorts of unconventional surfaces. Many techniques have been borrowed from campaigning or art. Campaigners spent the 1980s projecting laser messages onto the sides of ships and nuclear power stations, but by the 1990s it had become an advertising staple. Cliff- and island-wrapping artists such as Christo were co-opted into advertising, along with the natural environment itself.

</td></tr>
</table>

Advertisers went back to earlier eras by painting large parts of buildings – even entire streets – with slogans, in what Naomi Klein describes as 'building takeover'.[9] Invasion of the civic or public space by corporate messaging is now an issue worldwide.

'Ambient' media simply means carrying messages with everyday things around you. It stems from the same thought as word-of-mouth communication now popular in mainstream advertising. For example, attractive actors are paid to go into bars and talk loudly about the virtues of particular drinks.

Marketing consultant Sean Larkins[10] cites the use of London taxi drivers by the South African Tourist Authority. Rather than spend a limited budget on high-cost advertising, the South Africans took a group of these inveterate professional gossips on holiday to South Africa, then sent them home again. Of course, they talked about it to passengers in their cabs – again, and again and again. With a final twist, the drivers picked were those mainly working the route to London Heathrow, whose passengers were likely to be frequent fliers.

In *The Tipping Point*,[11] Malcolm Gladwell writes about the horse ride of Paul Revere, who alerted American colonists to the oncoming British Army with a dramatic 'ride through the night'. Two key factors in his effectiveness were drama (it was done at dead of night) and his role in the community – Gladwell says he was the man with the 'biggest Rolodex' – a networker extraordinaire, and a helping maven (expert). Revere was a member of all the relevant social groups – one of the very few super-connected people in the social network.

This is surely part of the explanation for why Paul Revere's message was so powerful on the night of his midnight ride. News of the British march did not come by fax, or by means of a group

155

email. It wasn't broadcast on the nightly news, surrounded by commercials. It was carried by a man, a volunteer, riding on a cold night with no personal agenda other than a concern for the liberty of his peers.

The less-well-known William Dawes also made a ride at the same time as Revere, but without as much success. He was a less-well-connected person, not as sociable, not a networker, and he rode in the afternoon (a bad move, since most of the people were out working in the fields). A ride in the afternoon also lacked drama.

Organized gossip

An example of word-of-mouth communications

As the public have trusted government and business less, and at the same time have become more aware that most 'messages' have a purpose behind them, suspicion of paid-for communication of any type increases. Consequently, there's more and more commercial interest in PR and 'word-of-mouth' communication.

Enticing the media to cover an issue in a particular way has long been a delicate speciality of campaign groups – the mainstream media industry is now having to catch up in order to reach a wised-up general public.

A 1990 case involved an illustrated toilet roll (subject: Britain – Dirty Man of Europe) and two reports. The toilet rolls were designed to stimulate gossip.

Green NGOs approached Media Natura to puncture UK government PR around a forthcoming environment White Paper: *This Common Inheritance*. In 1989, the government had proposed a programme of eco-taxes, to fight the next election on 'the quality of life in the broadest sense',[12] which would be 'the big issue of the next decade'.[13] Minister Chris Patten said his White Paper would 'set out our environmental agenda for the rest of this century'.

By February 1990, however, the idea of legislation was dropped until after the next election,[14] and by July, the *Daily Telegraph* had declared the draft content a 'damp squib'.[15] Amid worsening economic news, it had been subject to a thousand cuts by government departments such as energy, transport and industry. Having been loudly talked up, the White Paper was very quietly talked down. The general impression of sweeping change created in the first wave of publicity was still likely to frame public perceptions, however.

To ensure that it got a far more critical reception, Media Natura produced three pieces of communication aimed at different audiences.[16] To stimulate gossip, the 'chattering classes' were targeted using colour-illustrated toilet rolls, printed with '17 reasons why Britain is still the Dirty Man of Europe'. These used the very 1980s 'hook' of 'Britain – Dirty Man of Europe', to re-awaken an established framing and anchor the debate to actual environmental performance, rather than political spin. The rolls were distributed by hand to executive media offices, politicians, journalists, socialites and gossipmongers. Some were delivered with a neat label to the front desk, others were smuggled into ministerial toilets or boardrooms and left to be discovered. The objective was to stimulate conversation. As they were carefully packaged in a colourful design of European flags with a message that invited unwrapping, it was unlikely that anyone would simply throw them away.

Next, a plain, unpublicized report, published without a press release, entitled *The Great Car Economy and the Quality of Life* was distributed to political correspondents and editorial writers. It attempted an elite 'framing' in terms of the Conservative Party's own policy choices. It made no claims, but simply introduced an angle that, when the time came, might be echoed in media comment.

Lastly, published on the day before the White Paper so that it was in the press on the day, and to provide ammunition for questioning of the government by journalists, came a very detailed report fleshing out the 17 reasons in some 60 pages.[17]

A subsequent newspaper cartoon showed a man hesitating in front of a recycling bin, in which there were three slots: 'white paper', 'green paper' and 'government White Paper'.

Monitoring truth and bias in the media

Campaigning to save impartial journalism

Organizations that specifically set out to counteract media bias and to monitor standards include Fairness and Accuracy in Reporting (FAIR) (US) and Media Lens (UK).

Started in 1986, FAIR (www.fair.org) works with activists and journalists and says it maintains 'a regular dialogue with reporters at news outlets across the country ... to encourage the public to contact media with their concerns, to become media activists rather than passive consumers of news'.

FAIR aims to 'expose neglected news stories and defend working journalists when they are muzzled'. It believes that 'structural reform is ultimately needed to break up the dominant media conglomerates'.

CounterSpin[18] is FAIR's weekly radio show, broadcast on over 125 commercial radio stations across the US and Canada, and on the internet.

UK-based Media Lens – 'correcting for the distorted vision of the corporate media' – is at www.medialens.org (with many links and interesting free e-mail alerts). It pursues specific instances of what it sees as incomplete or inaccurate broadcasting, saying:

Media Lens is a response based on our conviction that mainstream newspapers and broadcasters provide a profoundly distorted picture of our world. We are convinced that the increasingly centralized, corporate nature of the media means that it acts as a de facto propaganda system for corporate and other establishment interests. The costs incurred as a result of this propaganda, in terms of human suffering and environmental degradation, are incalculable.

Most news 'sources' are owned by individuals or business consortia, and their editorial content and news agenda broadly reflects their political and business interests. Among UK newspapers, the only one owned by anything remotely similar to its readers is *The Guardian*, which is owned by a trust.

One of the best-known UK media studies team is probably the Glasgow University Media Group.[19] It takes issue with theoretical post-modernist communications studies that focus on how people 'construct their own meaning' for media. As a result of these ideas, say

Greg Philo and David Miller, 'there can be no assessments on grounds of accuracy/truth'.[20] They say:

> There is a silence in most media and cultural studies about the consequences of popular culture and the media. There are very few analyses of the content of the press or television, and of the influence which these can have on public belief and understanding. There is an absence of studies which address the real and often brutal relations of power which have shaped our cultural life.

Their own work has examined the influence of media on understanding of breast cancer, food hazards, BSE, migration and race.

New media

New media requires new campaign thinking

Digital media and interactivity[21] are fracturing audiences as they globalize. In the early 1990s, the average momentary audience per UK TV channel was 350,000, but by 2003 it was 23,000, and heading lower,[22] a tenfold reduction.

The network, or new, economy (originally called the information economy) refers to value created in trade of goods or services because they are networked – that is, connected together – or because of what is known rather than used up.

In a network economy, potential value increases with the network, the resource becoming both more valuable and cheaper the more it gets used; the reverse of non-networked resources. Business strategies differ from those for non-networked economies. Networks are not new, but information technology coupled with de-materialization[23] may transform much economic activity into a network economy. Thinking this would happen almost overnight promoted the dot.com bubble, but it would be a mistake to conclude from that that new media or the network economy will not happen.

In the past, most campaigns have conformed to the old industrial design model of design > build > sell (that is, design, build and launch). The newer 'info-com' model is sell > build > redesign. The best-known example is software floated onto the web in 'beta' form, for users to work with and redesign.

The classic engagement sequence is broadly: awareness > engagement > action. Direct action by groups such as Greenpeace and Earth First! broke with this format by making *action* the starting point. The internet now offers *engagement* as a starting point. This works where knowledge of cause and problem are saturated, but opportunity to take effective action is limited.

The channel primarily gives agency rather than information. This invites a completely different and non-linear style of campaign design. In the end, it changes most campaign communication from 'we've been' ('we did it, look what we achieved, give us your backing') to 'let's go together'. The immediacy, intimacy and interactivity of media such as e-mail invite a rethink of the temporal nature of campaigns – how they are planned and conducted in real time.

The Yes Men (www.theyesmen.org) and Stop Esso (www.stopesso.com) both provide extensive campaign toolkits, and then show the results. Helping supporters to participate as campaigners begins to turn the old closed-box office-based model of campaign organization inside out. The Yes Men also enable supporters to colonize web space and spoof major corporations, supplying tailor-made software at www.reamweaver.com.

New media's significance

New media is significant for campaigns because:

Campaigns are communication exercises

- It is often global – in the past, you switched on the old TV and you saw local TV. A local phone call was normal, while a call to the other side of the world was a novelty. Now with one click you are anywhere
- It is cheap and almost instant. E-mail and website interactions have reduced transaction costs to almost nothing. Newsletters, virtual communities and clubs have almost no cost to join
- It's interactive. Digital TV,[24] for example, allows more interaction than analogue TV
- It shrinks distance and equalizes time. Videoconferencing can eliminate some travel needs and e-mail exchanges across a waking day. It can include friends in other time zones without the dislocating effect of someone talking from a working morning

perspective to someone about to go to bed
- It is accessible. The technology needed to act as a source, as a sort of broadcaster, is now widespread and affordable by many people
- It is more transferable – what works on one platform can often easily cross to another, hence all forms of convergence
- It enables all information, libraries, databases to be shared globally
- It makes some previously specialist information or knowledge widely available.

All this has implications for campaigns because they are an exercise in communication.

New rules for campaigns

---
11 strategies for network campaigning

Many of the 'rules for the new economy'[25] popularized by writer Kevin Kelly, designed to describe economic transactions, also apply to campaigns. Indeed, in many ways it seems they apply better to campaigning than to business. They are at least useful in thinking about how to design network-based campaigns.

Here, paraphrased, are some of Kelly's 'Dependable principles for thriving in a turbulent world' with my ideas of possible applications shown as bullet points (reproduced with permission from Kevin Kelly).

1 The law of connection
Embrace dumb power. Dumb parts, properly connected, yield smart results (for example, embedded microchips networked together).

- Many supporters each taking small actions.

2 The law of plentitude
More gives more. The first fax machine cost millions but was worth nothing, as you could not communicate with it. The second one made the first one worth something, and each additional fax machine increases the value of all the ones operating before it. So strong is this network value that anyone purchasing a fax machine becomes an evangelist for the fax network. 'Do you have a fax?' fax-owners ask you. 'You should get one.'

- Establish campaign networks where there is an incentive for members to recruit others because each new one makes it work better.

3 The law of exponential value
Success is non-linear. For 20 years, fax machines spread slowly, and then, in the mid-1980s, they crossed a point of no return and 'the next thing you know, they are irreversibly everywhere'.

- Solution technologies.

4 The law of tipping points
Significance precedes momentum. The moment where contagion's momentum 'has tipped from pushing uphill against all odds to rolling downhill with all odds behind it'. Technologies are being taken seriously much earlier in their development.

- Trail the long-term consequences of achieving your campaign objective, or better still, get a third party to do so.

5 The law of increasing returns
Make virtuous circles. Value increases with membership of networks much quicker (exponentially) than the old economies of scale (linear). Hence, Microsoft is tolerated despite its huge profits because there are so many on-sellers.

- Ethically based NGOs could create large networks, giving political and social agency to participants.

6 The law of inverse pricing
Anticipate the cheap. The best things get cheaper each year. Computer chips have halved in price, doubling in power, every 18 months (Moore's Law).

- To lever changes in commercial systems, find ways to influence consumers rather than producers to pull development.

7 The law of generosity
Follow the free. Where services become more valuable the more plentiful they are, and if they cost less, the better and the more valuable they become, then the most valuable things of all should be those that are given away. For example, Microsoft gives away its web browser, Internet Explorer.

- Externalize some of your campaign tools and know-how and make your network accessible, for example the tools and website of www.stopesso.com.

8 The law of the allegiance

Feed the web first. The distinguishing characteristic of networks is that they have no clear centre and no clear outer boundaries. The vital distinction between the self (us) and the non-self (them) – once exemplified by the allegiance of the industrial-era organization man – becomes less meaningful in a network economy. Standard-setting becomes important.

A network is like a country but with three important differences:

1 No geographical or temporal boundaries exist – relations flow 24 by 7 by 365
2 Relations in the network economy are more tightly coupled, more intense, more persistent, and more intimate in many ways than those in a country
3 Multiple overlapping networks exist, with multiple overlapping allegiances.

- Ethically driven NGOs could create a global virtual country and thereby create a significant counterweight voice and alternative channel to profit-driven systems and profit-driven politics.

9 The law of devolution

Let go at the top. All organizations face two problems as they attempt to find their peak of optimal fit.

First, unlike the industrial arc's relatively simple environment, where it was fairly clear what an optimal product looked like and where on the slow-moving horizon a company should place itself, it is increasingly difficult in the network economy to discern which hills are highest and which summits are false.

You can easily get stuck on a local peak. There is only one way out: devolve – to go from one high peak to another, go downhill first and cross a valley before climbing uphill again. The company must reverse itself and become less adapted, less fit, less optimal.

The second problem is that organizations, like living beings, are hard-wired to optimize what they know and to not throw success away. Companies find devolving (a) unthinkable and (b) impossible. There is simply no room in the enterprise for the concept of letting go, – let alone the skill to let go – of something that is working, and trudge downhill toward chaos.

In the network economy, the ability to relinquish a product, occupation or industry at its peak will be priceless. Let go at the top.

- Big-brand NGOs that developed an effective strategy based on mass media are threatened unless they re-evolve, but start-ups may, in any case, take over.

10 The law of churn

Seek sustainable disequilibrium. Companies come and go quickly, careers are patchworks of vocations, industries are indefinite groupings of fluctuating firms. The network economy has moved from change to churn. Churn is more a creative force of destruction and genesis.

- Potential problems, solutions and allies are in constant flux, while campaign organisation needs to be constantly reinventing itself.

11 The law of inefficiencies

Don't solve problems. In a paradox, increasing technology has not led to measurable increases in productivity.

Productivity is exactly the wrong thing to care about. The only ones who should worry about productivity are robots. In the network economy, where machines do most of the inhumane work of manufacturing, the task for each worker is not 'how to do this job right' but 'what is the right job to do?' Wasting time and being inefficient are the way to discovery. In the words of Peter Drucker, 'Don't solve problems: seek opportunities.'

- Ethically driven organizations should question 'conventional' ideas of what useful work is, and propose new definitions as a way of targeting objectives – more on work objectives than policy objectives.

The media day

Marketing strategist Sean Larkins says: 'Media can be looked at according to share of display advertising by medium – for example, in March 2001, in the UK, TV accounted for around 40 per cent by value of all display advertising, radio 6 per cent, newspapers just under a third, magazines 15 per cent and outdoor the rest – which was about 8 per cent.'

Media menu for breakfast, lunch and tea

In terms of the average 'media day', or share of media consumption by time of day, says Larkins, 'TV advertising is dominant at over half, with internet at a few per cent but rapidly rising, magazines at 2 per cent, newspapers at 7 per cent, and radio very much larger than in terms of spend, at 31 per cent. Video is a 4 per cent'.[26] This means every other ad we are exposed to comes from TV – but that doesn't necessarily mean they are the effective ones.

So, in terms of time, radio is the dominant morning medium, TV dominates the evening, and newspapers are mostly consumed between breakfast and lunchtime. Until mid-afternoon, radio listening exceeds TV viewing among Britons.

Radio advertising is less 'avoided' than advertising in print or on TV. People may switch off or get up to make a coffee or tea when expensive ads run on TV (obvious exceptions are 'cult ads' which spill over into a real-life existence, such as GAP's khaki campaign run in 1999 and described in Naomi Klein's *No Logo*) but they tend not to react when radio ads are on. Sean Larkins says that responding to adverts follows the scheme below:

* First hearing – miss it altogether
* Second hearing – pick up the message
* Third hearing – take in the detail
* Fourth hearing pick up address/phone/internet address.

Nobody listens all day every day, so ads are usually played 30–40 times each week, or at least four times a day. The usual minimum length of a radio 'campaign' is one month.

Evening newspapers are, unsurprisingly, particularly read by home-bound (train or bus) commuters, while drive-time radio reaches motorists. The internet occupies its largest proportionate share at night, though within that generalization, there are many niche audiences, such as students and retired people. For global internet data, see www.glreach.com/globstats and the authoritative www.nua.com.

In the UK, more people listen to local than to national radio. Local radio reaches very specific audiences. These range station-by-station and, to a lesser extent, programme-to-programme, from hip hop to easy listening, and sometimes both. Local radio is good for both editorial and advertising. Being helpful to local radio will pay dividends, as they are very short of resources. This applies as much to offering news as to taking out paid advertising.

Which media work for which people

Tailoring communications

It pays to research your audience in terms of the media they consume. In the UK, for example, studies segment TV advertisement viewers into the following groups:

- Acceptors (22 per cent) – I find TV advertising interesting and quite often it gives me something to talk about
- Rejectors (20 per cent) – Nearly all TV advertising annoys me
- Players (35 per cent) – I find some TV advertising is OK, but I think quite a lot of it is devious
- Uninvolved (22 per cent) – Quite often I find TV advertising more entertaining than the programmes.[27]

Audiences segment in their media consumption according to social, psychological, lifestyle and other factors, and this area is heavily researched by commercial agencies. For most NGOs the best way to access such information is probably via a friendly contact in an advertising or PR agency, or a marketing department of a large company.

Young people may adopt completely different channels from their parents. Text messaging (SMS) became increasingly popular in many countries in the 1990s and 2000s, (and the main source of profit on the telephone network, exceeding internet usage in its penetration), first among the young. It was popularized by a role-playing game 'the Nokia game' invented by Finnish youth after Nokia introduced texting in 1992.[28]

Commercial and BBC local radio split the audience about evenly, but commercial radio mainly reaches younger people (an obvious national exception being stations such as Classic FM or Saga Radio.[29]

Beware though, of making generalizations such as 'young people use the internet'. In Britain this disguises the fact, for instance, that socially disadvantaged young people are disproportionately unlikely to use the internet,[30] and for many social issues they are the very people who need to be reached. Better channels for reaching them in the early 2000s included cheap video rental stores and the boxes of videos, as they frequently hire and watch a video in a group. Often, campaigns need to invent their own tailor-made communication channels.

Chapter 10

TO DO AND NOT TO DO

Be simple: Avoid 'the issue'

Be an expert of
change, not
issues

Campaign groups often organize 'by issue'. This feeds the illusion that you can campaign 'on issues'. In reality, a campaign has to change an issue by re-arranging its political landscape just one step at a time.

Few campaigns of any significance are achieved quickly. Most entail many steps, each a campaign in itself, often taking decades. Any that succeeds does so in jumps forward or single blows like a lapidary cutting a diamond. A perfect, multi-faceted jewel cannot be created in one step.

Issue mapping inevitably reveals, once you have a good look at it, that almost any issue is a complex beast. Its entrails will be a labyrinth with appendices that lead nowhere, and branches that split into too many choices to handle. Debate explores mature issues and expands them to fill the available space.

The complexity must be overcome or avoided, for a campaign to be planned. Issue 'experts' may misunderstand this. They know a lot about their subject – too much. They often know much less, however, about how it may be changed. If they cannot imagine how big changes could be brought about except by processes they know – which depend very much on knowing more than the next person – they assume this is how change must come. They then cannot imagine how anyone who does not 'grasp the complexity' of the issue, can work on it effectively. As for making progress by simplification; that is surely wrong.

In truth, every issue is complex. 'Drugs' (as in not taking illegal drugs) is a simple issue to anyone who abhors and abstains from them.

Nancy Reagan's wonderfully simple 'Just Say No' crusade is a famous example of a strategic communications failure – not just with the wrong messenger for the intended audience, but with a naive, presumably unresearched, if memorable, message.[1]

In practice, the reasons people do or don't use drugs are diverse and very complex, as anyone who has worked in that field knows. Yet to a drugs worker, something else will seem just as simple as drugs seemingly did to Mrs Reagan. A ballpoint pen, for example, might seem a very simple beast. But try standing up at the 15th Biennial International Pen and Writing Implement Conference and saying that the pen issue is simple. The delegates will laugh scornfully. Ask them what they think of the 'drugs' issue and they will probably not want to give it the time of day – 'it's simple – just say no – I don't take drugs – why should they?'

This is why you cannot campaign 'on an issue' or 'about an issue', only to *change* the issue.

Avoid black holes and elephants

_____

Things that can impede progress

_____

Communication 'black holes' are issue tarpits into which your campaign can fall and never escape. If you are starting a new campaign or trying to change an issue where previous campaigns have become bogged down, then these are things to steer clear of.

This is not as easy as it sounds, because established contentious 'frames' are the obvious place to go. After all, everyone else is there already. As Rick Le Coyte has put it, these are 'congested roundabouts', better avoided by breaking out across country. These are contemporary points of struggle between conflicting interests. They act like a honey pot for journalists and 'passing trade', because that's where the arguments are going on. But often it's where there isn't much scope for real movement.

Communicators also refer to the problem of 'pattern-matching', as in people thinking 'I know what this is; it looks/feels/sounds like a so-and-so', and 'I know what I think of it'. If this happens, your opportunity to frame understanding or begin a new, preconception-free conversation, is lost. When Greenpeace researched an expanded campaign on genetic engineering, we found several possible 'pattern-matching' problems that could have diverted the campaign into one of these tarpits:

- Animal testing (cued through the appearance of laboratories, with barbed wire fencing, lights, testing cages, white-coated scientists)
- E-numbers and additives (prompted by any reference to food labels)
- Food technology (yeast in vats or yoghurt) – the reason that the GM industry subsequently tried to call itself 'biotechnology', avoiding 'genetic engineering').

Other tarpits can be ideological disputes – in transport, for example, the public–private ownership issue, or the car-good/car-bad debate: these are so well rehearsed, and positions are so polarized and familiar, that any strategy that stumbles across them tends to get stuck there.

Lastly, to change minds or establish a new frame, don't trigger existing ones. This is the elephant problem (see www.frameworksintitute.org): a speaker tries to explain what a giraffe is. Unfortunately, he tells the audience about elephants – 'it's not an elephant' – and because they know something about elephants, they then focus on that and never do get a mental picture of a giraffe. If instead he had avoided mention of elephants and sketched a mental picture of a giraffe, its surrounding and activities, adding detail and colour in layers, they could have got there.

Don't be led by the press agenda

Journalists may have strong views, about 'what the issue is'. News likes to move along established tracks: use this but do not become trapped by it.

Don't rely on the news to do the campaigning

The best way to break *new* things into the news system is not by trying to make them 'news' but to get them into the work and social world of professional communicators. Then they can discover it for themselves.

Features pages are a good route, but one of the best is children's media, which comes with a helpful nag-factor. To get there, start from the real world, in public events, networks and direct person-to-person communication.

News mainly reflects the doings of the rich and powerful, such as politicians. Campaigners should be wary of following the agenda of day-to-day politics, both of government departments and of members of the legislature. As Andrew Marr wrote of the activities of MPs in the UK: 'The excitement is febrile – what seems at first sight to be important, is revealed, at second glance, to be merely self-important'.[2] The test should be, 'by doing this will we best progress our campaign plan – is it on our critical path?'

The media itself should not be the objective or the target for a campaign, unless it is a campaign about the media.

A few years ago, when asked 'where environmental problems exist', people had started to see them as 'on TV'. Environment and campaigning were becoming unreal media creatures, disconnected from real life. People would see a street scene on TV with children suffering asthma apparently associated with car fumes, and say 'how terrible', but not associate it with their own street. As a result, campaigns did not engage effectively and people did not see the need or opportunity for them to demand political action. Overemphasis on communicating through the mass media was also leading critics of environmental campaigns to blame the media for them, and encouraging a backlash against campaigners within the media establishment.

One response adopted by Greenpeace was to put effort into 'direct communication' in other words not simply relying on the press to do the campaigning communication.

Evaluation

However beautiful the strategy, you should occasionally look at the results

Winston Churchill

Assessing intended and unintended impacts

If you find yourself thinking 'we don't have the money for evaluation', start planning again. Without evaluation, success or failure can't be understood.

Formative evaluation involves doing research and testing ideas at the design stage. Professionals such as Pat Branigan[3] recommend three rounds of pre-planning and testing. Katie Aston,[4] an expert in public health campaigns, recommends setting aside 10–15 per cent of the budget for testing and evaluation, depending on the complexity of the communications.

Basic evaluation can consist of looking at:

Table 10.1 *How to evaluate a campaign's success*

Stage	Output	Intended impact	Unintended impact
Awareness	Output achieved yes/no	Objective achieved yes/no	Unintended impact
Alignment	Output achieved yes/no	Objective achieved yes/no	Unintended impact
Engagement	Output achieved yes/no	Objective achieved yes/no	Unintended impact
Action	Output achieved yes/no	Objective achieved yes/no	Unintended impact

Making such an evaluation requires a before and after assessment. A campaign project may only have an objective at one stage – say, awareness.

Too many campaign groups analyse 'process' and outputs, rather than the impacts of the campaign. It's important to evaluate whether the campaign achieved its objectives, but also, what other impact it had. Looking only at the objectives may miss the most important effects.

Judging the size of effect to look for is vital. Campaigners sometimes phrase objectives in terms of aims, if they haven't thought them through properly. It's important to assess change around an objective that is actually attainable, and to measure the activities it is hoped an intended audience will take, which actually make a direct contribution to that.

Don't believe your detractors

Use objective research to find out what is really going on

It's always a mistake to believe your own propaganda, if you have any. Equally, it's a mistake to believe that of your critics. There is an old parable about the devil that goes something like this:

A man is walking down the road. He meets another man – handsome, charming, well read. They talk. The first asks the second who he is. 'I am the devil,' comes the reply. 'But you can't be,' protests the first. 'I have heard about the devil, and he is ugly, stupid and offensive.' 'Aha', says the devil, 'you have been listening to my detractors.'

Don't volunteer yourself into this position. Don't believe the demonization of opponents by ill-informed supporters, or of yourself by opponents.

If your campaign suffers a loss of public support, for example, or a supporter leaves your organization, don't assume that this is because, as some critics have it, your campaign is 'wrong', or as others might say, 'badly targeted', 'this will lose you public support', or any other criticism. Don't accept the validity of widely or loudly expressed criticisms that predict a problem, just because some part of that problem seems to be occurring. Use objective research to find what is really going on.

Worry about the right things

Worry most about the impact of your communications

Organizations focused on not making mistakes with factual details and 'the line to take', are unlikely to succeed in visual communication. Yet this is often what will make all the difference. The most common causes of communications failure are not mistakes of fact, but communicating completely the wrong thing because of poor visuals, or simply being ignored altogether.

Worry most about the impact of your communication – which will be mostly visual – in target audiences, not the opinions of colleagues.

Of course, getting the words wrong can also have dire consequences. If you regularly address the same public groups, it is worth investing in the time of specialist writers, such as agencies that develop specific dictionaries – language that works for an audience – so you use words and terms that have the right effect. Internal language and jargon will never be the right language to use for an external audience. See www.burton-morris.com for an example of a word-based communications agency that offers a free trial of writing for tone and style. *The Invisible Grail* by John Simmons[5] makes the case for developing effective brands using written language.

Other things that are easily forgotten in the hurly-burly of running campaigns and demands for accountability (which can easily become accounting), include:

- The spirit of what you are trying to do – what keeps supporters loyal, what stops staff from leaving – each campaign should light that touchpaper, at least for a moment
- The community – an effective campaign organization is usually also a family, a conspiracy, a ruse, an adventure, not just a job
- Attitude – you can teach method, you can pick people with any number of qualifications, but as a friend of mine[6] once put it: 'To be any good as a campaigner, they need to want to act up.' If you're ever in any doubt about recruiting staff, follow your heart and instincts, and pick the person with the right attitude and track record over qualifications any day
- Who you are trying to influence – you can design a great tactic that is just so beautiful, you really want to use it – and forget that it won't do the job you have in hand
- Of the two main ways campaigns affect politics – through changing values and altering the balance of interests – values are softer and harder to evaluate, but are far more significant.

Common failures in choosing media

These include:

TV needs moving pictures

- Overemphasis of news media for persuasion, at the expense of human-interest stories on features pages
- Too much reliance on the media and publicity at the expense of business-to-business techniques and direct communication, especially face to face
- A too-academic or 'professional/policy community' approach – too many data and too much information, not enough empathy and emotion
- Trying to argue rather than to show: it is far better to set things up so people draw their own conclusions
- Website fixation (a problem in 2003, giving way to texting – before that it was video, but now video is underused, while soon it will be some other new medium) – trying to make websites do too many things
- Failing to think through the particular needs of TV – it must have *moving* pictures – a static event is really useless. The Pope is news if he just appears and stands there; you are almost certainly not

- Failing to think through the particular needs of radio – must have *sounds* – a silent event is really useless – best to have sounds of a *process* ('that's the sound of... ') and various voices
- Failing to be visual – for example, so pictures can accompany a newspaper story
- Targeting media that the staff of the organization read or watch or listen to, rather than those that the supposed target audience do.

Don't assume we need to change minds

Most campaigns succeed by mobilization, rather than changing beliefs or convictions. To change minds and *then* mobilize people is a two-stage process. If you only need to mobilize them, you don't need the mind-changing step: it's simpler. Not only that, but changing minds is hard. After we reach our early 20s, big changes in perspective generally come with major life stages, such as having children, and other instances are rare.

_____

Campaign success is not dependent on changing minds

_____

So beware the trap of analysing a problem and concluding that, because the problem would be solved if people 'changed their minds', that is what the campaign should do. Even worse is to make a hidden, embedded assumption that the campaign will do this, without knowing how.

You *can* set out to 'change minds' in a campaign, but to do so you must first understand views and motivations very well, and then set an achievable objective[7] – probably only a very small change of view.

Even if you do intend to change minds, then getting people's *attention* will probably involve starting from where they are. Using *channels* they use for instance, and *messengers* they like to hear from, and a *context* they are comfortable in – face to face perhaps – for example, a talk by a wine expert at a wine-tasting. Generally, if you can get to people 'where they are', physically, emotionally and intellectually, and then *show* them something or even better involve them in something that is a life-changing or world view-changing experience, you will have the best chance of changing minds.

Examples of jigsaw problems

Fuel taxes and protests

If communication jumps straight to the 'solution', without successfully selling the idea of the problem, it will be met with disinterest, blank puzzlement or polite but unengaged tolerance ('it's interesting you are doing that, but it's nothing to do with me'). Politicians in power often make this mistake. In many political systems, once elected they can introduce policies or measures that may have little specific backing. This doesn't become apparent until they hit an obstacle and try to appeal for public support.

Does your solution fit the problem?

In the 1990s, the UK government introduced a rising tax on petrol prices.[8] Ministers justified it (solution) on grounds that it would reduce climate-changing CO_2 emissions from road transport (problem). The public, however, didn't buy the connection – the pieces of jigsaw didn't fit. They suspected that a moral cause was being hijacked to justify taxes that would be used for other purposes. Environmentalists didn't feel they 'owned' the measure. When truckers later organized fuel-price protests, the public remained ambivalent. The government tried to play the climate card, and vented its frustration on environmentalists: 'Where were you?' MPs cried when news pictures remained dominated by the protests.

Eventually, the truckers were bought off by concessions,[9] deprived of their organizational spine, and with fuel prices once again dropping,[10] the protests died. In fact, all the major groups active on climate *had* supported the government, and some went much further. Greenpeace, for example, went to meet protestors face to face, and showed what it thought the real 'solution' was by giving away free biofuel (biodiesel). Nevertheless, these activities couldn't compete with the visual power of the protests, and did little to re-frame the debate (see framing, Chapter 1).

What does this tell us? That the 'solution' hadn't been sold to or bought by the public, so they weren't interested in defending it,[11] and that to really counter the price protests campaigners would need a solution which had a more convincing fit to the problem (in this case defined as cost).

UK backing for the 2003 US–Iraq war

In 2003, the UK went to war in Iraq, with the majority of its people unconvinced of the justification.[12] From late 2002 to early 2003, Tony Blair deployed a series of different rationales (problem), all designed to arrive at the same 'solution' (war). Here, the war was a pre-made solution. The problem for Mr Blair was the problem – there wasn't one. Or rather it kept changing[13] when it seemed that the public didn't buy it.

Changing your claims about which problems fit the solution, is as implausible as changing your mind about which solutions fit the problem, especially where the subsequent call to action has such drastic consequences. So the mistake in communication terms was to start from the 'solution' and then have to try and sell the problem. The difficulty for Blair was that he had hitched his policy to that of George Bush, who had much less need of justification.[14]

The chlorine campaign

In the 1980s and 1990s, Greenpeace conducted a lengthy war of attrition against the global chlorine (chemicals) industry. Some of this involved very direct and transparent action, such as stopping particular pollution streams leading into the Great Lakes or the Rhine. Some involved pulp and paper bleaching, or chemical plants themselves, or incineration of plastic wastes or solvents, or PVC manufacture.

The campaign secured bans and controls specific to industries, such as timber treatment, and waterway 'clean-ups'. In some cases, workers and communities had benefited, and a community understood why. In other cases, the specific role of chlorine, or chlorinated compounds, would not have been understood by the public, which just saw 'pollution' and maybe specific victims, ranging from pregnant mothers or babies to fish, where the visual 'fit' to chlorine was loose, at best.[15]

The campaign succeeded in mobilizing international bodies and governments to introduce controls on emission, production or disposal. The discussions involved were highly technical and almost totally outside the public realm. With a political appetite to do more for the environment all was fine, but when environment slipped down the scale of political priorities, problems arose. Industries organized and lobbied heavily to roll back controls.

Companies funded 'Astroturf' (artificial grass-roots) groups to campaign for the chlorine industry. Concrete job benefits were positioned against hard-to-understand environmental restrictions. Politicians faced a mobilized constituency against chlorine controls and almost no public understanding of the benefits of eliminating chlorine (for example to reduce the body burden of dioxins). 'Solutions' had been advanced too far ahead of public understanding, and without lock-ins to hold the policies in place.

Subsequent 'toxics' campaigns are now building the public engagement and understanding that some of the earlier advances lacked. Greenpeace Netherlands has sampled rainwater, and dust in homes, while in the UK, WWF has sampled blood from members of the public and analysed for over 70 chemicals.[16]

The earlier weakness of the chlorine campaign stemmed from taking a perfectly sound academic analysis of the problem – that chlorine chemistry and the organic chlorine industry was at the root of a vast swathe of the worst toxics problems – and transferring that analysis into the public domain as a broad, problem-led campaign. A series of narrower but more intelligible campaigns with the same industrial and environmental consequences might have proved more durable.

Consider failure

Campaign directors and boards should study failures, not look for blame. Failures usually provide the clearest lessons. The history of success, on the other hand, gets clouded by swarms of people claiming the credit. 'I was at the meeting where… ', 'I remember taking the call that… ', 'of course, what people don't realize, is that if it had not been for the work we did five years previously in… '.

Winning by losing

Blame prevents learning, and it only encourages the ingenious rewriting of objectives, post-hoc. To get maximum value from failure you need to persist. All good campaign groups don't give up, but adapt and try again. As Winston Churchill put it: 'Success consists of going from failure to failure without loss of enthusiasm.'

As campaigning is a form of public politics, failure may be widely noticed, though really miserable failure usually just goes quietly 'phut'. So try to design the campaign so that failure will not discourage key followers or allies in the medium term. With the right qualities, a deserving or particularly poignant campaign effort can not only fail and be forgiven, but actually succeed by changing the climate around what is at stake.

When the *explicit* message is failure, the *implicit* message has to be the hope or promise of greater success. A lower-league soccer team may have its fortunes transformed by reaching the quarter finals of an important competition and being beaten by Manchester United. To get so far and to be positioned alongside such a great team may change perceptions and exceed expectations.

The unintended message of failure may, however, be less helpful – incompetence or naivety, for example. One test of a strategy should be to ask: 'What are the consequences of failure in terms of support, allies and opponents?' It should at least meet, if not exceed expectations. This argues strongly for picking objectives that you think are just possible, and which others view as just about impossible. Engage enough support and you can bridge the gap.

Chapter 11

THE BIGGER PICTURE

Campaigns at organizational level

Campaign
strategy should fit
the organization

Each organization has a way of doing things,[1] a purpose in life (aka 'mission' or raison d'etre) and hopefully, a vision (the difference it's going to make). The 'organizational strategy' is the way of doing things – style, method and route.

Such strategy does not change easily or often. It's too fundamental for that – for example, The Sierra Club's strategy for *being* the Sierra Club and for being an environmental organization. It's mind, body and soul.

Organization-level strategy decides how the organization develops, retains and deploys its assets and resources, and the big choices about core business. It sets the tone, attracts or repels partners, stakeholders and supporters; and determines whether the organization acts alone or with others. All this is communicated.

Many NGOs and even some public bodies and companies include 'campaigns' but how? Is it recognizably, say, a WWF campaign, or a Save The Children Campaign? What are the consistent features that mark out your way of campaigning?

Possible functional organizational campaign strategies:

- problem-driver;
- solution-driver;
- advocate;
- catalyst;

- convenor;
- witness;
- investigator;
- intelligencer;
- inspirer;
- enforcer;
- whistle-blower;
- provider;
- fixer or deal-maker;
- instigator of discussions;
- researcher – primary provider of knowledge;
- editor – sifter of knowledge;
- network-maker;
- fund-raiser;
- organizer of people;
- standard-setter;
- standard-bearer;
- insider;
- outsider;
- dialoguer;
- adjudicator.

Campaign strategy should fit with, or 'resonate' with, organizational strategy. Dissonance makes the organization 'unhappy in its skin' with:

- disputes over 'whether we should be campaigning at all';
- fears that 'you are trying to turn us into something else';
- internal conflict between campaigns and other parts of the organization (attack from the organizational immune system);
- planning fever and evaluation mania;
- objective congestion – trying to 'fix' an uncomfortable campaign by bolting on lots of comforting objectives;
- under-resourcing by activities and resources, in relation to the objectives;
- limited participation across the organization;
- fears among the board and senior managers that things are 'out of hand';
- resentment among campaigners: 'we're not allowed to campaign';
- high turnover in campaign staff;
- failure to capitalize on successes;
- usually, low visibility or public recognition of campaign efforts (as the organizational brand negates campaign communication);
- feeling 'it's not us – we shouldn't be doing this'.

Organizational communications:
The glass onion

Expressing values and character is more likely to inspire

In the 'glass onion' brand metaphor, the organization is like a glass onion, arranged in layers, through which an outside observer can see to the core. If a campaign expresses the deeper layers, it's more likely to inspire supporters.

From *OUTSIDE*

- attributes – obvious things, surface appearances, tangible assets, activities;
- personality – its way of doing things – you find that out as you get to know it;
- character – what only becomes apparent when the organization is tested;
- values – beliefs which drive the organization;
- essence – hard to put into words, but you know it when you see it – almost indefinable, largely intuitive, paradoxical, not capable of rational analysis or reductionist dissection.

To *CENTRE*

To develop a 'glass onion' model for an organization, you need to know it well. Here's one we invented for Greenpeace UK in the mid-1990s:[2]

- attributes – ships, boats, familiar campaigns (for example, whales, Antarctica), direct actions, protests, solar, greenfreeze, name recognition;
- personality – confrontation, radical, dogged, charisma, tabloid, plus positive, enthusiastic, here's how, inspirational, leading;
- character – deep commitment to the environment, free spirit, integrity, elimination not management of environmental abuse, mythbound, forward looking, deep optimism, bravery;
- core values – love of nature (for example, expressed as defence and reinstatement of the natural environment), non-violence (including commitment to peace), independence (internationalism), commitment to action, bearing witness;
- essence – freedom, nature, truth (this could only be a stab at 'essence' – it's something like that but not literally these three things).

An example of organization-level communication was the design of a 1980s membership leaflet used by Greenpeace UK. The organization's communications guru Nick Gallie found from research that supporters and potential supporters saw the organization as a 'light in the darkness'. It was an era when UK Prime Minister Mrs Thatcher and her policies made many people feel fearful, depressed and powerless.

The Greenpeace leaflet didn't address itself to these feelings directly – it talked about the organization, its values, its work. It used the strapline 'Against All Odds', under a picture of a breaching humpback whale in Antarctica.

On the surface, the image was about well-known campaigns, but its impact stemmed from the way it resonated with both the deepest values and 'essence' of Greenpeace, and subtly identified with how many of the public felt: that they faced impossible odds. The breaching whale invoked freedom, optimism, nature. Because there was nothing else in the picture, it was pure and elemental – it could be about 'essence'. And 'against all odds' was an implicit promise, as well as an alignment of the organization with the mood of the time.

Any campaign organization can do this sort of exercise. A word of warning though – don't try to communicate the communications strategy. It's best kept as a reference – not on a shelf, but as a working tool to plan and test your work but not projected at 'audiences'. Your work should tell the story and that should express values, character, and so on.

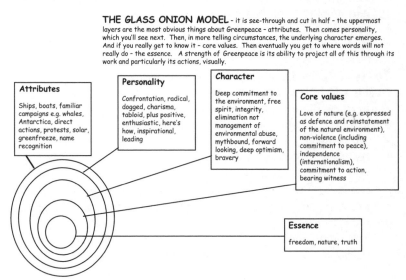

THE GLASS ONION MODEL – it is see-through and cut in half – the uppermost layers are the most obvious things about Greenpeace – attributes. Then comes personality, which you'll see next. Then, in more telling circumstances, the underlying character emerges. And if you really get to know it – core values. Then eventually you get to where words will not really do – the essence. A strength of Greenpeace is its ability to project all of this through its work and particularly its actions, visually.

Attributes

Ships, boats, familiar campaigns e.g. whales, Antarctica, direct actions, protests, solar, greenfreeze, name recognition

Personality

Confrontation, radical, dogged, charisma, tabloid, plus positive, enthusiastic, here's how, inspirational, leading

Character

Deep commitment to the environment, free spirit, integrity, elimination not management of environmental abuse, mythbound, forward looking, deep optimism, bravery

Core values

Love of nature (e.g. expressed as defence and reinstatement of the natural environment), non-violence (including commitment to peace), independence (internationalism), commitment to action, bearing witness

Essence

freedom, nature, truth

Figure 11.1 *The glass onion model*

Changing dynamics of awareness and action

When everyone agrees there's a problem, the solution is harder to implement

---

The value mode model (see Chapter 2) developed by Pat Dade of Cultural Dynamics[3] reveals significant changes in how 'environment' has changed as an issue, becoming newsworthy then 'credible', then 'not an issue' as it has normed. The communication, organizational and political implications of this for 'green' groups are profound, and may be a model for any other issue undergoing similar changes. Dade recognizes three stages:

Late 1960s to early 1980s – environmental concern (Stage 1)

- Pioneer issue. Very minority in uptake, but growing every year; not a fad, but a trend in society
- Typified as younger in age profile
- More educated than their age cohort and society in general
- Aware of unsatisfactory immediate consequences of economic growth on some localities and regions
- Aware of probable global long-term damage
- Favoured solution – Taking personal responsibility for not further harming the environment
- Secondary solution – Discover and practise methods of sustainably changing their own behaviour to enhance the environment.

Early 1980s to early 1990s – environmental action (Stage 2)

- Led by pioneers and attracting prospectors, becoming more mainstream, 'mainstream alternative'
- Still younger and more educated than society as a whole
- Explosive growth in the awareness of worldwide inter-relationships that seemed to be creating problems – for example, aerosols and ozone-layer depletion, or fossil fuel usage and global warming
- Favoured solution – Join together in groups that would highlight the problem
- Secondary solution – Take indirect or direct action against the despoilers of the environment.

Early 1990s to date – ozone-friendly (Stage 3)

- All groups – pioneer, prospector and settler – agree on the need to protect the environment from further damage. Accepted as a mainstream concern
- All ages agree (the 20-year-olds of 1970 are now the 50-year-olds of the 21st Century!)
- Levels of education still have an element of discrimination, but not nearly to the same extent as 30 years ago. Dozens of TV channels and 30 years of news and documentaries have created much of the increased awareness of the world as a set of worldwide inter-relationships
- Favoured solution – No longer a clear answer, as different value modes are often 'violently agreeing' with each other
- Secondary solution – The settlers have introduced a new dynamic into the mix of personal and group responsibility. This is to make governments, rather than individuals or corporations, responsible for the protection of the environment.

Dade says: 'As this awareness has increased over the last 30 years, the range of options for changing the "problems" that are attractive to those who are "aware" has changed in nature and increased in number.'

- 1960s/1970s – Pioneer-only answer. Simple. Personal responsibility
- 1980s/Early 1990s – Pioneer answer *and* prospector answer. Both simple. Prospector answer was about group responsibility
- 1990s to date – Pioneer, prospector and settler answers. All simple. Settler answer was about making government responsible.

He adds:

Over time, we have seen an increased set of simple solutions, which has lead to the complex set of responses we see to each issue today. As more people become aware of issues, the more different value sets will begin to generate solutions to the issues.

Ironically, as the dynamic changes, with the range of options increasing, the consensus among 'aware people' becomes less. All may agree as to the problem, but a lack of consensus exists as to the solution.

This is confusing to all but the most committed activists and creates the situation we have today, where the old adage 'knowledge is power' is almost 100 per cent wrong. With data and information at personal overload levels, the 'simple' answers of the past decades are less and less clear and empowering.

In fact, it isn't just the number of simple solutions that is presenting the problem, it is the nature of the people coming into awareness of the issues and their psychological predisposition to generate their own simple solutions that is creating a complexity to the solutions process that wasn't there in previous stages of development (see above).

As the settlers perceive the issues and generate solutions they will not do so from the psychological space of the pioneers and prospectors, who are more about personally taking responsibility, or being members of groups that take direct or indirect action. The settlers are happier to hand over 'power' to those who wish to exercise it, rather than use it themselves. In terms of awareness or concern about the environment, they are happy to hand over responsibility to their representatives, the governments of the countries they inhabit.

This passing of responsibility has many effects on the dynamics of people or groups taking responsibility for changing circumstances relating to the environment. The immediate effect is that new recruits are no longer available as activists. The newly aware will delegate this responsibility to a government department.

Another immediate effect is that there is no immediate effect! When pioneers and prospectors come to awareness they will tend to change behaviours. When the settlers come to awareness they abrogate the need for any self-responsibility and expect 'someone' to 'do something' about the issue. This 'someone' is usually defined as the government. Observation of the workings of the government both here and abroad, suggests that often governments will then work together with existing, or form new, NGOs to provide solutions to the issues raised. This dramatically increases the time to 'effect'.

This leads, says Dade, 'to a situation where one of the biggest drivers of social consciousness-raising in centuries, which has driven worldwide changes in perceptions and behaviours, (the "green movement"), has created a dynamic that will rob it of its energy as it becomes more successful at raising awareness of issues'.

Campaigners may recognize some of these consequences:

- Groups start off dominated by activists (inner-directeds) but as they succeed, the managers arrive and want structure, organization and 'credibility' (esteem-drivens), compartmentalizing and controlling action, and looking for signs (and measures) of success. Activism becomes more difficult
- The cause, once wacky, becomes newsworthy (rapidly changing and expanding relevance) and fashionable (attracting the esteem-driven, such as green consumers) and then normal (everyone agrees with it), not radical and not newsworthy

186

- The news media, seeing that it's not newsworthy any more, and that activism has declined, pronounce the issue dead and conclude that 'nobody cares' any longer – in fact, the opposite is true; everyone cares
- Once an issue is normed, only major aberrations are intrinsically newsworthy (for example, the Brent Spar). General concern is normal. In February 2004, UK Prime Minister Tony Blair said he thought climate change was the greatest problem facing the world. It got one sentence in a long press report on his views in *The Independent*
- Campaigns tend first to be inspirational, then aspirational, and finally normal – that is, not an issue at all.

Environment groups have yet to adapt their strategies to take account of these changes. Whether established groups can do so, is an open question.

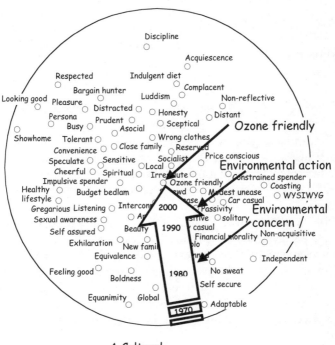

A Cultural
Values Model

Source: Pat Dade, Cultural Dynamics

Figure 11.2 *The three stages of environmental awareness*

Why campaigns need brands, organization and propositions

... the ad hoc group adopted the plan. Typical of those days, the anti-war crowd parted with the V-sign, saying 'peace'. A quiet 23-year-old Canadian carpenter, union organizer and ecologist, Bill Darnell, who rarely spoke at the meetings, added sheepishly, 'Make it a green peace.'

'The term had a nice ring to it', recalls Bob Hunter, one of the founders of Greenpeace. 'It worked better in a headline than The Don't-Make-a-Wave Committee. We decided to find a boat and call it Greenpeace.'

Rex Weyler, *Waves of Compassion*[4]

Providing handles for support

A brand – such as 'Oxfam' – acts as a rallying point, a flag hoist on the social battlefield. It is recognizable from a distance, it identifies whose side you are on.

A brand can help with trust. If I am an Oxfam supporter, I do not need to see the plan for its new campaign on fishing communities to know I will probably support it. A brand is a short cut to public engagement.

Brand[5] plus organization creates a mechanism for individuals to support campaigns without the campaign relying for its impact solely on the incremental effect of the actions of individuals. Instead, if they are well judged, campaigns exert leverage[6] – the brand acts as a multiplier.

If the brand says who we are, and organization makes it possible to sustain participation, the proposition gives supporters the reason to stay engaged, and offers opponents the terms on which to concede.

One of the best political campaign propositions comes from businessmen who supported free trade, so long as it suited their interests.[7] 'No taxation without representation' was a neat battle cry for the American colonists wanting to throw off the yoke of British colonial powers.

'No taxation' would have had far less traction. Even in the lightly taxed 18th century, no taxation might have seemed Utopian. How would essential public things get paid for?

Of course, 'give us representation' may be what you want, but it invites the response: 'Why should I?' The proposition 'no taxation without representation' answers that point. Provided a plausible tax revolt could be organized, it's a negotiating position.

Conventional campaigns have organization, a proposition and a brand. So far, attempts to run campaigns without these have only illustrated their value (but who knows how things may change in future?).

Winning and losing the roads campaign, with no brand and no organization

---
Giving your campaign staying power

With hallmark mass treetop or rooftop occupations and tunnelling, the UK 'roads protests' from Twyford Down (1992) through Newbury (1996) and maybe beyond, were run as networked gatherings.[8] Facilitated by mobile phones and e-mail – both new – they had no easily discernible leadership or structure. Partly this was tactical – to avoid punitive legal injunctions that could be served on conventional groups – and partly ideological – a rejection of brands, logos, and anything 'corporate'.

The 'movement' helped surface and then rode a breaking wave of public anxiety at the way society was going, with the roads programme, sold by the government as 'biggest since the Romans', a hubristic icon of much that was wrong. All party political pressure led the Major Conservative government to downsize the programme twice. The Blair Labour government came to power in 1997, claiming to be anti-road and pro-public transport. Battered by five years of intense conflict and with victory declared, the roads movement dissolved. Veterans got jobs or went gardening, neophytes moved to the anti-globalization agenda. Transport campaigning was once again the preserve of earnest but unexciting enthusiasts.

By 2000, however, Blair's Labour had planned 360 miles of new motorway and industry demanded 465 new bypasses. The great victory was swiftly reversed with hardly a murmur.

With few exceptions,[9] Britain was back on the road to road building. In 2003, Roger Higman of FoE, said:[10]

Following the big road protests of the early- to mid-1990s, the Tories reviewed the roads programme and cut 49 schemes in 1994, 77 schemes in 1995 and 110 schemes in 1996.

Labour came into power in 1997, carried out a rapid review of 18 schemes (of which they dropped three and gave the go ahead to, I think, seven). They carried out a broader review, gave the go-ahead to 37 and put another 150 or so on hold pending the results of multi-modal studies.

Since then, things have been harder. The 37 schemes have largely been built and the multi-modal studies are beginning to report. So far they have tended to recommend roads get built. Ministers have also tended to confirm the recommendations.

The failure of the roads 'movement' is not down to a single factor, but lack of organization meant it had no staying power. Its considerable energy was easily lost. It depended for its effect on the collective impact of many individual commitments and was thus vulnerable to every whim, pressure or fashion affecting individual members. It had no collective memory,[11] little means of speaking to the media when there was no action going on, and perhaps above all, no mechanism to convert the sympathy and admiration of what were probably many millions of people who had seen the protests on television, into resources that could be used to sustain a campaign.

With no brand,[12] there was no mechanism for vicarious involvement – no emotional equivalent of the card-carrying party member out there in Middle England to carry on the fight. There was no 'organizational weapon'.[13] Once gone, the activism was, in effect, impossible to recall.

A campaign without a proposition: Globalization

Lack of a coherent problem and solution meant failure

The 'anti-globalization' movement of the late 1990s and early 2000s shared some roots with the roads protests. Although most easily identified by set-piece protests – such as Seattle in 1999 – it was primarily intellectual, even narcissistically so, rather than activist like the roads movement. Like Greenpeace, the roads campaigners used direct action as a bargaining tool, as well as an influencing one: if they stayed up the trees long enough, if the M11 campaigners could have stayed on the roof in Claremont Road until the bulldozers went away, they would have won.

The protests of the anti-globalization movement, on the other hand, were merely that – protests. The 'problem' of globalization could not be stopped by the protests at Genoa or other gatherings of the G8 by a direct power grab or physical action, only by persuasion (and that is debatable) of the G8 leaders.

The anti-globalization movement has been dominated by writers and would-be politicians, keen to put their name to tracts, with even the celebrated Subcomandante Marcos enjoying high-profile anonymity. It has promoted the idea that its ideas will change the world, or are changing the world.

It succeeded in creating powerful events which generated news. It struck on a weakness in the opposition – the G8 and their ilk have a very weak case when the benefits of untrammelled marketization, globalization, privatization and other aspects of neo-liberal economics or the 'Washington consensus' are weighed against results. But as a campaign it failed to push home its advantage – it failed to supplant conventional political economic thinking with its ideas in the mainstream, it failed to engage the non-protesting public, it failed to pose a question that the G8 had to answer. It failed the chip shop queue test and failed to set a directional agenda.

If the 'movement', which has now 'moved on' to social justice, was a 'campaign', then it failed. If it was simply a seedbed for political ideas, then its significance has yet to be felt.

As a campaign it failed because it had no proposition. Paul Kingsnorth titles his account of the movement 'One No, Many Yeses',[14] but in reality, it had many different nos and many yeses. It had no proposition, and as a result could not split the opposition or call a division for supporters to rally behind. It generated a lot of talk and very little effect – which is fine for a political nursery but is no use for a campaign.

The causes of this were mainly cultural. First, many in the movement distrusted the mainstream media and they left others to provide commentary and explanation at major events they organized. One US commentator[15] called it a 'reverse Jesse Jackson phenomenon'. It allowed Tony Blair and the G8 to dismiss the movement's case, reversing it as an attack on democracy by invoking the frame of meaningless violence and anarchy. Second, as Kingsnorth relates, the movement talked mainly to itself, celebrated diversity, and was generally reluctant to propose a 'big yes' or a single answer – consequently, it had no answer, and not even a coherent view of what the problem was.

Lacking a RASPB proposition (see Chapter 6), there was nothing consistent for the media or public to hold politicians to, or debate among themselves. There was no equivalent for globalization of the qualified proposition 'no taxation without representation'.

Consequences of winning:
The Brent Spar campaign

If your campaign succeeds massively, expect revenge

In June 1995, the oil company Shell was towing the redundant 14,000-tonne oil storage buoy the Brent Spar towards a watery grave in the Atlantic, off Scotland. Backed strongly by the UK government, Shell had stuck by its plan to dump the Spar, despite a prolonged struggle with Greenpeace and massive opposition of European petrol consumers. Then, on 20 June, hours away from the intended sinking ground, Shell gave in, and turned the Spar around.

When at less than the 11th hour, Shell abandoned dumping, it handed Greenpeace one of its most spectacular and decisive campaign victories. As a director of campaigns sitting in a London office, I remember telling my staff to wait until it was formally confirmed before giving any media reaction, and having a considerable sense of foreboding. A 'radical' pressure group doesn't do that sort of thing and get off 'scot-free'.

With the benefit of hindsight, the Brent Spar clash, with its extraordinary volte-face by Shell, and the consequent humiliation of much of the UK political class and official scientific establishment, was a punishment by citizens (as consumers especially) for violating a social norm (don't litter, or dump in the sea). By turning normal power relations upside down, it provoked a two-year government-led backlash against Greenpeace that effectively ended only with the demise of the Conservative government of John Major in 1997.[16]

Vitriolic denunciation by the government and many press commentators began immediately. In a faithful pre-echo of the 2003 Iraq War affair over Dr David Kelly, enraged Ministers deployed the old trick of attacking the messenger, and in particular the BBC, for its part in 'supplying publicity'. Scientists from the official establishment joined the attack, not least because if public opinion decided issues like the Spar on ethical grounds, their established monopoly as bureaucratic arbiters of what was right or wrong for the environment would be eroded. Similar dynamics returned in the 2000s over the public rejection of GM foods: again a class of politicized scientists claimed to know better.

The propaganda onslaught against Greenpeace received a significant boost in September 1995 when the organization apologized to Shell over a mistaken estimate about how much oil might remain in the Spar. A loosely worded BBC report said Greenpeace had 'apologized for the campaign', and within hours that was the story worldwide. For years Greenpeace's critics then tried to rerun the campaign as 'Greenpeace were wrong – the campaign was wrong'. Even today, there are plenty who cling happily to this version of events.

In fact, the estimate played no part in mobilizing the public (being released only three days before the reversal) and got almost no press coverage. It wasn't even mentioned in the 37 major UK press stories about the Spar from 17–20 June. Neither did Greenpeace lie: it told the truth. Nonetheless, the BBC ran a series of knocking commentaries and programmes, ending only when the BBC itself had to issue an apology to Greenpeace, in 1999, over its broadcast of a claim by former Conservative Environment Minister John Gummer that Greenpeace had 'lied'.[17]

Apart from the obvious point 'don't make mistakes', there are at least two fundamental lessons in this for campaigns.

First, Greenpeace could have avoided the impact of the error if it had never allowed the toxicity of the Spar's contents[18] to become an issue, and had disciplined its communications better and stuck to dumping/littering. It now seems to me though, that this plurality was part of the price of scale – it brought campaigners 'on board' and made the Spar relevant to international processes, which helped the campaign develop. Big campaigns – like wars – have a lot of chaos within them.

Second, if your campaign succeeds massively and suddenly, it's unlikely that the losers will have time to save face, so expect them to seek revenge. Shell decided to do a U-turn, but the UK government didn't. Shell learned a lesson and modernized – it found a new way to listen to the public and consumers. The longer-term damage to the UK government and its system was greater. They learned few lessons and committed many of the same errors – remaining out of step with public values, not putting environmental rhetoric into practice, not standing by promises, not protecting public goods in the public interest, hiding political decisions behind a debased use of science, and denying the politics of risk – over issues such as GM foods.

Risk politics

More and more campaigns revolve around issues of risk, particularly the types of hard-to-define risks, such as those from novel processes, which will come about in the future or where you need science to detect them. Writer Ulrick Beck has described how having moved beyond the simple risks of agricultural and industrial societies, the controversial creation and distribution of *new* risks is a defining condition of materially well-off societies.[19]

> The creation and distribution of risk is a political issue that politicians find tricky

Yet, especially it seems in the UK, many professional politicians have a hard time dealing with risk. The old left–right culture omits risk and science, and is based on competing ideologies about economic production. Many politicians and journalists are lawyers, who notoriously tend to believe that risk is a technical issue that can be quantified, whereas, in fact, many significant risks are indeterminate.

'Science' has been comprehensively co-opted to legitimize and mystify technological development, and help dismiss public concerns about risk as irrational and unfounded 'anxieties'.

In an increasingly scientifically literate world, the public does not buy this line, and it leads to repeated bruising encounters between officialdom and the citizens (in the UK for example, over GM foods, BSE, foot and mouth disease, MMR and the Brent Spar). Science writer Colin Tudge lists five reasons why the UK public now tends to distrust scientists or 'experts'.[20]

Risk, and particularly the creation and distribution of risk, is a political issue, including one of distributive justice, in the same way that creation and distribution of wealth is. A useful guide to the types of risk and appropriate ways to make public decisions about them, and hence how to frame risk-based campaigns, is given in Andrew Stirling's 1999 study *On Science and Precaution in the Management of Technological Risk*.[21]

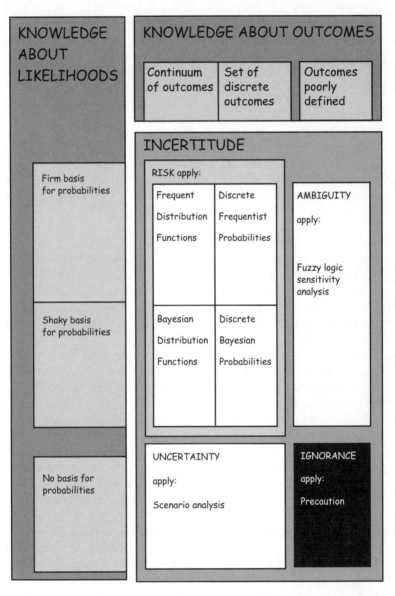

Figure 11.3 *The concepts of 'incertitude', 'risk', 'uncertainty' and 'ignorance' (after Stirling)*

How campaigns became politics

Politics sometimes takes new forms

Since the 1990s, campaigns have developed as a form of politics. There were five main steps in this process:

1 New concerns were politically excluded
2 The mass media developed dominance
3 Government retreated from leadership
4 Business advanced into the vacuum
5 Politics developed without politicians – involving NGOs, citizens (often as consumers), and other social actors, such as supermarket retailers.

Campaigns defined new concerns, but politicians, from the conventional right and left, often resisted them. Examples include sexual equality, environmentalism, human rights, animal rights and globalization. In the case of the environment, science – particularly the 'new' science of ecology – provided a new language, completely independent of established political ideology. Political parties called these 'fringe' or 'single-issue' concerns.

Governments reluctantly had to accommodate them, but they have mostly remained marginal, often treated with lip-service, rather than becoming organizing ideas. However, they laid the first foundation for the rise of campaigns as a political force.

TV brought occasional power to the excluded campaigners in the 1960s, 1970s and 1980s. Then, from the 1980s, governments began to retreat from *doing* things. Privatization, liberalization, tax cuts, 'less government' and replacement of the public with the private sector, came into political fashion. One writer said in 2003 that, in the US, political liberalism and collective action have 'declined into oblivion'.[22]

The response to the Brent Spar and GM shows that, in Europe, this is far from the case, though politics now sometimes takes new forms, which professional politicians veer between denying, decrying and following. At Greenpeace in the 1990s, we called it 'unpolitics', and others have called it 'New Politics'[23] or simply, 'politics without politicians'.[24]

Politicians in power worry themselves over dwindling voter participation, and focus on spin or engagement mechanism such as easier voting, but the root problem is that they have failed to respond to public concerns, abandoned defence of the public interest, and made government less and less useful. It's only logical in these circumstances for people to seek agency elsewhere.

Reading the weather and the tea leaves

To plan or run a campaign you need to read the social 'weather conditions'. A drop of rain lands on your window-pane. Does it presage a squall, a day rained off, or a storm that could wash your foundations away? Or even a long-term shift in the climate? If your campaign is surrounded by waves of controversy, hit by unanticipated pressures, or comes across unforeseen opportunities, are these temporary, short term or significant?

Deal with the significant, not the urgent

Campaigners may distinguish:

- Social climate change – a complete transformation of societies
- Major currents – significant structural trends in society
- Storm waves – social upheavals
- Wind waves – controversies.

Climate change is a change from these long-term conditions. Naturally, you cannot see it easily – we need measurements or indicators. Social equivalents are the underlying conditions of society. Some are so slow that they are like continental drift; others are fast enough to have identifiable effects on institutions, companies, states or inter-generational perceptions. A change may involve sudden earth-shaking realignments after a long build-up of pressure.

Possible examples of social change on the scale of 'climate' are:

- getting materially richer – in absolute terms in almost all societies;
- ending the Cold War;
- living longer;
- industrialization;
- post-industrialization;
- seeing the Earth as limited in space (triggered by 'going to the moon' – the one event, some say, that the 20th century will be remembered for);
- secularization;
- the global network economy

In no case can you do anything about these things, though it may well be that your entire organization's existence be down to one of them.

Major currents are frequently caused by the interaction of ideas, technologies and interests.[25]

In the physical world, such huge currents include the global conveyor by which the oceans recirculate water. Major currents that dominate society might include:

- the spread and then fracturing of mass media;
- the development of environmentalism;
- the growth of NGOs and civil society;
- economic refugees;
- questioning of global free market capitalism;
- the shrinking of state functionality and ceding power to business;
- shrinking numbers of 'security-driven' people and growth in esteem-seekers and inner-directed types;
- development of the US as a super-rich, super-power society (and then its decline relative to Asia?);
- corresponding political intolerance of inequity and US cultural hegemony, including 'culture-wars' or unconventional post-geo politics (state versus non-state etc.);
- bio-technologies, artificial intelligence and nanotechnologies?
- the spread of numeracy.

With increasing material well-being, most societies have a shrinking population of the security-driven (see Chapter 2) and a growing number of inner-directeds.[26] The strain this places on social assumptions and institutions are at the root of many campaigns and many forced political adjustments.[27]

A campaign may ride such currents or push things into them to demonstrate that they are there. More likely, it will *use* them to try and redirect events, but it certainly shouldn't ignore them.

Campaigns and 'movements' can make waves. Very successful ones may start or redirect a current in society.

Storm waves

A really big campaign success can create formative 'events': things people will recall as a way to remember what they think about an issue.

By and large, though, it's not campaigns that cause such perception – changing events. Some may occur as a result of currents coming up against some notable obstacle and suddenly toppling it. The collapse of the Berlin Wall is perhaps the best example. At the time of writing, the jury is out on the many meanings of September 11, 2001, but it was definitely such an event.

Such signal events are usually much more important as icons or reference points that can be *used* in communication.

Campaigns that might have a claim to having provided such pivotal moments include:

- Martin Luther King's speech 'I have a dream', delivered on the steps at the Lincoln Memorial in Washington DC on August 28, 1963
- The New York march of Earth Day, 1970
- David McTaggart's 1972 'voyage into the bomb' in the Pacific on the Greenpeace yacht Vega to oppose atmospheric nuclear tests, during which he was beaten up by the French military – and the pictures smuggled out and televised[28]
- The Green Party's electoral success in Germany in 1981, triggered by forest decline or 'Waldsterben', because of the number of small, private forest owners
- Jubilee 2000's campaign for debt cancellation from 1996–2000[29]
- The campaign to have the Antarctic declared a world park (ending 1991 with the 50-year mining moratorium)
- The Brent Spar campaign of 1995, which many say 'rewrote the rule book' on corporate accountability,[30] together with the simultaneous campaign against Shell over the Ogoni of Nigeria, and the execution of writer Ken Sarowiwa
- 'Save The Whale' – the campaign to end commercial exploitation of the great whales, culminating in the 1983 moratorium by the International Whaling Commission
- The Daintree rainforest campaign in Tasmania – Franklin River Dam halted in 1983 after a blockade, during which 1400 people were arrested and many jailed
- Chico Mendes – shot by hired killers in 1988, Xapuri, Acre, a rubber tapper who fought for the Amazon forest and the people who used it sustainably
- Chipko Movement – Hindi for 'tree-huggers'. The Chipko Movement of 1973 was the most famous of several similar campaigns, along with Himalayan community resistance movement against state-condoned logging[31]
- The McLibel campaign against McDonald's, which became a trial of corporate values and accountability and changed the McDonald's brand into a political cipher[32]
- The anti-apartheid campaign of the 1970s and 1980s, including the boycott of Barclays Bank by the National Union of Students, culminating in the release of Nelson Mandela, symbolically

converted from a 'terrorist' into a global statesman.

It is said that there are three steps in creating a norm: First it's like a benchmark, a positive standard. Second, social pressure is applied to violations. Third, it is accepted and becomes the normal thing to do. Look at civil rights, sexual rights or health and safety – achieving such 'norms' took decades. Environment as a global concern was accepted by leaders of countries such as Sweden in 1972, but it took the 1985 hole in the ozone layer and the announcement of global warming in 1988 to swing laggards like Margaret Thatcher in the UK. As of 2004, US President G. W. Bush remains unmoved.

Wind waves

News is history shot on the wing. The huntsmen from the Fourth Estate seek to bag only the peacock or the eagle of the swifting day.
Gene Fowler

The same cannot be said of 'wind waves', the product of tempests that blow up 'out of nowhere' and often die down just as quickly. Campaigners must not mistake news squalls for major events, and end up dealing with the urgent rather than the significant. Wind waves are driven by argument, not commitments. Without the 'oxygen of publicity', they die.

The daily manoeuvrings of politics are in close synergy with the short-term requirements of news. Even in democracies, and especially in highly centralized ones,[33] a huge amount of press coverage consists of political gossip dressed up as significant developments. Much of it relates to what politicians are interested in; who is going up or down the 'greasy pole' and who will get which job, or lose a job. In such countries politics is mainly reported as a sort of blood sport, based on personalities and power, rather than 'issues'. This is one reason why the electorate takes less and less interest in politics.

AFTERWORD

Although I favour campaigns planned as projects with critical paths, it has to be recognized that each path affects the landscape of an issue and gradually changes it. Your campaign is therefore benefiting (it is to be hoped) from previous efforts. Rick Le Coyte writes:

> *We shorten the odds by the day-to-day, year-on-year campaigning that not only exploits the consequences of [previous] actions but also help create the context where ... actions lead to significant repercussions. Put more simply, opportunities arise partly because they are created.*

NOTES

Introduction

1 Rose, C. (2004) 'Changing times, changing strategies', *Inside Track*, vol 7, available at www.campaignstrategy.org

2 One of the best is Amnesty International (1997) *Campaigning Manual*, Amnesty International, London

3 Lattimer, M. (2000) *The Campaigning Handbook*, Directory of Social Change, London; Dodds, F. and Strauss, M. (2004) *How To Lobby At Intergovernmental Meetings*, Earthscan, London

4 In the UK, for instance, the excellent Friends of the Earth library of 'campaign guides', see www.foe.co.uk

5 www.frameworksinstitute.org

6 Depending on the situation, many other forms of communication may be more important – for example, direct communication person to person, directly from an advertisement, from your campaign group via the internet, or by e-mail directly to an individual

7 'Dramatic polarities of the most unsubtle kind', journalist Simon Barnes describing the Brent Spar Campaign

8 We used to use this with NGO clients at Media Natura, based on a system introduced to me by John Wyatt (johnwyatt@wyattandwyatt.com)

9 Tzu, S. (1981) *The Art of War*, Hodder and Stoughton, London; Wing, R. L. (1988) *The Art of Strategy*, new translation, Doubleday, London

10 The popular version of the story behind this saying is that the founder of the Salvation Army, William Booth, 'resolved to capture the hits of the day and turn them into choruses of salvation' after a visit to a revivalist meeting in a Worcester theatre in 1883. According to the Salvation Army:

There he enjoyed a song performed by converted sea captain George 'Sailor' Field – 'Bless His Name, He Sets Me Free'. He was surprised to be told afterwards that the tune was that of the popular music-hall song 'Champagne Charlie is My Name'. After reflecting on the impact it had had on the audience, the general turned to Bramwell Booth and said, famously, 'That settles it. Why should the devil have all the best tunes?' What is not so well-known, however, is that he was not the first to use that

phrase. Rowland Hill, an 18th-century preacher, said the same a century earlier when turning 'Rule Britannia' into a sacred song which began, 'When Jesus first at Heaven's command'.
www.salvationarmy.org.uk/music/VictHymn.html

11 Public goods were first defined by economist Adam Smith in 1776, who noted that there were products 'which though they may be in the highest advantageous to a great society are, however, of such a nature that the profits could never repay the expenses to any individual or small number of individuals, and which it therefore cannot be expected that any individual or small number of individuals should erect' (from Musgrave, R. A. and Musgrave P. B. (2003) 'Prologue', in Kaul, I. et al (eds), *Providing Public Goods: Managing Globalization*, UNDP, Oxford University Press, Oxford

12 Muir is celebrated in a small way but his legacy is largely overlooked, maybe because of two weaknesses in the environmental and campaigning organizations. First, campaign organizations set more store by 'elite' communication with institutions such as governments than by communication with the public. Muir engaged with important people but he was first and foremost a communicator to a 'mass' audience, and a maverick. Second, the dominant form of campaign communication stresses the economic, the political, the scientific, the rationalistic realms, rather than the psychological and the emotional ones. Consequently, campaigning lacks heroes and, the environment movement at least, is much the weaker for it.

 You might argue that the closest it has come in the last 50 years have been interpreters of nature and disaster and television advocates such as Jacques Cousteau or David Attenborough on the BBC, and David Suzuki on CBC. In addition, there are organizations such as Greenpeace, often seen as heroic, but for the most part studiously anonymous. An exception was the German campaigner Monica Griefhan who became a national TV figure (aka 'Mrs Greenpeace') in the 1980s and is now a minister in the German government. Among political 'greens', Petra Kelly is perhaps the most heroic figure. David Brower, founder of Friends of the Earth (FoE) in the US, and David McTaggart of Greenpeace are also heroes to some

13 Obviously, numbers are important. Six is half a dozen, which always sounds a bit arbitrary and as if it's a half-measure. Hollywood didn't go for the Magnificent Six. Nobody ever has useful lists of eight. Three is the magic constructor of speeches, answers and arguments. Seven is a good upper limit for something to actually remember. Ten is good for a 10-point plan and ticks the box 'comprehensive' but is not intended to be opened at the first sitting. Anything more than 10 in a 'plan' implies a failure to prioritize ('An 11-point plan' would only be OK if implementation wasn't urgent – who remembers the Eleventh Commandment?). Nine might be seen as pedantic

Chapter 1

1   Smith, P. R., Berry, C. and Pulford, A. (1997) *Strategic Marketing Communications*, Kogan Page, London, p23
2   Traci Madison of Unicorn Promotions, for example, claims we are exposed to 16,000 advertising messages every day. Others say hundreds of visual messages
3   Wilson, D. and Andrews, L. (1993) *Campaigning: The A–Z of Public Advocacy*, Hawksmere, London
4   You *can* start without the victim but this only really works in policy or academic circles, where the ground rules for defining a problem already exist – for instance, when a pollutant or a social effect reaches a certain level. For public campaigning, though, you need to be able to show a victim, so start with the victim + problem
5   I developed this sequence when working with WWF International in the 1980s but many communicators use something like it and they didn't all get it from me
6   Whether it played much of a role in the vote is debatable, but it's a great example of the sequence
7   That's why the image became so famous. The woman, Carolina Mabuiango, and her daughter Rosita, subsequently toured Western countries supporting aid work – just by turning up at one US church they raised UK£8000 for Mozambique (source: Duval Smith, A. (5 September 2000) 'This baby was born in a tree', *The Independent*)
8   Tom Burke
9   Leipold, Gerd (August 2000) 'Campaigning: a fashion or the best way to change the global agenda?', *Development in Practice*, vol 10, nos 3 and 4
10 Ayerman, R. and Jamison, A. (1989) 'Environmental knowledge as an organizational weapon: The case of Greenpeace', *Social Science Information*, vol 28, pp99–119
11 If you doubt this, try the group exercise used by Ed Gyde, a Director of Munro and Forster Public Relations. Ask people if they saw local TV news the night before. If they did, can they remember a story? If they can, do they recall the spokesperson/interviewee? And if they do, what was he or she saying?
12 Katie Aston, pers comm, katie.aston@ukgateway.net
13 I recently told this story and a woman said to me that her mother came from a part of Tanzania that used chickens as currency, so perhaps it is true. I don't remember where I first heard it
14 As a Friends of the Earth campaigner in a BBC radio show, Tony Burton of the CPRE and I assisted Chris Hall, then editor of *The Countryman* to make a case for planning controls to be extended to protect hedges, woods, ancient meadows and other features of the environment from agricultural intensification
15 Lippmann, W. (1921) *Public Opinion* (reissue available: Lippmann, W. (1997) *Public Opinion*, Free Press, New York)

16 'To be ten times richer in 2100 versus 2102 would hardly be noticed', and to meet the terms of the Kyoto Protocol would mean industrialized countries 'get 20 per cent richer by June 2010 rather than January 2010', when the costs of climate action are added to conventional 2 per cent growth forecasts. Pearce, F. (2002) 'Miserly attitude to climate rubbished' *New Scientist*, 15 June

17 O'Connor, J. and Seymour, J. (1990) *Introducing Neuro-Linguistic Programming: Psychological Skills for Understanding and Influencing People*, Thorsons, London.

18 Le Coyte, R. (October 1998) Campaign Guide, Greenpeace UK, unpublished, rick@lecoyte.co.uk

19 For more see www.climateark.org or the Climate Action Network, www.cne.org

20 For example, see www.panda.org/about_wwf/what_we_do/climate_change/what_we_do/index.cfm

21 www.awea.org – 'According to *Our Ecological Footprint*, (Wackemagel and Rees, 1996), a forest absorbs approximately 3 tonnes of CO_2 per acre of trees per year. Thus, a single 750kW wind turbine prevents as much CO_2 from being emitted each year as could be absorbed by 500 acres of forest. And the roughly 3 billion kW that are produced each year by California's windpower plants displace CO_2 emissions of 4.5 billion pounds (2.25 million tonnes), or as much as could be absorbed by a forest covering more than 1100 square miles

22 See Harem B., *Fossil Fuels and Climate Protection: The Carbon Logic*, Greenpeace International – http://archive.greenpeace.org/~climate/science/reports/fossil.html

23 Randerson, J. (2003) 'Nature's best buys', *New Scientist*, 1 March

24 Dan Archer, a character in the long-running BBC Radio series *The Archers*, which for decades idealized farming as a benign and entirely wholesome activity. *The Archers* was originally started to promote farming after World War II, at the prompting of the UK Ministry of Agriculture

25 One of the few examples of a campaign organization being wound up was Des Wilson's not quite one-man Campaign for Lead-free Air (CLEAR). This set out to eliminate leaded petrol in the UK, and once that had become inevitable, Des had it wound up. Few organizations have such a specific rationale or constitution, with such a domineering and incisive leader. Most will always find something else to do if an aim is fulfilled or an objective is achieved

Chapter 2

1 Stewart, J., *The Basic Theory of Learning with Stories*, www.tms.com.au/tms10r.html

2 Richard Dawkins, author of *The Selfish Gene*, coined the term 'meme' for a contagious information pattern that replicates by parasitically 'infecting'

human minds and altering their behaviour, causing them to propagate the pattern (by analogy with 'gene'). Slogans, catchphrases, melodies, icons, inventions and fashions are all said to be memes. An idea or information pattern is not a meme until it causes someone to replicate it, to repeat it to someone else, like a gene

3   Stewart quotes from Nelson Mandela's book, *Long Walk To Freedom*, to show the process: www.tms.com.au/tms10r.html

4   www.tms.com.au/tms10r.html

5   www.knoxvilleopera.com/msgboard/read.php?action=print&TID=1

6   McKee, R. (1999) *Story – Substance, Structure, Style and the Principles of Storytelling*, Methuen, London

7   Rose, C. (1984) *The First Incidents Report*, Friends of the Earth, London, work now carried on by PAN-UK (Pesticides Action Network). PAN has an established system for helping people who become victims of pesticides. Anyone so affected should contact Alison Craig (alisoncraig@pan-uk.org), or visit the PAN website: www.pan-uk.org to complete an online form and get the *PEX briefings – Pesticide exposure and Health*

8   Neuro-Linguistic Programming, (NLP) identifies the main 'learning preferences' for receiving and taking in information as visual (by seeing), auditory (by hearing) or kinaesthetic (by touch). In the US, 60–72 per cent of the population are said to generally prefer the visual route, 12–18 per cent the auditory and 18–30 per cent the kinaesthetic, route – www.russellmartin.com/foodforbrain.asp

    A very useful NLP website is www.new-oceans.co.uk – NLP practitioners stress that these are not 'types' of people – you are not one or another. NLP also looks at how we evaluate information, whether our attention is generally attracted to problems or solutions, and a host of other factors very relevant to campaigns

9   NLP practitioners say that people with an auditory preference tend to say things like: 'I can hear what you are saying', while those with a kinaesthetic preference – communicating best through touch, such as using 3D models – may say 'I get it'.

10 Starting with his 1983 book *Frames of the Mind* (Gardner, H. (1983) *Frames of the Mind*, Basic Books, New York)

11 www.new-oceans.co.uk, NLP consultants New Oceans

12 Gardner says most of us are comfortable in three or four (but not others) of the various forms of communication that are used to evaluate information

13 Prescriptions from www.new-oceans.co.uk

14 Known as Doctors without Borders in North America

15 Dutch psychologist Frank van Marwijk notes that 'body language codes also differ between (sub) cultures'. He cites a story from Desmond Morris who, in *The Naked Ape*, describes a tragic incident in which people from another culture interpreted a simple hand gesture meaning 'come here' in the wrong way. According to van Marwijk: 'Northern Europeans signal in a different manner than southern Europeans. In the North they signal with the palm of the hand upwards and in the South this is done with the

palm downwards. Morris gives an example of two northern European men who were swimming in the sea and misinterpreted the hand gestures of several armed soldiers. The soldiers gestured that they had to come out of the water while they thought that they had to leave. The militaries shot them because they thought they were spies. This is a tragic example of miscommunication through a different frame of reference.' See *Bodycom* Lichaamscommunicatie, The Netherlands – www.lichaamstaal.com/english/2main.html

16 www.kaaj.com/psych/index.html – personality & emotion tests & software; psychological resources for researchers, clinicians, & businesses, Albert Mehrabian, PhD, www.kaaj.com/psych/

17 In fact the studies on which this is based are very limited and it has been reshaped to have a wider firmer meaning (for example that it relates to receiving *information*, implying that most of that is non-verbal) than he originally intended, some say to become an NLP myth. See www.neurosemantics.com/Articles/Non-Verbal_Communication.htm 'Blasting away an old NLP myth about non-verbal dominance'. It's a good example of something that is too entertaining to be questioned. As Richard Ingrams, the editor of the satirical magazine *Private Eye* once said, 'This story is too good to check'

18 He said something like this. There is a lot of debate about exactly what he did say, but I am sure he would have agreed to be quoted

19 Activation of this model came about in a dramatic (and unexpected) way when a Greenpeace occupation of the redundant Shell North Sea oil installation the Brent Spar was supported by a massive Europe-wide boycott of Shell petrol stations

20 It would be interesting to know if this hypothesis is borne out by more academic study, but it does seem to apply in many cases, and may be useful in designing campaigns

21 UK examples include Bed Zed, currently Britain's largest 'carbon-neutral' housing project, with its own locally sourced wood-powered Combined Heat and Power (CHP) scheme, solar power, ecologically sensitive building materials and its own waste water system. Others include Tinkers Bubble near Yeovil, Somerset, described in Simon Fairlie's book *Low Impact Development Planning and People in a Sustainable Countryside* – see www.tlio.demon.co.uk/tinkers.htm – and the Hockerton project in London – www.hockerton.demon.co.uk. *Eurotopia* is a European directory of 336 intentional communities, many 'sustainable', in 23 countries throughout Europe – see www.eurotopia.de/englindex.html. Dozens of US communities, projects and networks are listed at www.ecobusinesslinks.com/sustainable_communities

22 Some supermarkets originally saw GM foods as a profitable new line but quickly reacted to consumer hostility and became helpful to campaigners against it. This was not the case with all subjects

23 Lewis, J. (2001) *Constructing Public Opinion: How Political Elites Do What They Like and Why We Seem to Go Along With It*, Columbia Press, New York

24 Jane Wildblood, pers comm
25 www.rprogress.org
26 See also www.gpiatlantic.org for a Canadian version and the 17 October 1995, Senate speech of Senator Byron Dorgan – www.emagazine.com/may-june_1999/0599feat2.html
27 *David Copperfield*, Chapter xii
28 *Listen With Mother* – a 1950s BBC radio programme which began with the phrase that has now entered into popular culture, continued until 1980 on television as *Watch with Mother*
29 There are many critics of 'using Maslow' and it can't be said to express all human experience or diversity. To me, however, it is convincing in the way that Newtonian physics enables you to navigate the Solar System even though we know it breaks down as an explanation of fundamental matter and energy
30 These are continually revised

Chapter 3

Notes for Figure 3.1

1 WRI Green power development group ■■■■■■
   Focuses on developing use of renewable power by corporates
2 WRI www.climatesafe.net ■■■■■■
   Focuses on reducing emissions from commerce and offices
3 Fabclimate www.fabclimate.org ■■■■■■
   Consumer pressure on US companies to support Kyoto Protocol
4 Climate voice www.climatevoice.org ■■■■■■
   Internet lobbying exercise on the Climate Convention (for the Sixth Conference of Parties at the Hague 2001), organized with coalition of 16 environmental organizations led by WWF Greenpeace FoE, also including Climate Action Network Australia (CANA), David Suzuki Foundation, German NGO Forum on Environment and Development (Forum Umwelt and Entwicklung), HELIO International, EURONATURA, Ozone Action, The Clean Air Network, Climate Solutions, The Climate Alliance of European Cities with Indigenous Rainforest Peoples (Klima-Buendnis/Alianza del Clima e.V.), The Center for International Environmental Law, Save Our World, Natural Resources Defense Council (NRDC) and National Environmental Trust. 'The first international web-based initiative to give citizens around the world a voice in demanding a halt to global warming'. Collected over 11 million 'signatures'.
   The website www.climatevoice.org has been launched by 16 organizations.
5 Carbon frontier campaigns ■■■■■■
   e.g. in the arctic and on the Atlantic Frontier, http://www.gpuk.org/atlantic/.

6 Fuel efficient vehicle campaigns in the US: ■ ■ ■
   Ford fuel economy campaign: US national day of action by 'Greenpeace,
   Rainforest Action Network, Public Interest Research Group, Friends of
   the Earth, the Sierra Student Coalition, and other groups, please call
   Ford today, April 2, 2003, and tell them it's time to increase fuel
   economy, for their customer's wallets, and to address global warming
   emissions. Just Dial 1-800-392-3673, Press 3, and at the next prompt press
   either 1 or 2.
      Once you have a customer representative on the phone, ask them why
   Ford isn't using current technologies that would reduce gas consumption,
   and tell them that it's about time they did' (Greenpeace e-mail action
   alert), and http://www.detroitproject.com, which argues that oil
   dependence 'helps terrorists buy guns'.
      A 'grass-roots project by Americans for fuel efficient cars'. 'Let the car
   corporations in Detroit know that fuel efficiency is important to our
   national security.' Americans for Fuel Efficient Cars (AFEC). And
   'Drive For America' by the Alliance To Save Energy, at
   http://www.driveforamerica.org/moreInfo/index.asp 'Showing Our
   Patriotism One Gallon At A Time'
7 http://www.cleanair-coolplanet.org ⁞ ■ ■ ■
   Regional US group that specializes in mobilizing around 'New England's
   dramatic ecological diversity that we risk losing as temperatures rise in
   our region'
8 www.mipiggs.org ■■■■■■
   Dedicated to eliminating potent industrial greenhouse gases
9 Friends of the Earth (in the UK) ━ ━ ━
   http://www.foe.co.uk/campaigns/transport
   Opposing a new london airport, on climate grounds
10 Tree planting to try and compensate for fossil fuel emissions ■■■■■■■
   e.g. http://www.stichtingface.nl/ and http://www.futureforests.com
11 Global commons Institute http://www.gci.org.uk/ ∿∿∿∿∿∿∿
   promotes the emissions scenario of contraction and convergence – as a
   negotiation strategy
12 Energy conservation ⁄⁄⁄⁄⁄⁄⁄⁄⁄
   Association for the Conservation of Energy (UK) www.ukace.org
13 Many organizations simply promote the use of renewable energy ■■■■■■
   e.g. Montana Renewable Energy Association
   www.montanagreenpower.com/mrea and Friends of the Earth in the UK,
   which has an online comparator of energy companies
   www.foe.co.uk/campaigns/climate/press_for_change/choose_green_energy,
   and at the time of writing promotes good energy, www.good.energy.co.uk

1 In its analysis, WWF UK sent a survey to over 300 organizations, from
   house builders to local authorities and social NGOs, and held dozens of
   meetings with government and industry, to distil the information in the
   problem map. This was then tested and refined at a workshop with

representatives of house builders, industry research bodies, social housing providers, investors and developers

2   When I worked for WWF International we were kept well supplied with intelligence on the European timber trade by a small NGO that seemed to specialize in such trawls

3   A cardinal rule for interviewees is to beware the moment that the interview 'ends' and the journalist lays down their pad, closes it and puts away the pen, or switches off the TV camera. At this point it is natural for your guard to drop and to lapse into friendly chat mode. This is often when the interviewee lets drop some key point which they had been careful not to state in the actual interview. If interviewed in your office, try to have someone else show the journalist out, for exactly this reason

4   At this time I was running the consultancy and charity Media Natura. Greenpeace asked us to look into what might change and explain the UK policy

5   For example, MOx – mixed oxide fuel – instead of uranium

6   Or perhaps not, and that is the industry's greatest asset: it is so bizarre and ridiculous that it makes its critics sound implausible. 'It can't really be that bad …' but it is. And being impossible to believe, few politicians get the true measure of it. Not surprisingly, when the UK government authorized the MOx plant to start in October 2001, thereby putting more plutonium into circulation, few politicians seemed to notice. The Royal United Services Institute said it 'beggars belief' that UK ministers could take 'a reckless decision' to launch an export business expanding global trade in plutonium 'at such a time of global insecurity' (*Environment Watch* 12 October 2001 p3)

7   Aerial emissions from, for example, the THORP plant have become a growing part of Sellafield's emissions

8   Dry storage is the least polluting option for nuclear waste, holding it in stores where it is recoverable and can be monitored and, if necessary, moved and repackaged. The industry is gradually moving to this position, and reprocessing at Sellafield will eventually shut down. Subterranean 'out-of-sight-out-of-mind' options, such as pursued by the nuclear dump-makers Nirex, in which waste would be deposited in caverns and then glued in using a high-tech version of tile grout, are also gradually losing credibility

9   See, for example, Lewis, J. (2001) *Constructing Public Opinion: How Political Elites Do What They Like and Why We Seem to Go Along With It*, Columbia Press, New York.

10   MORI (April 1986) *Public Attitudes Towards Charities and the Environment*, MORI, for WWF

11   The newspaper's chosen topic was animals, and it gave extensive coverage to the seal distemper virus epidemic in the North Sea, which was linked by many to pollution. This, along with dramatic pictures of algal red tides encouraged by nutrient pollution, undoubtedly helped sensitize Conservative Party opinion on the environment. Combined with news of

global warming and back-bench disquiet over new road building, it helped convince Mrs Thatcher to go 'green'. A year later (14 November 1988) *The Daily Telegraph* reported that Gallup found damage to the environment ranked as 'the greatest threat facing mankind'

12   www.environics.ca and www.environicsinternational.com

13   A useful website is at www.mapfornonprofits.org where Carter McNamara has compiled a large resource of papers. www.mapnp.org/library/grp_skll/focusgrp/focusgrp.htm#anchor365840. Another helpful site is the commercial Market Navigator of George Silverman and Eve Zukergood at www.mnav.com

14   *Client Guide To The Focus Group* at www.mnav.com

15   I was told this by a researcher – I think he was serious

16   It produced and lobbied heavily for chlorofluorocarbons (CFCs) and hydrochlorofluorocarbons (HCFCs)

17   'Focus groups' have a bad name because of their abuse and misuse in politics. Many political focus group exercises are hopelessly superficial, but the real problem is where they are used to create propositions irrespective of the values of an organization

18   John Scott pers comm, john.scott@ksbr.co.uk

19   Matthews, R. (1999) 'Get connected', *New Scientist*, vol 164, issue 2215, 4 December, p24

20   Cohen, D. (2002) 'All the world's a net', *New Scientist*, vol 174, issue 2338, 13 April, p24; and Matthews, R. (1999) 'Get connected', *New Scientist*, vol 164, issue 2215, 4 December, p24

21   The Ozone Campaign – research by Diagnostics for Greenpeace UK, unpublished

22   Source: Steve Park of the UK Crime and Disorder Reduction Partnership

Chapter 4

1   A good one is SOSTAC; standing for Situation, Objectives, Strategy, Tactics, Action, Control (source: Smith, P. R., Berry, C. and Pulford, A. (1997) *Strategic Marketing Communications: New Ways To Build and Integrate Communications*, Kogan Page, London). Their system is intended for commercial marketing. A difference between most commercial organizations and some campaign groups is that the values and methods of NGOs are closely entwined. What they *are* determines how they work. What they deliver is as much intangible – maybe a spiritual touchstone, an icon, sustaining a hope – as it is a tangible service or product. Their choice of strategy and tactics then becomes constrained by who and what they are. They may pick objectives with principles, plan them with strategy and then run them with tactics that express the values that supporters share with the organization. In this sense they may be more comparable to religions than businesses

Another is the 10-point plan invented by Steve Shalhorn (steve.shallhorn@dialb.greenpeace.org) and Jo Dufay (my extracts only):

0   choose what your work is on (a kind of precondition)
1   Claim moral ground. Present a persuasive moral argument – choose your ground carefully so as to deny the opponent any moral ground
2   Clarify goal and message. Your goal may not be the same as outright victory – you may just want to weaken your opponent. Getting your message out might be the most important thing. Your campaign may be just one element in a long-term struggle
4   Know what a win looks like. Who has the power to make the changes you need – exactly how can they yield to your campaign demands?
3   Organizational context. Be aware of your weaknesses. It is usually easier for your opponent to attack your organization and its credibility than your moral ground
5   Assess the players. If you can, try to deny your opponent the support of its allies. Try to enlist neutral organizations to your cause
6   Choose target. Your target is not necessarily the same player as your opponent but should be in a position to deliver the change you want, or a significant part of it
7   Strategy. A plan that integrates goals, policies and actions into a cohesive campaign
8   Tactics. A finite event or activity, used towards achieving your goal. Leave your opponent little room for counteraction
9   Win. Assess a win realistically. In issue campaigns, unlike elections, an outright win is rare. Refuse false offers of compromise but be looking to take a win – people are attracted to victors. Celebrate
10 Evaluate. What worked well, what didn't meet expectations, what could be improved next time

2   Unless, of course, they devote their time solely to this. The need is to avoid uninformed interference in what should be an evidence-based design process
3   Critical path planning has its origins in the oil industry. Engineers wanted to know which steps were critical – those that absolutely had to take place, and in which order, to complete a project safely and on time. Campaign planning usually deals with softer, less-predictable material than an engineering project made of steel and concrete, but critical paths are an extremely useful tool in sorting out what has to happen and in which order
4   Rose, C. (1998) *The Turning of the Spar*, Greenpeace, London, available from info@greenpeace.uk.org
5   Currently enjoying archived status at http://archive.greenpeace.org/~odumping, see also Brent Spar pages at http://archive.greenpeace.org/~comms/brent/brent.html and photo library at http://archive.greenpeace.org/~comms/brent/phopho.html
6   Michael Brown and John May in *The Greenpeace Story* (Brown, M. and May, J. (1989) *The Greenpeace Story*, Dorling Kindersley, London) give an account of how Pete Wilkinson first came across ocean dumping of radioactive waste, off the south west of the UK

7   In this as in many other campaigns the perceived awfulness or wrongness of the act is as much down to the irresponsibility of those causing it, as it is down to impact of the act. Campaigns are about responsibility not just impacts

8   Controlling dumping in the NE Atlantic area

9   Although many others such as WWF and Friends of the Earth were also involved in this and in preventing POPs

10   Now with consultants Varda – www.vardagroup.org

11   The Spar was a floating storage unit in the Brent field, used before that field was served by pipelines, shaped like a vast vertical biscuit tin

12   Rather than oil installations, the main agenda focused on pollution entering the sea from rivers and the air. Greenpeace argued that as direct dumping was prohibited, the next logical step was to stop the same pollutants entering by direct discharges via rivers, and so on. This became the next successful campaign objective in the OSPAR-level critical path. On 23 July 1998 in Lisbon, Portugal, the Oslo-Paris Commission environment ministers voted for a full ban on the dumping of steel oil installations at sea, to avoid the production of new chemicals, and to remove hazardous toxic chemicals from the marine environment within a generation. Substantial reductions in radioactive discharges had to be made by the 2000 and by 2020, while radioactive concentrations added to the seabed must be close to zero

13   See note 4

14   The Spar was a huge structure, twice the height of London's Nelson's Column, weighing over 14,000 tonnes empty, including 7700 tonnes of steel and 6800 tonnes of haematite (iron ore) mixed with concrete and used for ballast. It had six tanks that stored 43,000 tonnes of crude oil altogether, which it would receive from rigs on the Brent oil field, before passing it on to tankers for shipment. In 1991 it ceased operation. The top end of its 137 metres height emerged from the sea like a vast steel turret, while 109 metres remained iceberg-like below the waves. Huge chains and concrete blocks held it in place. A number of men had died in accidents on the Spar, and life on board couldn't have been much fun in winter – a wave height recorder on board suggested waves had sometimes reached almost a hundred feet in height, and in any sort of swell, the structure groaned and creaked and swayed

15   This had been the plan when it was first anchored in the mid-North Sea, before changes to UK Petroleum Revenue Tax had tipped the balance in favour of dumping instead of a return to shore. That, coupled with a spat between oil companies and the heavy-lifting firms over pricing for removal, had set Shell on a collision course with Greenpeace, when it opted for the largest single act of littering ever seen in the Western world

16   Gladwell, M. (2000) *The Tipping Point: How Little Things Can Make a Big Difference*, Little, Brown and Co, Boston, New York and London

17   Colegreave, S. (2002) 'The Brent Spar story', *Critical Marketing: Cause Related Marketing*, winter issue. Colegreave writes: 'From 1995 onwards

there was a change in corporate and pressure-group marketing, advertising and PR. The following years were to see the introduction of cause-related marketing and 'green' summits and conferences that brought corporations and interest groups together for the first time. This development was a direct result of a confrontation between the environmental pressure group Greenpeace and the multinational oil company Shell'

18   For an example of change in a commercial context see the useful website at www.mindtools.com/pages/article/newTED_06.htm

Chapter 5

1   www.commonground.org.uk – specializing in the celebration of place and localness

2   1997–2000 – see website http://archive.greenpeace.org/climate, the 1999–2000 campaign at www.greenpeace.org.uk and note 4

3   Hare, B. (1997) *Fossil Fuels and Climate Protection: The Carbon Logic*, Greenpeace, London

4   At the June 1997 UN General Assembly Special Session on the environment – unfortunately, internal differences in Greenpeace meant this didn't happen, robbing the campaign of some political salience

5   With other NGOs

6   The campaign suffered several shortcomings. Public engagement mechanisms never developed very effectively, and it was ended before it became widely known in the UK outside Scotland. Among its successes the campaign put the term 'fossil fuels' into the political dictionary used in discussing climate change for the first time, and led to significantly increased political backing for renewables in Scotland

7   The 2001/2002 London 'countryside marches' mobilized a pro-hunting lobby around the classic security-driven proposition of 'defend our (rural) way of life'. The first march made politicians panic at its size, but the second underlined that almost the whole lobby, well-organized, had been bussed to London – a 'that's-all-there-is' moment – which was unimpressive

8   Ward, B. (1966) *Spaceship Earth*, Columbia University Press, New York

9   Was any of this deliberate? If so, it was impeccable use of visual language for PR

10   George Lakoff is professor of linguistics at the University of California at Berkeley. He is the author of *Moral Politics*, a study of how conservatives and liberals see the world, and *Metaphor and War*, a critique of the Gulf War (Lakoff, G. 'Metaphor and war: The metaphor system used to justify war in the Gulf', University of California, Berkeley, CA. See www.frameworksinstitute.org

11   Ed Gyde of Munro and Forster – ed_gyde@munroforster.com

12   While I was director from 1988 to 1992, we undertook hundreds of projects for NGOs large and small. I have also seen similar results from other studies of NGO support

13   Take John Pilger's book and update of the imperialist 'great game', *The New Rulers of the World*, Pilger, J. (2003, Verso, London). Pilger is a journalist for whom I have great respect, but in *The New Rulers of the World*, I reached the bit about the continuing refusal of the Australian prime minister to apologize for a century of degrading treatment of Aboriginals by the white Australian establishment, the theft of their land, the denial of human rights, the withholding of reparations called for by the British, the children torn from families by police in a programme to 'breed out' colour from mixed-race families, the continuing underfunding of aboriginal health as opposed to whites' – this came after the 1967 carve-up of Indonesia's economy by the US, UK and multinationals, doling out the tropical forests of Sumatra (mostly gone now) to US, French and Japanese companies, the copper, gold and bauxite to the Americans; and after the 35,000-strong CIA training programme Operation Cyclone, which helped form al-Qa'eda and the Taliban, the US White House activities of Paul Wolfowitz, Richard Perle and others in planning 'total war' to 'let our vision of the world go forward' and achieve 'full-spectrum dominance' of the planet; after the mass murders in Indonesia and East Timor for long disguised as good news by the media of Australia and the US; after the use of 300 tonnes of depleted uranium in the 1991 Gulf War and the cancer wave that has followed – and there was still more to come in the book

14   It was this realization that led Greenpeace UK to initiate systematic 'solutions campaigning' in 1993. See Rose, C. (1994) 'Beyond the struggle for proof: Factors changing the environmental movement', *Environmental Values*, vol 2, pp285–298

15   The campaign against chlorine bleaching converted much of the industry to 'ECF' paper – which is 'elemental chlorine-free' and significantly reduces the total load of pollutants. Fewer users, however, have opted for totally chlorine-free paper. This emphasizes that, while commercial and market mechanisms may create rapid and innovative change where industrial-political regulations were deadlocked, they are relatively unreliable at delivering a complete solution. For that, government regulation is still required

16   UK prime minister's speech to CBI/Green Alliance, 24 October 2000

17   For recent developments regarding HFCs, see www.mipiggs.org the website of the Multisectoral Initiative on Potent Industrial Greenhouse Gases. It is the dominant domestic refrigeration technology in Europe. Yet in the US, the chemicals industry had succeeded in using supposed safety concerns over hydrocarbon flammability to keep out the technology – this in a country so enthusiastic about gasoline, and despite the fact that there had been a million accident-free fridge years of operation in Europe by 2000. The US Environment Protection Agency has actually given out prizes to HFC manufacturers on 'environmental' grounds

18   The first Greenpeace boat

19 Brown, M. and May, J. (1989) *The Greenpeace Story*, Dorling Kindersley, London

20 During the Amchitka voyage, for example, Bob Hunter of the *Vancouver Sun* and Bob Metcalfe of the CBC, were both on board, along with a photographer. Like marine versions of John Muir, they made regular reports to radio stations and newspapers. Later, Greenpeace broke new ground in the techniques and technology of 'running film' and, eventually, transmitting still and TV pictures by satellite with its 'squisher', technology, now in commercial use worldwide

21 This formulation was invented by Nick Gallie, a small Scotsman whose contributions included the famous David Bailey 'fur coat' advertisement 'It takes up to 40 dumb animals to make a fur coat. But only one to wear it'

22 This also implies that emotional and rational are exclusive, and that there is only one form of rationality; both of which are obviously untrue

23 These are preferences not absolutes, but are reflected in the number of neural net connections in the brain – so individuals really are more one than the other. Visit www.mtsu.edu/~devstud/advisor/hemis.html for a description and an online right/left brain hemispheric dominance inventory to test yourself

24 Speech by Heinz Rothermund, Managing Director of Shell UK exploration and Production at the 1997 Celebrity Lecture for the Institute of Petroleum at Strathclyde University, 20 May 1997

25 In 1996, Professor John Shepherd, chairman of the UK Natural Environmental Research Council was asked by the UK government to report on the arguments over the 'science' of the Brent Spar. Unusually for an 'official scientist' Shepherd wrote: 'if people have an emotional response to pristine areas like Antarctica or the deep sea, and want them to remain unpolluted, it is not up to scientists to say this is irrational'. This stood in great contrast to the gales of political and media criticism that lashed Greenpeace on grounds that it was 'unscientific' or 'wrong'. Perhaps Shepherd could do this because he was the boss and didn't feel threatened by the idea that emotion (including aesthetics, morals, ethics) and rationality were not opposites, or maybe he'd just thought about it more?

Chapter 6

1 I am indebted to media trainer Sara Jones, smcjones@blueyonder.co.uk, for pointing this out

2 New Oceans say: 'Perceptual Filters are patterns of behaviour, not types of people'. You can try its sample online 'personality profilers' for learning and sorting preferences (NLP), and the psychometric MBTI (Myers Briggs Type Indicator) and right/left brain tools at the same website www.new-oceans.co.uk

3 www.new-oceans.co.uk

4   www.wyattandwyatt.com
5   They included alkylphenols, phthalates, brominated flame retardants, chlorinated paraffins and organotin compounds
6   Britain's biggest-ever protest
7   Palast, G. (2003) *The Best Democracy Money Can Buy: The Truth About Corporate Cons, Globalization and High-finance Fraudsters*, Plume Books, New York
8   Which took over the Union [Carbide] plant
9   Roszak, T. (1992) *The Voice of the Earth*, Touchstone, New York

Chapter 7

1   By which I mean the edited media, the press, news wire, TV, radio and internet channels where someone else owns and controls the communication channel, which you may influence but can't directly control unless you buy advertising. In contrast, direct communication involves no intermediaries between you and the audience, for example, direct mail, events, face-to-face, telephone calls
2   As Dan Rather, US news anchor put it, 'as addictive as crack cocaine'
3   From Basic Media Briefing, developed for local groups – you can contact FoE via www.foe.co.uk
4   Cohen, N. (5 May 2003) 'The defeat of the left', *New Statesman*, pp16–17
5   Underwood, M., Communication Cultural and Media Studies Infobase at www.cultsock.ndirect.co.uk/MUHome/cshtml/index.html
6   *The Observer*, 11 June 2000
7   BBC Today Programme, 12 May 2003
8   Fiske J. (1987) *Film, TV and the Popular*, Bell, P. and Hanet, K. (eds), *Continuum: The Australian Journal of Media & Culture*, vol 12 (http://kali.murdoch.edu.au/continuum) (see note 5)
9   McShane, D. (1979) *Using the Media*, Pluto Press – now out of print
10   Based on material from Ed Gyde, pers comm ed_gyde@munroforster.com
11   I was once talking to Charles Clover, now environment editor of the *Daily Telegraph*, outside the dockland offices of that newspaper, when his then editor, Bill Deedes, came up. 'Good editorial, Clover' he said. 'Thank you sir,' said Charles. 'Know what was wrong with it though?' asked Deedes. Clover intimated that he didn't. 'Two facts, Clover – that's one too many. The readers don't like more than one fact – confuses 'em' – and with that he walked off. One number, not more. What's true of *Daily Telegraph* readers is true of most of us
12   Public Affairs consultant Peter Sandman has a formula for 'outrage' that he supplies to corporations wanting to understand why the public gets upset with them (and how to avoid that)
13   Cohen, N. (2 December 2002) 'National parks, state schools and hospitals, laws against pollution: All could be under threat from the World Trade Organisation', *New Statesman*, p20–22

14 Figures from www.drugscope.org.uk 'Deaths From Drug Use' 2000 data for England and Wales, using IDC 10 and not double counting, is available from the National Programme on Substance Abuse Deaths (np-SAD). The data found the following: cocaine 57 deaths, amphetamine 19, ecstasy 27, opiates 486, alcohol 353, GHB 2

15 Which became the London Wildlife Trust

16 Example taken from my website: www.campaignstrategy.org

Chapter 8

1 I was accused of this by the *Evening Standard* over a campaign by the London Wildlife Trust to stop an office block being built on the 'Chiswick Triangle', now a nature reserve

2 In 2003, WWF International's ingenious web and real-life lobbying campaign for fisheries, organized by Martin Hiller and Karl Wagner, took the sea to Brussels with a rather magnificent lighthouse constructed just outside the main conference, and set up a virtual protest that attracted 20,000 participants. What effect it had beyond good press pictures is harder to pin down

3 BBC news website: Saturday, 21 December, 2002, 'Fisheries cuts spell disaster – www.bbc.co.uk

4 BBC news website: Saturday, 21 December, 2002, 'EU ministers agree fishing reform', www.bbc.co.uk

5 'Fishing for trouble' (2003) *The Ecologist*, April, pp18–19

6 Leipold, G. (August 2000) 'Campaigning: A fashion or the best way to change the global agenda?' in Eade, D. (ed) *Debating Development: NGOs and the Future*, Oxfam, Oxford, p234

7 A friend, Andy Stirling says: 'Guessing off the top of the head and slightly conservatively that about a quarter of stations are interconnections (say 60) and that these typically link to an average of one tenth of the interconnections (say 6), my final total guess is therefore that the final number lies somewhere between a lower bound of 60 x 6! (= 43,200) and the boggling upper bound of 272! Factorial 272! Is larger than the number of elementary particles in the Universe ('Q' = $10^{\wedge}80$) and would apparently be the number of possible journeys if you could move in any sequence between stations without using the lines

8 Although these studies did not look at motivation, it's a fair assumption that many of this 'sensitive' group are the prospectors in Dade's model. By and large, NGOs have not been very successful with these people, partly because their engagement mechanisms have been designed to encourage a 'ladder of activism'. To involve these people requires alternative chains of engagement such as lifestyle change, rather than activism

9 This picture is a composite impression based on many surveys and research projects I saw conducted for groups such as WWF, Greenpeace

and a renewables company. For some published data in this area see www.mori.com and, internationally, www.environics.com

10 The 'supporter' numbers are not comparable as organizations differ in what they count. Some count each family member as a member, while others do not, and some count any sort of a donation as support

Chapter 9

1 Friday, 1 November 2002, 'News audiences 'declining' in UK' http://news.bbc.co.uk/1/hi/entertainment/tv_and_radio/2385625.stm – 'New news, old news', report conducted for the Independent Television Commission (ITC) and Broadcasting Standards Council (BSC) by Ian Hargreaves and James Thomas
2 British Market Research Bureau
3 www.thisisbournemouth.co.uk/dorset/bournemouth/media/07.pdf
4 www.naa.org/marketscope/databank/tdnpr1299.htm
5 According to the Federation of International Editors of Journals, www.ulsterbusiness.com/current/items/item-16.htm
6 http://abcnews.go.com/sections/scitech/DailyNews/onlinenews_poll 011017.html
7 Burgess, J. (1987) 'Landscapes in the living room', *Landscape Research Group*, vol 12, no 3
8 True at least with Greenpeace UK
9 Klein, N. (2000) *No Logo*, Flamingo, London
10 Sean Larkins (larkins.miah@btinternet.com)
11 Gladwell, M. (2000) *The Tipping Point: How Little Things Can Make a Big Difference*, Little, Brown and Company, London, New York
12 Conservative Party Chairman Kenneth Baker, quoted p5 in *The Great Car Economy Versus the Quality of Life* (1990) Greenpeace
13 Hurd, D. (12 November 1989) 'Quality of life: The big issue of the next decade', *Sunday Correspondent*
14 Comfort, N. & Nicholson-Lord, D. (11 February 1990) 'Tories put green slant on next election', *Independent on Sunday*
15 Jones G. & Clover, C. (27 July 1990) 'Veto on plan for carbon tax to cut pollution', *Daily Telegraph*
16 Rose, C. (1993) 'An Example of a Campaign', in Goldsmith F. B. and Warren A. (eds) *Conservation in Progress*, John Wiley, New York, London pp182–183
17 Rose, C. (1990) *Why Britain Remains the Dirty Man of Europe* Greenpeace, London
18 www.fair.org/counterspin/index.html
19 www.gla.ac.uk/Acad/Sociology/media.html
20 Summary of their book *Market Killing* at www.gla.ac.uk/Acad/Sociology/Market.htm

21 'New media' is often taken to include such technologies as websites, including interactive chat sites and newsgroups, the internet, weblogs, bots/robots, web crawlers and browsers, intelligent agents, e-mail, (including sound messages, pictures), video-telephony, local networks such as Bluetooth, combining interfaces, digital TV, webTV, DVD, databases, extranets and intranets, all seen in the context of the network economy, and the growing application of artificial intelligence

22 Cox, D. (2003) *New Statesman*, 20 January, p49

23 Replacement of materials with design or information value

24 In the UK, households with digital TV grew from 20 per cent in 1999 to 40 per cent in 2002 – Corry, D. (April 2003) 'Communications bill: inside story', *Prospect*, pp48–53

25 See www.wired.com/wired/archive/5.09/newrules_pr.html and Kelly, K. (1998) *New Rules for the New Economy: 10 Radical Strategies for a Connected World*, Viking Press, London

26 These figures were for the period 1999–2001 and will change rapidly. Many commercial agencies publish data on who watches what and when

27 www.nfoeurope.com/ib/ThoughtLeadership.cfm?lan=en

28 www.wired.com/wired/archive/7.09/nokia.html

29 www.saga.co.uk/radio 'music and lifestyle-oriented speech catering for today's over-50s'

30 Sean Larkins, pers comm, study COI/Mediavest March 2001, Sean Larkins (larkins.miah@btinternet.com)

Chapter 10

1 See the study *Now Hear This* at www.fenton.com

2 Marr, A. (1995) *Ruling Britannia: Failure and Future of British Democracy*, Michael Joseph, London

3 patrick.branigan@homeoffice.gsi.gov.uk

4 katie.aston@ukgateway.net

5 Simmons, J. (2003) *The Invisible Grail*, Texere, London

6 The late John Grey, chairman of Media Natura, director of Halpin Grey Vermier, who taught me about visual language and who was a great communicator

7 Apply triage: is what you are assuming as a critical path or final objective simply too difficult to be practically achievable? Focus not on what will change anyway, or is impossibly hard to change, but on things that may change if you act on them

8 The fuel duty escalator introduced by the UK John Major government government as a 'carbon tax' measure. Retained by the 1997 Tony Blair government, it yielded large revenues for the treasury, which were not spent specifically for either transport or climate-change measures, such as renewable energy – although it was 'counted in' by the environment

department of the government as one of its climate policy measures designed to help meet international commitments for the UK to reduce CO_2 emissions. It was never clear that the tax was set at levels that actually deterred use of fuel. Petrol prices rose as a result of world oil price rises, and an aggressive campaign of direct action was organized by truckers and farmers

9 Organizer Brynle Williams told the BBC in 2002 that protests had achieved 'the reduction of some fuel duty in this year's budget, as well as big reductions in licence costs for hauliers. The wagon-owners had a dramatic reduction, the cost of fuel has come down by approximately 10 per cent,' he said. http://news.bbc.co.uk/1/hi/uk/1533218.stm Fuel duty was subsequently frozen in two budgets

10 Between September 2000 and January 2001, the price of Brent crude oil dropped by 30 per cent and petrol prices followed, though dropping much less – Wednesday, 3 January, 2001, 'Should petrol be cheaper?' http://news.bbc.co.uk/hi/english/business/newsid_1098000/1098985.stm

11 A few weeks after protests dominated the headlines, polls showed that attitudes to environment and fuel on the one hand, and the price of fuel and the protests on the other, were not aligned on the same axis. MORI, for instance, found 58 per cent supporting protest action, while the RSPB found 51 per cent believing petrol should be taxed for environmental reasons, with 46 per cent wanting taxation to limit greenhouse gas emissions. 'The public's intimate relationship with their car as a second skin' is what drives their irrational fuel protests – Coward, R (7 November, 2000) 'Special report: the petrol war', *The Guardian*

12 A 'pro war' swing began after the war started, but the choice and consequences of 'no war' or stopping the war once begun, are very different and incomparable

13 Terrorist threat to countries outside Iraq, weapons of mass destruction inside Iraq, the same but maybe exported from Iraq, the intention to use them or the potential to use them, threats to the region, contacts with al-Qa'eda, harbouring al-Qa'eda, and the 'failure' of the United Nations to resolve various Iraq-related problems, ending up with humanitarian abuses by the Iraqi regime

14 President Bush had a much less critical and a more poorly informed public and media, along with a popular desire for revenge, almost any sort of revenge, post 9/11. The subtext rationale for Blair's position was to contain or moderate Bush, and that might have been a more effective explanation to use if it had not been for the fact that war without a convincing rationale seemed to many to be at least unwise (that is, he had failed to moderate Bush beyond the US waiting for the UK to join in the war)

15 One could argue that chlorine never had a visual identity in the campaign

16 www.wwf.org.uk/chemicals

Chapter 11

1   There are a host of mostly very dull books about this. For me, one of the more interesting approaches, and one that can be applied to non-governmental organizations, is organizational psychology, such as William Bridges' book – Bridges, W. (1992) *The Character Of Organizations: Using Jungian Type in Organizational Development*, Davies-Black Publishers, Palo Alto, CA

2   'We' in this case was Chris Williams, then marketing director, Nick Gallie, then creative director, and myself, but the process of developing an organizational communications strategy also involved dozens of other people, such as Annie Moreton

3   Pat Dade thegurupat@aol.com pers comm – see also www.cultdyn.co.uk

4   www.utne.com/web_special/web_specials_archives/ articles/2246-1.html

5   I don't mean to encourage the invention of brands for specific campaigns. That's usually a mistake. Brands are what define you as different, and trying to define one campaign as different from the rest of your organization only raises questions and doubts about both of them. Resist the temptation to establish vanity brands for individual campaigns – stand out by what you do, not by superficial things like new logos or graphic design. The real campaign value of a brand lies in its heritage of past accomplishments and journeys that you and its supporters have been on

6   Psychological, political, corporate, and so on, often by acting as indicators of what may come if they are ignored

7   In *Cod* (Jonathan Cape, 1998), his history of the cod, Mark Kurlansky writes: 'the real revolutionaries were middle-class Massachusetts merchants with commercial interests, and their revolution was about the right to make money ... the ability to make decisions about their own economy... Massachusetts radicals sought an economic, not a social revolution. They were not thinking of the hungry masses and their salaries. They were thinking of the right of every man to be middle-class, to be an entrepreneur, to conduct commerce and make money. Men of no particular skill, with very little capital, had made fortunes in the cod fishery. That was the system they believed in (p93). Some may say that the more recent American practice of demanding free access for its goods abroad while protecting its own markets at home, is evidence that this tradition is alive and well

8   Conventional NGOs were present on the sidelines – for example, FoE – or behind the scenes, as with Greenpeace, which gave limited help but exterted no control

9   One remarkable success for FoE was in 2002 at Hastings, where a bypass scheme was defeated. The A556(M) in Cheshire has also been scrapped

10   Roger Higman, pers comm rogerh@foe.co.uk

11   Although any internet search will retrieve large amounts of material from Schnews and elsewhere

12 Of course within 'their' world, the campaigns did have brands, such as – in Britain at least – Reclaim the Streets, the magazine Schnews, and the Union Jill, a rainbow version of the Union Jack. But these were not used to recruit or lever support from outside the activist circle, so are not campaign brands in the sense used here

13 This term may date from a book by Philip Selznik published in 1952: *The Organizational Weapon: A Study of Bolshevik Strategy and Tactics* (Rand series), McGraw-Hill

14 Kingsworth, P (2003) *One No, Many Yeses*, Free Press, London

15 'Communicating Global Interdependence', A FrameWorks Message Memo, www.frameworksinstitute.org

16 Rose, C. (1998) *The Turning of the Spar*, Greenpeace, London

17 http://news.bbc.co.uk/1/hi/uk/536533.stm *Thursday, 25 November, 1999* – BBC apologizes to Greenpeace

18 Despite conventional wisdom in environmental circles, that was considerable. The Ministry of Agriculture's laboratory at Burnham-on-Crouch, Essex, wrote about the contents of the Spar in a memo leaked to Greenpeace: 'The chemistry of this water is such that it has to be considered very toxic to marine biota (life). It should be treated as hazardous waste and any discharge prohibited.' Clearly, this could not be done if it was dumped at sea. One of the scientists added a comment: 'The bottom line is that the waste cannot be dumped at sea. The only option is to take ashore and treat'

19 Beck, U., *Risk Society* (1986), *Counterpoison* (1991), *Ecological Enlightenment* (1992) and *Ecological Politics in an Age of Risk* (1994)

20 Tudge, C., 'Mad, bad and dangerous', *New Statesman*, 4 March 2002

21 Stirling, A. (1999) *On Science and Precaution in the Management of Technological Risk*, University of Sussex, Brighton. A synthesis report of studies conducted by Professor Ortwin Renn and Dr Andreas Klinke of AFTA Stuttgart, Professor Arie Rip of CSS Twente, Professor Ahti Salo of HUT, Helsinki and Dr Andrew Stirling of SPRU Sussex. EC Forward Studies Unit Final Report of a project for the EC Forward Studies Unit under the auspices of the ESTO Network,commissioned by Dr Michael Rogers, CdP, Brussels; oversight by Silvio Funtowicz, JRC, Ispra. Final Report, May 1999

22 Milliband, E. (10 March 2003) 'The house Jack couldn't build', *New Statesman*, pp16–17

23 Marr, A. (1996) *Ruling Britannia*, Penguin, London

24 Reinicke, W. H. (1998) *Global Public Policy: Governing Without Government?* Brookings Institute, Washington, DC

25 See, for example, Burke, J. and Ornstein, R. (1997) *The Axemaker's Gift*, Tarcher Putnam, New York

26 But not in the US. The proportion of security-driven people has increased rapidly in recent decades. It seems because deteriorating real prospects have caused many formerly esteem-driven people to 'retreat' to a security-driven state. See more at www.campaignstrategy.org

27 For example, the loss of old social allegiances based on security-driven politics has reordered the power base of both left and right in Britain, resulting in a shift towards the centre, which fails to satisfy the inner-directeds, and an overemphasis on esteem-driven voter propositions, which annoys the others

28 http://archive.greenpeace.org/~comms/vrml/rw/text/z02.html

29 See 'The world will never be the same again ... because of Jubilee 2000', a justifiably self-congratulatory report at www.jubilee2000uk.org

30 For example, John Elkington at Sustainability, www.sustainability.com

31 http://travelindia.com/TI_Guides/garhwal/garhwal_html/chipko_movement.html

32 McSpotlight – www.mcspotlight.org – gets well over a million hits a month. The McLibel trial was an infamous British court case between McDonald's and Helen Steel and Dave Morris, a postman and a gardener from London. It took two-and-a-half years; the longest-ever English trial. The judge declared in June 1997 that McDonald's 'exploits children' with its advertising, produces 'misleading' advertising, is 'culpably responsible' for cruelty to animals, is 'antipathetic' to unionization and pays its workers low wages. But he also ruled that the campaigners libelled McDonald's and they should pay £60,000 damages. They refused to pay, and McDonald's did not pursue it

33 Compare the centralized UK or US with highly federal Switzerland, for example

INDEX